Microsoft ISA Server 2000

Zubair Alexander

800 East 96th St., Indianapolis, Indiana, 46240 USA

Microsoft ISA Server 2000

Copyright © 2002 by Sams Publishing

International Standard Book Number: 0672321009

Library of Congress Catalog Card Number: 2001086074

Printed in the United States of America

First Printing: December 2001

This product is printed digitally on demand.

Trademarks

Warning and Disclaimer

ASSOCIATE PUBLISHER
Jeff Koch

ACQUISITIONS EDITOR
Terry Neal

DEVELOPMENT EDITOR
Steve Rowe

MANAGING EDITOR
Matt Purcell

PROJECT EDITOR
Natalie Harris

PRODUCTION EDITOR
Seth Kerney

INDEXER
Sharon Shock

TECHNICAL EDITOR
Ronald Beekelaar

TEAM COORDINATOR
Chris Feather
Vicki Harding

INTERIOR DESIGNER
Dan Armstrong

COVER DESIGNER
Aren Howell

PAGE LAYOUT
Octal Publishing, Inc.

Contents at a Glance

Introduction **1**

1 Introducing ISA Server: Moving Beyond Proxy Server 2.0 **3**

2 ISA Server Installation and Configuration **29**

3 ISA Security Concepts Part I **69**

4 ISA Security Concepts Part II **99**

5 ISA Acceleration Concepts **121**

6 Configuring Policy Elements **143**

7 Implementing Publishing **175**

8 Monitoring, Alerts, and Reporting **205**

9 Troubleshooting **237**

A Bug Fixes and Patches for ISA Server 2000 **261**

B Microsoft Knowledge Base Articles **267**

C TCP/IP Port Assignments **285**

D Default MIME Types in Internet Information Services **291**

Glossary **297**

Index **311**

Contents

Introduction   1

1   Introducing ISA Server: Moving Beyond Proxy Server 2.0   3
  ISA Server's Extensibility 4
  Internet Acceleration Updates from Proxy 2.0 4
    RAM Caching 5
    Scheduled Content Downloads 5
    Streaming Media Support 6
  Extending Windows 2000 Services 6
  ISA Server Architecture 7
    Standard Edition 9
    Enterprise Edition 9
    Deciding Between Standard and Enterprise Editions 11
  Server Installation Modes 12
    Firewall Mode 12
    Cache Mode 13
    Integrated Mode 13
    Switching Modes 13
    Clients 14
    Client Mode Comparisons 16
  Web Proxy Autodiscovery Protocol 17
    Configuring DNS for Automatic Discovery 17
    Configuring DHCP for Automatic Discovery 18
    Publishing Automatic Discovery on the ISA Server 20
  Web Caching Services 21
    Forward Caching Web Content 22
    Reverse Caching Web Content 22
    Scheduled Caching of Web Content 23
    Distributed Caching 23
    Hierarchical Caching 23
  Firewall Services 24
    Packet Filtering 24
    Application Filtering 25
    Stateful Inspection 25
    VPN Support 25
    Intrusion Detection 26
  Hosting Services 27
  Summary 28

2   ISA Server Installation and Configuration   29

ISA Server Hardware Requirements 30
Additional Considerations 32
Pre-Installation Considerations 33
Installing the ISA Server Schema Step-By-Step 35
Installing ISA Server on a Windows 2000 Terminal Server 37
Installing ISA Server Step-By-Step 37
The CD KEY and EULA 38
Installation Options 38
Array Selection 41
Stopping IIS 44
Cache Configuration 45
LAT Configuration 45
The ISA Server Getting Started Wizard 48
Uninstalling or Reinstalling ISA Server Step-By-Step 48
Running an Unattended Server Installation 49
Default ISA Server Settings 50
Migrating from Proxy Server 2.0 50
Migrating Proxy Server 2.0 from Windows NT 4.0 51
The Effects of Migration 51
Migrating Proxy Server 2.0 from Windows 2000 52
How Proxy Server 2.0 Tasks are Performed in ISA Server 53
ISA Server Clients 53
Configuring Firewall Clients 54
Configuring SecureNAT Clients 58
Configuring Web Proxy Clients 60
Configuring Direct Access 61
Accessing the Internet from the ISA Server Computer 62
Additional Tips 62
Configuring the H.323 Gatekeeper Service 63
H.323 Overview 63
Adding H.323 Gatekeeper to ISA 64
Working with the H.323 Protocol 66
Configuring H.323 Permissions 67
Working with Clients and H.323 67
Summary 68

3   ISA Security Concepts Part I   69

Emphasizing Network Security 70
Running the Security Wizard 71
ISA Server Rules 74
Site and Content Rules 74
Protocol Rules 77

Bandwidth Rules 79

Publishing Policy Rules 82

VPN Support 87

PPTP, L2TP, and IPSec 88

Setting Up a Local ISA VPN Server 89

Setting Up a Remote ISA VPN Server 92

Setting Up ISA Server to Accept Client VPN Requests 92

Allowing Outbound PPTP Access 93

Comparison of Existing Security Solutions 93

DMZ Overview 94

DMZ Scenarios 95

Summary 96

4 ISA Security Concepts Part II   99

Packet Filtering 100

Creating an IP Packet Filter 101

Applying an IP Packet Filter to a Server 103

Configuring a Protocol for an IP Filter 104

Configuring IP Fragment Filtering 105

Static Versus Dynamic Packet Filtering 107

Application Filtering 107

Exploring Built-in Application Filters 108

Summary 119

5 ISA Acceleration Concepts   121

Forward Caching 122

Forward Caching Requirements 122

Advantages of Caching 123

Understanding TTL 124

ISA Server Cache—Behind the Scenes 126

Reverse Caching 127

Reverse Caching Requirements 127

Advantages of Reverse Caching 128

Scheduled Caching 128

Creating a Scheduled Cache Download Job 128

Advantages of Scheduled Caching 131

Active Caching 131

Configuring Active Caching 132

How Active Caching Works 133

Negative Caching 133

Configuring Negative Caching 134

Distributed Caching 135

Hierarchical Caching 136

Typical Hierarchical Caching Scenario 136

Introduction to CARP 137

    Understanding CARP 137

    Difference Between ICP and CARP 138

    CARP's Use in ISA Server 139

    CARP's Use in Distributed and Hierarchical Caching 140

Cache Drives 140

    Cache Requirements 140

.cdat Files 141

Summary 142

6   Configuring Policy Elements   143

Policy Elements Overview 144

Bandwidth Priorities 145

    Windows 2000 QoS 145

    Creating a Bandwidth Priority 146

    Modifying and Deleting a Bandwidth Priority 149

Client Address Sets 149

    Creating a Client Address Set 150

    Modifying and Deleting a Client Address Set 150

Content Groups 152

    Adding a Content Group 154

    Modifying and Deleting a Content Group 155

Destination Sets 156

    Creating a Destination Set 156

    Modifying and Deleting a Destination Set 157

Dial-up Entries 158

    Creating a Dial-up Entry 158

    Modifying and Deleting a Dial-up Entry 159

    Setting an Active Dial-up Entry 159

Protocol Definitions 159

    Built-in Protocol Definitions 160

    Adding a Protocol Definition 168

    Modifying and Deleting a Protocol Definition 169

Schedules 170

    Adding a Schedule 170

    Modifying and Deleting a Schedule 170

Using Array and Enterprise Policy Elements Together 172

Summary 172

7   Implementing Publishing   175

Hardware Requirements for Publishing 176

Web Publishing Concepts 177

    Web Publishing Rules 177

    Web Publishing Scenarios 180

Redirecting HTTP and SSL Requests 184
Server Publishing Concepts 186
    Configuring Server Publishing 187
    Server Publishing Rules 187
    Server Publishing Scenarios 189
    Establishing Listeners for Inbound Web Requests 193
Running Additional Services on an ISA Server Computer 195
    Configuring IIS to Run On an ISA Server Computer 196
    Configuring Outlook Express to Run On an ISA
        Server Computer 197
Publishing a Mail Server 198
    Configuring Message Screener 200
Summary 203

8 Monitoring, Alerts, and Reporting 205
Monitoring Performance 206
    Establishing a Baseline 206
    Performance Counters 207
Tips for Monitoring Performance 211
    Memory Bottlenecks 212
    Hard Disk Bottlenecks 212
    Processor Bottlenecks 213
    Network Bottlenecks 213
Using Alerts 214
    Creating Alerts 215
    Modifying Alerts 219
    Configuring Alert Thresholds 219
    Configuring Alert Conditions 221
    Configuring Alert Actions 221
Logging and Reporting 222
    Configuring Logging 223
    Log Formats Supported by ISA Server 224
    Logging to a File 225
    Logging to a Database 226
    Working with Reports 227
    Steps Required to Generate and View Reports 228
    Managing Reports 232
    Viewing Predefined Reports 233
Summary 236

9 Troubleshooting 237
Troubleshooting Services 238
    ISA Server Control Service 239
    Web Proxy Service 241

Firewall Service 241

H.323 Gatekeeper Service 242

Using the Event Viewer to Help Troubleshoot ISA Events 243

Troubleshooting Caching 246

Troubleshooting Sessions 249

Troubleshooting Connections 250

Troubleshooting Access 252

Troubleshooting Authentication 255

Troubleshooting Publishing 258

Troubleshooting Dial-Up 259

Summary 260

A   Bug Fixes and Patches for ISA Server 2000   261

Windows 2000 Service Pack 2 Updates for ISA Server 2000 262

Web Requests Can Cause Access Violations in ISA Server

    Web Proxy Service 263

ISA Server 2000 Fix for Packet Filter Log 264

ISA Server 2000 Fix for UDP Log 264

Security Mailing Lists and Other Resources 265

B   Microsoft Knowledge Base Articles   267

C   TCP/IP Port Assignments   285

D   Default MIME Types in Internet Information Services   291

Glossary   297

Index   311

About the Author

Zubair Alexander (MCSE, MCT, MCP+I, CNA, A+, Network+, CTT+, CIW) works as a trainer and consultant in Seattle, Washington. He has over ten years of experience as a trainer, consultant, network administrator, author, contributing editor, college instructor, and public speaker. He teaches Microsoft ISA Server 2000 and other Microsoft BackOffice products and has written extensively on Microsoft products for several years. When he is not busy training or writing, he finds time for consulting engagements. He excels in troubleshooting hardware and software problems and his real-world experience is one of his greatest strengths.

Zubair is known worldwide for his articles on Windows NT/2000, written as a contributing editor and online columnist for Windows 2000 Magazine. He reviews technical books and articles for various publishers and has co-authored a book on Windows 2000 networking services.

As a Microsoft EST-endorsed trainer, he trains Microsoft Consulting Services (MCS) and Microsoft Product Support Services (PSS) engineers. In addition to writing Professor Windows columns for Microsoft TechNet, he has been involved in writing Windows 2000 exam questions for Microsoft. He has been recognized by Microsoft as a Charter Member 2000, honoring his early achievement as an MCSE for Windows 2000. Zubair was one of only 13 Microsoft Certified Trainers in United States that were endorsed by Microsoft to teach Train-the-Trainer courses for the Windows XP initiative.

Zubair was awarded a Bachelor of Science (B.S.) in Aeronautics and Astronautics Engineering from the University of Washington in Seattle. He also holds a B.S. in Mathematics. He taught at North Seattle Community College after he earned his Computer Information Systems (CIS) degree. Zubair specializes in design, implementation, and engineering of enterprise network services. He speaks publicly at technical seminars and conferences on a wide range of topics, from network security and DNS to Active Directory design and Terminal Services.

Computers are not his only passion. Zubair considers himself to be one of the biggest sports fans in the world. He likes to participate in sports and watches just about every sport under the sun. Before he decided to jump into the technology field in the early 90s, Zubair won five trophies at the Northwest Roller-Skating championship, including the overall championship. He was also a winner of the Washington State Open Table Tennis championship. If you ask him for his favorite sport, he will name at least a dozen. His other interests include mind-challenging activities, IQ tests, puzzles, card games, chess, and performing magic tricks.

What does Zubair think about his work in the high-tech industry? He likes to tell his friends he doesn't have a job; he gets paid for his hobbies.

Dedication

This book is dedicated to my Dad who passed away in April 2001.

Tell Us What You Think!

As the reader of this book, *you* are our most important critic and commentator. We value your opinion and want to know what we're doing right, what we could do better, what areas you'd like to see us publish in, and any other words of wisdom you're willing to pass our way.

As an Associate Publisher for Sams Publishing, I welcome your comments. You can e-mail or write me directly to let me know what you did or didn't like about this book—as well as what we can do to make our books stronger.

Please note that I cannot help you with technical problems related to the topic of this book, and that due to the high volume of mail I receive, I might not be able to reply to every message.

When you write, please be sure to include this book's title and author as well as your name and phone or fax number. I will carefully review your comments and share them with the author and editors who worked on the book.

E-mail: `feedback@samspublishing.com`

Mail: Associate Publisher
          Sams Publishing
          800 East 96th Street
          Indianapolis, IN 46240 USA

Introduction

This ISA Server book is targeted towards ISA Server administrators, IT support professionals, trainers, and anyone who wants to set up an ISA Server in a small-to-medium size business.

I've tried to write the book so that everyone from the novices to the advanced readers can get something out of this book. However, the book is primarily focused on readers that fit in the beginning-to-intermediate category. If you are planning to implement an ISA Server solution, or you already have an ISA Server in place and want to use its more advanced features such as server publishing rules, application filtering, or the H.323 Gatekeeper service, this book is for you. You do not need to be an MCSE, but you will get much more out of this book if you have some networking, TCP/IP, and Proxy/Firewall background.

Being a trainer, it was natural for me to keep my students in mind when writing this book. What would they like to read? What are the questions that they ask me when I teach ISA Server classes? I also considered what I would like to know if I were to purchase an ISA Server book. Well, frankly I would like to purchase a book that explains the concepts, but also includes step-by-step instructions. I also prefer a book that I can use as a reference in the future, rather than reading it just once. That's exactly what you will get with this book.

Throughout the book, you will find tips and tricks, notes, and cautions. Instead of simply passing on Microsoft's requirements for ISA Server hardware to you, I've included my own recommendations. You will also find useful tables that summarize important topics. I find tables especially useful when I pick up a book and use it as a reference. For example, you will find a table that includes the services that you can disable to improve ISA Server's performance. For those of you who are familiar with Proxy Server 2.0, you'll find a table that shows you how you will perform Proxy Server 2.0's common tasks in ISA Server 2000.

Troubleshooting ISA Server is one area that is covered in great detail in this book with lots of tips. In addition to the chapter on troubleshooting, you'll discover that the information in the appendices is also very beneficial in troubleshooting ISA Server.

Speaking of appendices, you can use the appendices as a quick reference to some important information. Appendix A, "Bug Fixes and Patches for ISA Server 2000," lists the latest bug fixes and patches available at the time of writing. Take a close look at Appendix B, "Microsoft Knowledge Base Articles." You'll find a wealth of information in these Q-articles. You can learn how to perform tasks such as configuring ISA Server to open ICQ ports, or configuring the Gatekeeper service to allow inbound NetMeeting calls.

If you are responsible for securing your network with ISA Server, it's imperative that you know the TCP/IP port assignments for common services. Appendix C, "TCP/IP Port Assignments," lists most of the common port numbers used with Windows 2000 and ISA Server.

I have also tried to make the information in the Glossary more useful. For example, instead of simply stating that CARP stands for Cache Array Routing Protocol, which is great to know but doesn't really tell you anything, I've explained the glossary item in more detail. You'll notice that the description includes what CARP stands for, what it does, how it is used, and what its advantages are.

One thing you will appreciate is that I have included only the screen shots that I think are useful. Although I kept the beginners in mind and have included enough graphics to help you out, I made sure that I do not include useless screen shots that only tell you to click Next. In fact, you won't see the final screen shots in wizards in this book where you are told to click Finish. If you do, it will be only because there is some pertinent information that you need to pay close attention to. I can already hear the applause (and a sigh of relief) from you guys.

Finally, I've tried to stick to the technical information and left the tangential stories to other authors. Although I use examples, I don't like to go off the subject and my writing style keeps me focused on the topic. I could have written an 800 page book filled with stories, jokes, and "click Next" graphics, but because I am too busy to read the fluff, I assume that you are too.

I hope you will enjoy this book. If you are interested in my articles and publications, visit my Web site at `http://www.techgalaxy.net`.

Also, for the error log, corrections, updated URLs, and other information related to this book, visit `http://www.techgalaxy.net/isaserver.htm`.

Introducing ISA Server: Moving Beyond Proxy Server 2.0

IN THIS CHAPTER

- ISA Server's Extensibility   4
- Internet Acceleration Updates from Proxy 2.0   4
- Extending Windows 2000 Services   6
- ISA Server Architecture   7
- Server Installation Modes   12
- Web Proxy Autodiscovery Protocol   17
- Web Caching Services   21
- Firewall Services   24
- Hosting Services   27
- Summary   28

Microsoft's Internet Security and Acceleration (ISA) Server is not just a successor to Proxy Server 2.0. It is an enterprise firewall, a SecureNAT server, and a Web cache server. While many consider it a "Proxy Server 3.0," it takes the best capabilities of Proxy Server 2.0 and adds the built-in security and network functionality of Windows 2000. Furthermore, ISA Server adds new features such as stateful inspection, RAM caching, and a multi-layered firewall.

ISA Server also updates scalability features. Whether you are installing on a standalone machine, or setting up an enterprise-wide configuration, you can rest assured that your network will not outgrow your software.

This first chapter offers an overview of Microsoft's ISA Server 2000. In this chapter, you will discover how ISA Server interacts with the new features included in Windows 2000. ISA Server architecture, as well as how it can be utilized on any size LAN or WAN will also be presented. Finally, information on the types of ISA Server modes and client modes will be provided.

ISA Server's Extensibility

In a software product such as ISA Server that provides Firewall features, Web caching functionality, and Proxy services, ensuring its extensibility is essential. Microsoft recognized its importance and included a Software Development Kit (SDK) for developers to create customized solutions. In addition, third party vendors are offering solutions that integrate with ISA Server and extend its capabilities. The tools include security and management tools, reporting, virus scanning, and remote administration tools and much more. From Web filters to user interfaces, from alerts to extensible storage, vendors are coming out with complementary solutions to extend ISA Server's functionalities.

NOTE

Check out http://www.techgalaxy.net/isaserver.htm for a listing of ISA Server add-on products.

Internet Acceleration Updates from Proxy 2.0

Proxy Server 2.0 provided active and passive caching to accelerate network users' experience on the Internet. ISA Server provides a complete overhaul of the acceleration features that were present in Proxy Server 2.0.

As more and more network users request Internet access from their desktops, the Internet experience for these users will continue to be slower unless one of two things occurs. Either you will need to purchase more bandwidth, or purchase a software product that provides accelerated access. However, depending upon the access methods, purchasing faster bandwidth may prove to be quite expensive. Therefore, purchasing a product such as ISA Server that provides accelerated access could be a better choice in a lot of situations. ISA Server's caching technology and support for multiprocessors provides the improved performance that can save bandwidth and speed up your access to the Internet.

According to Microsoft's benchmark testing, the 2,083 requests per second filled by ISA Server eclipsed the 180 requests per second of Proxy Server 2.0 by more than a factor of 10.

NOTE

For information on how ISA Server performed in the "Third Industry Cache-Off" held by The Measurement Factory (TMF) in Houston, Texas, check out `http://www.microsoft.com/isaserver/evaluation/competitive/TMFcacheoff.asp`. Microsoft's ISA Server went head-to-head with Novell, IBM, Compaq, and other vendors and came out number one in price/performance ratio and number five in performance. For an unbiased official report from TMF, go to `http://www.measurement-factory.com/results/public/cacheoff/N03/report.by-meas.html`.

From smart caching to distributed caching, ISA Server provides a rich set of features that will accelerate network users' experience on the Internet, regardless of the size of the network. The following are some of the new acceleration features provided by ISA Server that were not available in Proxy Server 2.0.

RAM Caching

Compared to Proxy Server 2.0, ISA Server has the capability to cache objects in RAM, in addition to caching them on the hard drive. This feature, one of the several on Microsoft enthusiasts' wish list, provides much faster access to stored Web objects on the ISA Server computer. The disk access time on a typical hard disk is around 9 milliseconds, compared to the access time for an average memory chip, which is around 60 nanoseconds or faster. Obviously, accessing objects in RAM is incredibly faster. By default, ISA Server caches smaller objects in RAM and on the hard disk. Larger objects are stored only on the hard disk.

Scheduled Content Downloads

Another new feature of ISA Server is the capability to download frequently accessed Web objects during a specific schedule. For example, if users frequently access information from a particular Web site, this information can be downloaded to the ISA Server machine every morning, let's say at 2 a.m., when no one is in the office. This allows for faster access during peak hours. Scheduled content downloads differ from active caching because active caching only retrieves Web objects when the Time to Live (TTL) is near expiration. More information on scheduled content downloads can be found in Chapter 5, "ISA Acceleration Concepts."

Streaming Media Support

Another great feature of ISA Server is its capability to provide streaming media support. To understand streaming media support, take the following scenario: Your company is providing a Webcast over the Internet, and your corporate network has 150 users, all of whom are watching the Webcast simultaneously. There is a possibility of bandwidth saturation. With streaming media support on ISA Server, the media is downloaded just once to the ISA Server machine, and then sent to each client computer. This is achieved by a feature known as *live-stream splitting*.

Live stream splitting is a function performed by streaming media filters to offer network users enhanced network performance. The filters gather the information once, and then make it available to the users on a Microsoft Windows Media Technology (WMT) server.

ISA Server includes a streaming media filter that enables Firewall and SecureNAT clients to access several streaming media protocols. Support for the following streaming media protocols is included in ISA Server:

- Microsoft Windows Media (MMS)—MMS is used for Windows Media Player client access.
- Progressive Networks protocol (PNM)—PNM is used for RealPlayer client access.
- Real Time Streaming Protocol (RTSP)—RTSP is used for RealPlayer G2 and QuickTime 4 client access.

You can use these protocols to access streaming media servers such as Microsoft's WMT server. Streaming media servers can be published—meaning the users from the Internet can access these servers on the local network via ISA Server.

NOTE

The Windows Media Technology server must be installed on the same computer as the ISA Server computer.

Extending Windows 2000 Services

Windows 2000 by itself provides many advantages over Windows NT when it comes to its built-in networking and security services, such as Routing and Remote Access Service and

Network Address Translation. ISA Server takes these advantages and extends these services to provide for a full-featured firewall and Web cache server.

> **NOTE**
>
> If you are using Windows 2000 Advanced Server configured with Network Load Balancing (NLB), ISA Server can benefit from the NLB features automatically. These features not only provide fault tolerance, but they also enhance performance.

For example, before ISA Server, you might have used Routing and Remote Access service for remote connectivity. Compared to Routing and Remote Access, ISA Server offers more extensive features. It also provides more flexible administration and security, so you have more control over your network. Although ISA Server uses Routing and Remote Access' dial-up entries, it uses its own packet filtering. Routing and Remote Access can coexist with the ISA Server. In fact, ISA Server uses Routing and Remote Access to create and maintain virtual private networks (VPNs).

ISA Server can also extend Windows 2000's Network Address Translation (NAT) services. Even though NAT doesn't offer an authentication mechanism for NAT clients, you can apply ISA Server's rules and policies to the SecureNAT clients that are available in ISA Server. SecureNAT clients are covered in detail later in this chapter.

ISA Server Architecture

Whether you are using ISA Server on a standalone computer, a group of computers, or deploying enterprise-wide, it is important to understand the architecture behind the product. Understanding the architecture is important for three main reasons. First, installing and configuring ISA Server correctly the first time is a lot easier than having to redo everything all over again, especially after everything has been installed already. Second, it is important to install it in such a way so that if your company grows, additional ISA Server installations can be more easily integrated into your existing network. Finally, if you understand the architecture, you will be able to properly secure your network. After all, ISA Server is a firewall product, and it is imperative that you secure your network.

Every network is different, and ISA Server was built on the notion that it can provide services to your network whether it is large or small. An understanding of how standalone servers, arrays, and the enterprise interact with ISA Server is essential in planning your installation.

Figure 1.1 shows the ISA Server architecture. The server implements packet filtering at the packet layer. The three types of clients supported by the ISA Server communicate with the services running on the server. The Web Proxy client goes through the Web Proxy service. The Firewall and SecureNAT clients send requests to the Firewall service. The Firewall client can pass the information to the Web Proxy service through the HTTP redirector. The services can apply various types of filters to the inbound and outbound requests; for example, HTTP, FTP, SMTP, H.323, or some third party filters can be applied.

The types of clients supported by the ISA Server are discussed in more detail later in this chapter.

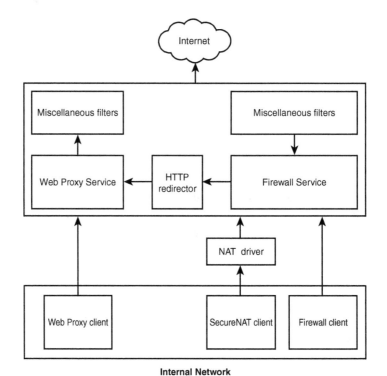

FIGURE 1.1
The ISA Server architecture.

Standard Edition

The Standard Edition provides the capability to install ISA Server in a standalone server environment. The Standard Edition only enables you to install ISA Server on one computer with a maximum of four processors. This is most suitable for a LAN, or a Small Office/Home Office (SOHO) network that does not expect much expansion. An example of a standalone server setup is shown in Figure 1.2. This method of installation does not provide for any type of expansion—ever. If you do expect any type of expansion, however, you should set up the ISA Server in an array, which requires the Enterprise Edition, and is described in the next section.

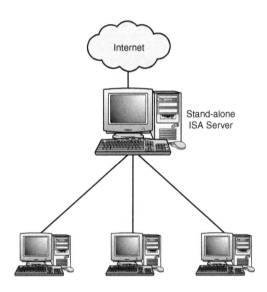

FIGURE 1.2
The ISA Server Standard Edition scenario.

Enterprise Edition

The Enterprise Edition provides the functionality to set up arrays. An ISA Server array is a group of ISA Server computers located at the same site, where each server provides the same security and acceleration services. Arrays from a management perspective are treated as a single entity, as opposed to a group of separate computers. An example of an array setup is shown in Figure 1.3.

ISA Server arrays provide the following advantages over standalone servers:

- Administration of an array is much easier than administration of multiple, separate machines.

- Arrays automatically provide load balancing and fault tolerance.

- Arrays provide increased performance because of load distribution.
- Arrays result in better security practices, because all security information in an array is stored in one location.

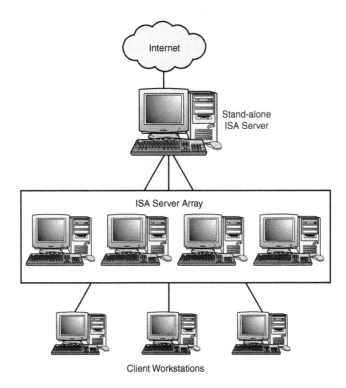

FIGURE 1.3
The ISA Server Enterprise Edition scenario.

There are certain requirements for computers belonging to an array. Each array member must be in the same Windows 2000 domain and site. In addition, each member must be in the same Active Directory site. An Active Directory site is defined as one or more well-connected IP subnets. The word *site* in this context does not necessarily refer to the location of these computers.

Within an array, you create rules and filters that will be applicable to all computers within that array. These rules and filters together determine what is known as an *array policy*. An array policy is applied once, and then it is propagated to all ISA Servers in the array.

An array policy in effect controls all inbound and outbound network traffic. For example, you can create a rule denying outbound access to a specific IP address. This rule can be applied to an array policy, and will be distributed to all ISA Servers in the array.

> **TIP**
>
> All servers in an ISA Server array should be installed in the same server mode: Firewall, Cache, or Integrated. Server modes are covered later in this chapter. For example, if the servers in your existing array were installed in Integrated mode, you should also install the new server in Integrated mode. The same is true for add-ins. To be consistent, install the same set of add-ins on all the members of an array.

Deciding Between Standard and Enterprise Editions

With the Standard Edition, standalone servers are limited to allowing only one member, while an array can have practically an unlimited number of servers. Unlike array members, where the configuration information is stored in Active Directory, standalone servers store their configuration information in the server's registry. This can result in potential problems, especially if your registry becomes corrupted, because you will have no fault tolerance. In the case of an array, you have the configuration information stored on multiple computers, which, besides other advantages, provides redundancy. The Enterprise Edition supports both enterprise and array-level policies and has no hardware limitation.

Unless you are absolutely sure that no future growth will affect your network, I highly recommend that you install your first ISA Server using the Enterprise Edition and create a new array. Should circumstances force you to add a new machine later on, it will be a much easier task to add the new computer to the existing array. When this happens, all the configuration settings will apply automatically to the new computer.

Of course, this requires that you (or your company) purchase the Enterprise Edition of the product. You might encounter budgetary concerns from higher-ups when making such a purchase request. However, the costs of labor, technical assistance, and administration can easily outweigh the costs of purchasing the Enterprise Edition up front.

Table 1.1 lists the prices for ISA Server in US dollars, as provided by Microsoft.

> **NOTE**
>
> For the latest price listing, go to http://www.microsoft.com/isaserver/howtobuy/pricing/default.asp.

TABLE 1.1 Estimated Retail Prices for ISA Server 2000

ISA Server 2000	Enterprise Edition	Standard Edition	Developer Edition
Single processor license	$5,999 per processor	$1,499 per processor	
Licensed per developer	N/A	N/A	Included with MSDN universal subscription

Server Installation Modes

ISA Server provides, as its own name implies, Internet security and acceleration. You can set up ISA to act as a security server, an acceleration server, or both. Microsoft defines these modes as Firewall, Cache, and Integrated mode.

Table 1.2 denotes what features are available for which mode of installation.

TABLE 1.2 Server Mode Comparisons

ISA Feature	Firewall	Cache	Integrated
Access Policies	Y	Y	Y
Packet Filtering	Y	N	Y
Application Filtering	Y	N	Y
Web Caching	N	Y	Y
Routing	Y	Y	Y
Chaining	Y	N	Y
Server Publishing	Y	N	Y
Web Publishing	Y	Y	Y
Alerts & Reports	Y	Y	Y
Virtual Private Networks	Y	N	Y

Please note that access policies in Cache mode can only be used for the HTTP and FTP protocols.

Firewall Mode

Firewall mode is self-explanatory. Just like a firewall between your garage and the rest of your house can protect your house in case of a fire in the garage, ISA Server installed in Firewall mode enables your system to prevent intruders from accessing your internal network from the outside world. Likewise, it enables outbound access only to the Internet content that you specify as acceptable.

Introducing ISA Server: Moving Beyond Proxy Server 2.0

CHAPTER 1

13

1

INTRODUCING ISA
SERVER: MOVING
BEYOND PROXY
SERVER 2.0

In addition, Firewall mode enables you to *publish* internal servers. Publishing is the process by which you permit external users the capability to view information on your internal servers. This can be useful for organizations that want to allow their business partners or customers access to their local area network.

You control access to your network by configuring rules. Rules can permit or deny access to certain objects. Protocol rules, as well as site and content rules, work at the application level so you can configure rules to permit or deny access to the users. For example, you might configure a rule to allow internal clients access to FTP sites on the Internet.

Application filters provide additional security in Firewall mode. They can be configured to perform various system-related tasks, such as checking for viruses or authenticating clients.

Cache Mode

In Cache mode, you provide acceleration for the users on your internal network. Caching provides the capability to store frequently accessed Web objects on the ISA Server.

Installing an ISA Server in Cache mode does not provide the capability to do server publishing, packet filtering, or working with application filters. In addition, there is no support for chaining (discussed later in this chapter) or VPNs.

NOTE

Distributed caching is only available in ISA Server Enterprise Edition.

Integrated Mode

Integrated mode gives you the best of both worlds. All firewall and caching features will be available to you if you install ISA Server in Integrated mode. As an organization, administering both of these services from one place can be beneficial to you.

Switching Modes

After ISA Server is installed in a particular mode, you can't change the mode without re-installing the product. For example, if you've installed ISA Server in Cache mode and later want to switch to Integrated mode, you'll have to re-install ISA Server. Furthermore, keep in mind that after you've backed up the server configuration in one mode, restoring it will restore the backup in that mode. Therefore, backing up ISA Server in Cache mode and restoring the backup after you've re-installed it in Integrated mode will result in restoring the Cache mode configuration. It would make sense to backup the configuration in every mode so that the appropriate configuration can be restored.

Clients

One of the biggest complaints about Proxy Server was the fact that in addition to installing the server software, software also had to be installed on every client. Depending upon the network setup, it is possible to use ISA Server without installing any software on the client.

There are three types of client installations: Firewall, SecureNAT, and Web Proxy. This section will delve into these three types, as well as the differences between them.

Firewall Client

The ISA Firewall client is an update to the Proxy 2.0 client that was installed on workstations. Firewall clients only work on Windows 2000, Windows 9x, Windows NT 4.0, and Windows ME. The Firewall client supports all Winsock-based applications, except that the 16-bit Winsock applications are only supported on Windows 2000 and Windows NT 4.0 computers.

Unlike SecureNAT clients, Firewall clients do not require the re-routing of their default gateway. In addition, user-level authentication is supported with this client. However, when using certain types of protocols, application filters will need to be installed on the ISA Server computer.

Depending on how you've configured your Web applications, the Firewall clients can also be Web Proxy clients. If the applications are configured to use the ISA Server, then all HTTPS, HTTP, FTP, and Gopher requests go through the Web Proxy service. All requests other than the aforementioned will go through the Firewall service.

The Firewall clients require the installation of client software. Once installed, you can enable or disable the client from the Control Panel using the Firewall Client icon. Deploying Firewall client, or any client software for that matter, on a large number of computers can be a monumental task. Luckily, ISA Server enables us to configure automatic discovery for Firewall (and Web Proxy) clients. The automatic discovery protocol is discussed later in this chapter.

SecureNAT Client

Windows 2000 provides Network Address Translation (NAT) technology as part of the base operating system. In its most basic form, NAT translates your IP addresses on your internal network to a public IP address provided to you by your ISP. This allows for enhanced security when your internal users are accessing the Internet.

There are some drawbacks to the Windows 2000 version of NAT, however. First, Routing and Remote Access must be installed on the server computer. Second, configuration can be tedious, especially on large networks. Finally, NAT only works properly with certain protocols where the IP address and port information are contained in the header.

> **NOTE**
>
> For more information on Windows 2000's NAT Server, check out my article at
> http://www.win2000mag.com/Articles/Print.cfm?Action=Print&ArticleID=7882.
> The article compares NAT with ICS and Proxy Server, and includes troubleshooting
> tips.

SecureNAT extends NAT functionality by intercepting traffic and applying ISA policy to the data, all without installation of any additional software or browser configuration on the client. However, Windows 2000 is not a requirement on the client machine. SecureNAT will work on any machine that has a network operating system that supports TCP/IP.

Configuring a SecureNAT client requires configuration of a default gateway on the client. The default gateway of the computer must be changed so that all Internet traffic passes through the ISA Server. This generally is done one of two ways. Either the default gateway is config-ured to point to the ISA Server machine, or it will point to a router that can forward the requests to the ISA Server. If you are using DHCP on your network and configure default gate-ways with this method, you can speed up the client installation process dramatically.

If you are currently using another NAT service to provide Internet connectivity for your net-work users, you should disable or uninstall the service before installing ISA Server. ISA Server does not work well with third party NAT programs.

There is a potential drawback of SecureNAT, however. If you are using user-level authentica-tion for Internet access, SecureNAT will not fit your needs. Firewall clients and/or Web Proxy clients are what you will need. In other words, ISA Server does not support user authentication for SecureNAT clients.

Web Proxy Client

This Web Proxy client is similar to the Web Proxy client that was included with Proxy Server. Because most current Web browsers support configuration of a proxy server, this is the method used to configure a Web Proxy client. In this case, regardless of the operating system, a com-puter must have a CERN-compatible browser in order for the configuration to work properly.

> ### CERN Compliance
>
> CERN, the European Organization for Nuclear Physics, is the world's largest particle
> physics center. One of its computer scientists named Tim Berners-Lee wrote the first
>
> *continues*

Web browser in 1990. At that time, it was called WorldWideWeb—all one word, which later became "World Wide Web." The original CERN browsers didn't have today's fancy graphical user interface. Instead, they simply offered a line-mode interface. Today, most of the popular browsers, such as Internet Explorer and Netscape, take pride in complying with CERN standards, and are therefore known as CERN-compatible browsers. CERN-Proxy protocol is yet another widely accepted industry standard. ISA Server's Web Proxy services are CERN-compatible.

No network reconfiguration is required on the client side, except for the browser configuration. User authentication works, but only if Microsoft Internet Explorer is used. Furthermore, with the Web Proxy client installed, only HTTP, secure HTTP, FTP, and Gopher are supported.

Client Mode Comparisons

A client cannot be both a Firewall client and a SecureNAT client simultaneously, because both services provide some of the same functionality. However, a client can be a Firewall client and a Web Proxy client, or a SecureNAT client and a Web Proxy client. In this case, all Web-based requests are handled by the Web Proxy client. Meanwhile, all other requests are handled by either the Firewall client or the SecureNAT client.

Deciding upon which type of client to install usually depends upon three factors. First, the types of operating systems you use on your computers; second, the types of protocols you will be supporting; and third, whether or not you will need user authentication.

If you are using UNIX or other non-Microsoft operating systems, you will not be able to use the Firewall client. Web Proxy and SecureNAT clients work with all TCP/IP clients. If you plan on supporting multiple protocols, the Web Proxy client is not a good idea, as it only supports Web-based protocols (HTTP, HTTPS, and FTP). However, you could use both Web Proxy and Firewall clients, provided your operating system supports Firewall clients. Finally, if you need user authentication, the SecureNAT client will not be an option you can consider. You should use the Web Proxy or Firewall client.

TIP

For SecureNAT or Firewall clients to be supported properly, the ISA Server must be installed in Firewall or Integrated mode. If you choose to install your servers in Cache mode, you must use the Web Proxy clients.

Web Proxy Autodiscovery Protocol

Firewall and Web Proxy clients use Web Proxy Autodiscovery Protocol (WPAD) to automatically discover ISA Server computers. You can use Dynamic Host Configuration Protocol (DHCP) to configure automatic discovery for Windows 2000, Windows Me, and Windows 98 clients. You can also use Domain Name System (DNS) to configure automatic discovery for Windows 2000, Windows Me, and Windows 98. ISA Server Help incorrectly states that you can use DNS to configure WPAD for Windows NT 4.0 and Windows 95. See readme.htm in the root directory of ISA Server CD for updated information.

You might choose to use either DNS or DHCP to configure WPAD. Microsoft decided to use DHCP to deploy WPAD on its network because it had far more DHCP scopes than DNS zones. With more than 130,000 clients distributed throughout the world in more than 90 subsidiaries, DHCP offers more granularity in its environment. With DHCP, Microsoft can configure clients to use the ISA Server array that's closest to them.

The ISA Server uses a WPAD entry to locate a Winsock Proxy Autodetect (WSPAD) entry. The WSPAD entry is not something that you need to specifically configure in DNS. You only configure the WPAD entry. When either a Firewall or a Web Proxy client makes a Winsock request and connects to a DNS or a DHCP server, the server (DNS or DHCP) contains the appropriate WPAD entry that points to the ISA Server computer. The client is therefore able to locate the ISA Server.

The following section shows you how to configure DNS for the automatic discovery of ISA Server.

Configuring DNS for Automatic Discovery

To configure DNS so that the clients can automatically discover an ISA Server, use the following procedure:

1. Open the DNS management console in Administrative Tools.
2. Locate the appropriate forward lookup zone, right-click on the zone, and select New Alias.
3. In the Alias Name box, enter WPAD, as shown in Figure 1.4.
4. In the Fully Qualified Name for Target Host box, enter the FQDN of the ISA server or array. I prefer to use the Browse button to locate the entry to eliminate any chances of entering incorrect information.

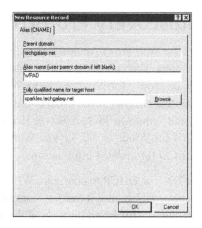

FIGURE 1.4
Configuring DNS for automatic discovery.

The next section shows you how to configure DHCP for the automatic discovery of ISA Server.

Configuring DHCP for Automatic Discovery

To configure DHCP so that the clients can automatically discover an ISA Server, use the following procedure:

1. Open the DHCP management console in Administrative Tools.
2. Right-click the name of the server and select Set Predefined Options, as shown in Figure 1.5.

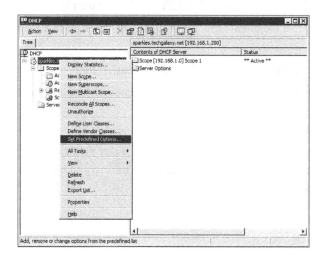

FIGURE 1.5
Setting predefined options in DHCP.

3. In the Predefined Options and Values screen, click Add.

4. Enter the options as shown in Figure 1.6. Pay special attention to the data type and code values and click OK.

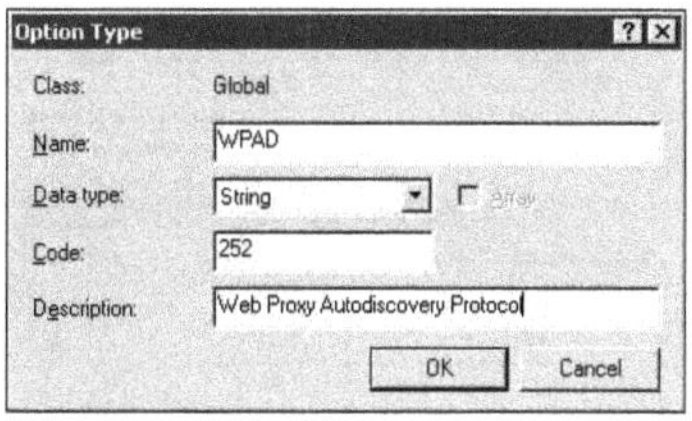

FIGURE 1.6
Configuring the option type for auto-discovery.

5. You are back at the Predefined Options and Values screen. Enter the following in the string box:

`http://server_name:AutoDiscoveryPort/wpad.dat`

where *server_name* is the FQDN of the ISA Server computer and *AutoDiscoveryPort* is the port number used for publishing automatic discovery, as shown in Figure 1.7.

FIGURE 1.7
Configuring the string value for auto-discovery.

6. Right-click Server Options in the DHCP console and select Configure Options.

7. On the General tab, check the 252 WPAD option, as shown in Figure 1.8.

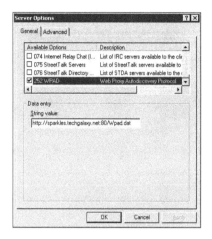

FIGURE 1.8
Configuring server options for WPAD.

Publishing Automatic Discovery on the ISA Server

Now that you know how to configure DNS and DHCP for automatic discovery, let's look at configuring the ISA Server to publish this information. Here's the procedure:

1. Go to the ISA Server Management console, Servers and Arrays, highlight the name of the server or array, right-click and select Properties.

2. On the Auto Discovery tab, check the box Publish Automatic Discovery Information, as shown in Figure 1.9.

3. Verify that the correct port number is used in the Use This Port for Automatic Discovery Requests box.

TIP

If you are going to use DNS to publish WPAD, make sure that you configure automatic discovery to use the standard HTTP port 80.

---

4. ISA Server warns you that the Web Proxy service needs to be restarted, as shown in Figure 1.10. You can either restart the services now or later.

Introducing ISA Server: Moving Beyond Proxy Server 2.0

CHAPTER 1

21

1

INTRODUCING ISA
SERVER: MOVING
BEYOND PROXY
SERVER 2.0

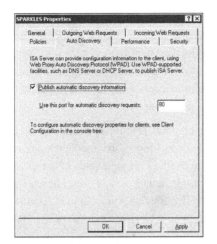

FIGURE 1.9

Configuring ISA Server for publishing automatic discovery.

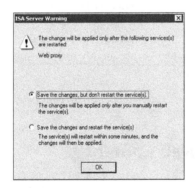

FIGURE 1.10

Options for restarting the Web Proxy service.

Web Caching Services

ISA Server provides powerful Web caching services that are used to store frequently down-loaded Web objects, including HTML pages, images, and files. Web caching increases the speed with which the clients can retrieve these objects, and decreases bandwidth on the Internet connection. The reason for this is that the client is able to retrieve objects from the local network, rather than downloading them every time from the Internet.

Web caching is especially useful in situations where a large number of clients are accessing a common location, such as a vendor Web site. Similar to other services, Web caching services are bound by the rules and cache policy that you configure. The Web publishing rules control the type of contents that the Internet clients will be accessing on your internal Web servers. The routing rules determine how the client requests are routed, and whether the clients are permitted to retrieve information from the Internet or supplied cached objects on the ISA Server. Similarly, the site and content rules control the sites that the clients are permitted to surf and the type of contents that they can access.

The next few sections will explain different types of caching available in ISA Server. The concepts of forward caching, reverse caching, distributed caching, and hierarchical caching will be discussed. Forward and reverse caching are opposites of each other. One caches Web contents for internal clients, while the other caches objects for external clients. Distributed and hierarchical caching extends the caching concept to multiple ISA Servers and arrays. You will also learn about scheduled caching, which allows you to download Web contents at specific intervals.

Forward Caching Web Content

Forward caching stores requested Web objects in a local cache. This increases the speed with which internal clients can access these objects, and reduces outbound bandwidth usage, because the object only needs to be downloaded once. Forward caching is very effective for static, or rarely changed, Web sites. For frequently updated sites, such as news or stock market quotes, it is not as effective.

Chapter 2 covers all the hardware recommendations for forward caching that you will find useful.

Reverse Caching Web Content

Reverse caching stores objects from internal Web servers in a central location for Internet clients to access. This is done by publishing the internal Web servers on the ISA server. This can help reduce internal network traffic for common objects, such as company logos.

NOTE

Forward caching is configured for outgoing Web requests so that internal clients can have quicker access to Web objects on the Internet. Reverse caching is configured for incoming Web requests so that the Internet clients can have quicker access to Web objects on internal Web servers.

Scheduled Caching of Web Content

Scheduled caching enables the ISA Server administrator to download Web objects to a local cache at a specific time. For example, if all the clients in your company's marketing department check a vendor's site every morning for updates when they come in, you could schedule the site to be cached overnight or during off-peak hours to speed up access and reduce bandwidth usage.

The best thing to do is to monitor Internet access and see what type of contents are required and at what time. Then you can schedule the downloading of contents at a predetermined time. You can download a single URL, several URLs, or even an entire Web site so that the clients can access the information from the ISA Server cache instead of downloading it from the Internet.

For example, if you were to configure forward caching, you could configure a scheduled download of Microsoft TechNet pages that are relevant to your users. In a reverse caching scenario, if you were a training organization, you could cache the course catalog for the external users. Your customers will be able to quickly access information about the courses that they can take from your company.

> **TIP**
>
> Do not configure scheduled cache content downloading from Web sites that require user authentication, because the scheduled download will fail.

Distributed Caching

Distributed caching is used in enterprise ISA arrays and uses the Cache Array Routing Protocol (CARP) to store the local cache across multiple servers, using a hash-based algorithm to determine the location. CARP then uses hash-based routing to respond to an object's request. The routing enables ISA to determine exactly where in the distributed cache an object resides, rather than having to query every server in the array.

Hierarchical Caching

Hierarchical caching, or *chaining*, is typically used in a multi-layered enterprise ISA array environment. Chaining replicates the stored cache from the array connected to the Internet to arrays lower in the hierarchy. This enables client requests to be serviced at the low-level arrays, rather than being passed up to the top-level array. Unlike distributed caching, hierarchical caching doesn't require an array. You could create hierarchical connections either between individual ISA Server computers or between ISA Server arrays.

For example, if you have your top-level array connected to the Internet in Seattle, and have your lower-level arrays in Sacramento and San Diego configured to use hierarchical caching, the objects are initially routed to the Internet through Seattle. The array in Seattle caches the objects and returns it to the branch office, for example in Sacramento. The Sacramento array caches the object and sends it to its client. This enables clients in Sacramento to only have to query the Sacramento array next time, rather than going across the WAN to Seattle to retrieve the same objects. In this sense, hierarchical caching brings caching closer to the clients.

Firewall Services

ISA Server provides packet and application filtering capabilities. Having been available in competing products for some time (and long waited by Microsoft aficionados), this multi-layered filtering technology grants managers the flexibility they need to provide firewall services for their network. You will discover the features of firewall services in the upcoming sections, such as application filtering, stateful inspection, VPN support, and intrusion detection.

The firewall service works with applications that are compatible with Winsock (Windows sockets) 1.1. The applications can be standard applications that use Winsock, such as RealAudio, IRC, or Telnet; or they can be custom Internet applications that you've developed. As a result, applications that do not have built-in support for proxy services can take advantage of the firewall service and connect to the Internet as if they were directly connected to it. The client applications make a request to connect to an application residing on the Internet, and the firewall service grabs the request and redirects it to the ISA Server, which in turn can forward the request to the application.

What is Winsock?

Winsock is Microsoft's implementation of sockets. Sockets are a set of Application Programming Interfaces (APIs) that enable applications to communicate using a TCP/IP address and a port number. TCP/IP addresses are used to uniquely identify a host on a TCP/IP network. The port number is used by TCP/IP internally to route the packets to the proper destination. For example, SMTP uses port 25. Therefore, when packets are sent to port 25, they are automatically routed to the SMTP service. In short, sockets enable you to open the channels, transfer the data, and then close the channels.

Packet Filtering

With *packet filtering*, ISA Server reads the protocol, port number, destination, and source address of each packet when it reaches the server. Only packets going to valid addresses and valid ports are allowed to proceed.

There are two types of packet filters: *allow filters* and *block filters*. Allow filters are exception filters, meaning all packet types are automatically blocked unless you specifically allow them. Block filters simply block specific ports. For example, you can create an allow filter for TCP port 110 to allow Post Office Protocol version 3 (POP3) traffic. Then you can create a block filter to block access for certain Internet clients so they can't communicate on port 110 of your ISA Server.

Application Filtering

Application filtering enables each packet in an application's data stream to be inspected as it passes through the firewall. This enables ISA Server to determine whether the packet contains any harmful commands, such as denial-of-service attacks oriented to a specific service or port. If the packets are harmful, they can be discarded.

At this point, it might be helpful to revisit Figure 1.1 depicting the ISA Server architecture. As you can see, the miscellaneous filters such as FTP, SMTP, and so on, inspect packets as they go through the service (Firewall or Web Proxy) to the Internet. The same is true for inbound traffic coming into the internal network as it goes through the service.

Filtering is covered in more detail in Chapter 4, "ISA Security Concepts Part II."

Stateful Inspection

Stateful inspection not only examines packets that are passing through the ISA Server computer, but also examines the data inside the packets as they are passing through. Let's look at the differences between standard packet filtering and stateful inspection. If you are going to a large arena to see a circus, there will be someone at the gate to make sure that you have a ticket to get inside. This is the same concept as packet filtering. It determines whether or not you (the data) should be permitted to enter the arena (internal network).

However, if you are going to a major rock concert, not only will you need a ticket, there is also the possibility that you will be patted down by the security guards at the gate checking for the possibility of weapons. This is the same concept as stateful inspection. Stateful inspection, in addition to only allowing the proper data types inside your corporate network, also 'pats down' the data to verify that the data means no harm.

VPN Support

A *virtual private network (VPN)* simply extends the capabilities of your private network (intranet) to a public network (the Internet). In a typical VPN scenario, you will create a secure VPN tunnel from your home network to your corporate network, using the Internet as a backbone. After you are connected to your corporate network, you will be able to perform several functions that you normally perform while you are at work, such as accessing documents on a file server, printing, accessing the Internet, using e-mail, and running various applications.

Windows 2000 includes support for VPN technology. ISA Server provides three wizards to establish VPN connections.

- Local ISA VPN Wizard
- Remote ISA VPN Wizard
- Setup Clients to ISA Server VPN Wizard

VPNs are covered in more detail in Chapter 3, "ISA Security Concepts Part I."

Intrusion Detection

ISA Server provides a built-in *intrusion detection* mechanism. Microsoft licensed the intrusion detection functionality from an Atlanta-based company called Internet Security Systems, Inc. One of the issues with Proxy Server 2.0 was that its functionality did not provide for real-world issues, such as dealing with "ping of death" attacks or port scans. ISA Server not only identifies these common attacks, but can also send alerts via e-mail to the network administrator when these attacks occur. In addition, you can log information and provide reports on these log files.

There are several attacks that ISA Server considers "intrusions." These events include the following:

- Windows out of band
- Land
- Ping of death
- IP half scan
- UDP bomb
- Port scan

As you can see in Figure 1.11, if you ask ISA Server to detect port scans, then you can also configure the number of attacks on well-known ports and the number of ports that are attacked before ISA Server will send you an alert.

NOTE

The well-known ports are assigned and managed by Internet Assigned Named Authority (IANA). Port numbers between 0 and 1023 are considered well-known ports. For more detailed information on port number ranges and TCP/IP port assignments, check out Appendix C.

Intrusion detection is covered in more detail in Chapter 4.

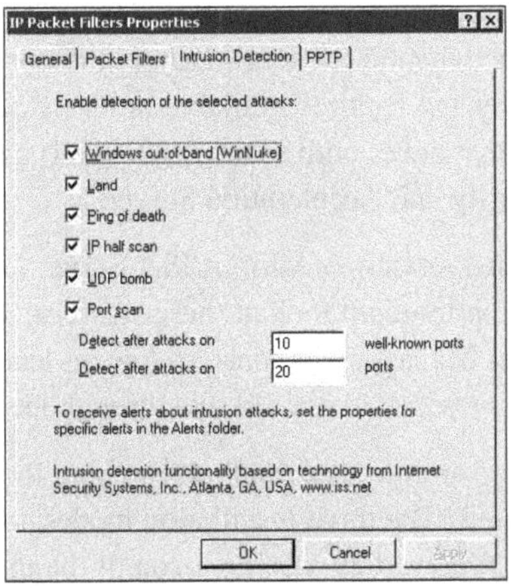

FIGURE 1.11
Events considered "intrusions" by ISA Server.

Hosting Services

ISA Server provides the capability to publish both Web and server services (for example, mail servers) to the Internet. This provides an extra level of protection, because Internet access is only allowed to the ISA Server, instead of multiple servers that reside inside the firewall.

Access to the servers can be controlled by using publishing rules. The rules control access to the published resource by Active Directory users or computers. These rules can also be used to set which authentication method is used, and whether Secure Sockets Layer (SSL) and server certificates are required. For example, you might permit anonymous, or guest, access to your public Web site, but require a user to log in using an Active Directory user account to access a secure Web area.

Server publishing rules control inbound access from external clients to the servers located behind the ISA Server computer. Web publishing rules offer the same functionality, but for inbound Web-based requests to the Web servers located behind the ISA Server. Web publishing rules are available in all three ISA Server modes. Server publishing rules apply only in Firewall and Integrated mode.

Summary

In Chapter 1, you were introduced to Microsoft's ISA Server 2000, an integrated firewall and caching solution that supports dynamic packet filtering, intrusion detection, and scheduled caching. ISA Server 2000 takes the features available in Proxy Server 2.0 to the next level. It adds a host of other features that cover both security (firewall) and acceleration (caching), hence the name Internet Security and Acceleration Server.

This first chapter presented an overview of various ISA Server features and services. In subsequent chapters, you will take an in-depth look at these services, and also learn how to configure them using the ISA Server Management console. As you learn how to install, configure, and manage these services, you will find helpful tips throughout the book.

We also looked at ISA Server's architecture, and talked about the differences between the Standard and Enterprise editions. The three installation modes—Firewall, Cache, and Integrated— were explained, followed by a comparison of the three ISA Server clients: Firewall, SecureNAT, and Web Proxy.

We covered the firewall services, such as packet filtering, application filtering, stateful inspection, intrusion detection, and the support for VPNs. These services form the foundation for ISA Server's firewall capabilities. In the last section, hosting services were addressed. These services enable you to host (or publish) servers on your private network to the outside world without compromising your security.

In the next chapter, you will learn how to install ISA Server. From hardware requirements to step-by-step installation process, you'll find in-depth information on not only installing ISA Server, but also configuring various types of clients.

ISA Server Installation and Configuration

IN THIS CHAPTER

- **ISA Server Hardware Requirements** 30

- **Pre-Installation Considerations** 33

- **Installing ISA Server Step-By-Step** 37

- **Uninstalling or Reinstalling ISA Server Step-By-Step** 48

- **Running an Unattended Server Installation** 49

- **Default ISA Server Settings** 50

- **Migrating from Proxy Server 2.0** 50

- **How Proxy Server 2.0 Tasks are Performed in ISA Server** 53

- **ISA Server Clients** 53

- **Configuring the H.323 Gatekeeper Service** 63

- **Summary** 68

This chapter will provide you with step-by-step instructions on how to install Microsoft's ISA Server 2000. The instructions assume that you are installing the Enterprise Edition of ISA Server, and that you are installing it in Integrated mode. If you are not, then you will need to skip some portions of this chapter.

> **NOTE**
>
> Microsoft offers a free 120-day trial version of ISA Server 2000. Downloading this free evaluation version will give you the opportunity to check out the product for four months before you purchase it. Download a free version at `http://www.microsoft.com/isaserver/evaluation/trial/default.asp`.

ISA Server Hardware Requirements

Before you jump into the installation of ISA Server, let's first talk about the hardware requirements. According to Microsoft, the minimum requirements for both the Enterprise Edition and the Standard Edition are as follows:

- 300MHz or higher Intel Pentium II-compatible CPU
- Windows 2000 Server and Advanced Server with Service Pack 2 or later; or Windows 2000 Datacenter Server
- 256MB of RAM
- 20MB of hard disk space
- Local hard disk formatted with NTFS
- One network card for internal interface
- One network card, analog modem, ISDN adapter, or DSL adapter for external interface

Enterprise Edition, which supports arrays, has an additional requirement—for arrays and advanced configuration options, Active Directory must be available on the network.

> **NOTE**
>
> At the time of this writing, Microsoft's Web site incorrectly stated that on Windows 2000 Server and Advanced Server, Service Pack 2 is required. You can successfully install ISA Server after installing Windows 2000 Service Pack 1. Although Service Pack 1 is the minimum requirement for ISA Server, Service Pack 2 or later is highly recommended.

So now you know what the minimum hardware requirements are for ISA Server computer, as advertised by Microsoft. However, the "minimum" hardware requirements are usually different, and always lower, than "recommended" requirements. Although the actual hardware requirements for ISA Server will depend on several factors, such as your deployment configuration, network bandwidth, number of clients, and the installed features, a good place to start will be the recommended hardware requirements for Windows 2000 Server.

With the cost of hardware dropping drastically, especially the cost of memory and hard drives, even in a small business environment I suggest you start with a 1GHz Pentium III with 512MB of RAM to run ISA Server. Needless to say, your mileage may vary, so you need to monitor your server's performance and adjust accordingly. Most businesses tend to run ISA Server in Integrated mode, which puts a lot more load on the server than if you were to choose, for instance, Cache mode.

Table 2.1 lists Microsoft's official requirements for forward caching. Table 2.2 lists my own recommendations.

TABLE 2.1 Microsoft's Forward Caching Requirements

Number of users	ISA Server computer	RAM	Disk space allocated for caching
< = 500	Pentium II, 300MHz	256MB	2–4GB
500–1,000	Dual Pentium III, 550MHz	256MB	10GB
> 1,000	Two ISA Server computers with Pentium III, 550MHz	256MB for each server	10GB for each server

TABLE 2.2 Author's Forward Caching Recommendations

Number of users	ISA Server computer	RAM	Disk space allocated for caching
< = 500	Pentium III, 1GHz	512MB	20GB
500–1,000	Dual Pentium III, 1GHz	512MB	40GB
> 1,000	Two ISA Server computers with Dual Pentium III, 1GHz	1GB for each server	20GB for each server

As you can see from these tables, Microsoft suggests that for up to 1000 users you use a Pentium III 550Mhz with only 256MB of RAM for forward caching. If I may borrow a phrase from John McEnroe: "You can *not* be serious!" I don't recommend using less than 512MB of

RAM on any Windows 2000 server—period. With memory prices falling, you can buy 512MB for about the cost of dinner at a decent restaurant.

For reverse caching, your goal should be to ensure that the objects you are caching for Internet clients fit in ISA Server's RAM. Therefore, depending on the size of the contents that you are publishing, you may require a large amount of memory. For reverse caching, I suggest you use at least a Pentium III 1GHz processor for up to 250 hits per second. Thereafter, for each additional 250 hits per second, add another ISA Server.

For Firewall and SecureNAT clients, a Pentium III with 1GB RAM should be the starting point to handle a rate of data transfer of about 50 megabits per second (Mbps) for your internal clients. For anything more than that, I recommend that you add an additional ISA Server for each 50 Mbps of data transfer rate.

If you are using arrays, use the following guidelines in Table 2.3.

TABLE 2.3   Author's Recommendations for Arrays

Number of concurrent users per array	ISA Server computer	Number of ISA Servers per array	RAM per Server	Disk space for cache per server
1000	Dual Pentium III, 1GHz	2	512MB	40GB
5,000	Dual Pentium III, 1GHz or faster	4	1GB	60GB
20,000	Quad Pentium III, 1GHz or faster	10	1GB	80GB

As I've stated before, your mileage may vary—depending on a lot of factors. You'll have to monitor your ISA Server's performance in your particular environment to get more realistic numbers. If you are budgeting for ISA Server hardware, these numbers can be helpful as a starting point.

Additional Considerations

Here are some additional considerations. It is best to put system, cache, and log files on separate physical partitions. For redundancy, you should implement Redundant Array of Inexpensive Disks (RAID). Even if you use RAID Level 1 for system partition, I suggest you use RAID Level 5 for your ISA cache and log file partitions.

For security reasons, it's best to disable the services that you don't need. Table 2.4 lists some of the services that can be disabled on the ISA Server computer, unless you really need them.

TABLE 2.4 Services That Can Be Disabled

Service	Description
Computer Browser	Keeps track of computers on the network. Provides a list of resources to the network clients.
Distributed File System	Manages volumes across a network.
Distributed Link Tracking (Server)	Keeps track of files moved between NTFS volumes in a domain.
Distributed Link Tracking (client)	Notifies you of files moved between NTFS volumes in a domain.
Fax	Responsible for sending and receiving faxes.
Internet Information Service 5.0	Provides Web services—consists of several components. ISA Server doesn't require IIS, so you can remove it if you don't need it.
License Logging	Keeps track of software licenses. Make sure you are complying with the licensing requirements and disable this service.
Telephony	Provides support for Telephony API (TAPI).

I recommend that you install Terminal Services in administration mode on every Windows 2000 Server in your network for remote administration. The licensing requirements for Terminal Services can be complicated. Even if you aren't running Terminal Server in Application Server mode, it will be to your advantage to learn about the Terminal Services licensing. Check out my article "Terminal Services Licensing for Windows 2000" on the Microsoft TechNet CD or online at http://www.microsoft.com/technet/treeview/default.asp?url=/technet/columns/profwin/pw0601.asp.

Pre-Installation Considerations

If you are installing ISA Server in an array for the first time in your Windows 2000 domain, you need to install the ISA Server schema to the Active Directory. You only have to install the schema once. All future ISA Server installations in your domain can use this schema.

Now that we've got the hardware requirements out of the way, let's talk about the ISA Server installation. If you have the ISA Server CD, insert it so you can get familiar with the ISA Server autorun console, as shown in Figure 2.1.

2

ISA SERVER INSTALLATION AND CONFIGURATION

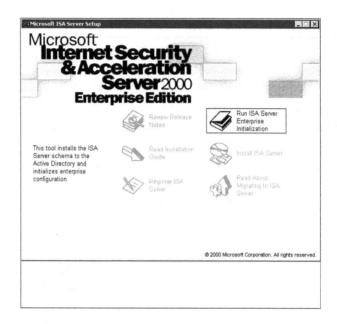

FIGURE 2.1

The ISA Server installation autorun console.

TIP

If you have copied the ISA Server CD-ROM to a shared network drive, running
`%path%:\ISAautorun.exe` will open the autorun screen, where `%path%` is the network
path where you have copied the files.

The autorun screen presents the following six choices:

- Review Release Notes—Additionally, you can open this file at `%path%:\readme.htm`.
- Read Installation and Deployment Guide—Found at `%path%:\isa\isastart.htm`.
- Register ISA Server—To be done after installation.
- Run ISA Server Enterprise Initialization—Performed later in this chapter.
- Install ISA Server—Performed later in this chapter.
- Read About Migrating to ISA Server—Found at `%path%:\Pre-Migration-Considerations.htm`.

> **TIP**
>
> Although ISA Server can be installed on Windows 2000 Advanced Server, which will support up to 8 processors, and Windows 2000 Datacenter Server, which will support up to 32 processors, ISA Server Standard Edition will only install on these servers if they have no more than 4 CPUs. The Enterprise Edition doesn't have this limitation and it can be installed on computers with more than 4 CPUs.

Installing the ISA Server Schema Step-By-Step

To install the ISA Server schema, select Run ISA Server Enterprise Initialization from the ISA Server autorun menu. Alternatively, you can run %path%:\isa\i386\msisaent.exe, where %path% is the location of your installation files.

To perform the installation correctly, make sure that you are a member of the administrators group on the local machine. Additionally, you must be a member of the Enterprise Admins and Schema Admins groups on the domain where you are updating the schema.

> **TIP**
>
> Installing the schema is only available on ISA Server Enterprise Edition.

When you choose to install the schema, the message in Figure 2.2 appears. Please note that Active Directory schema does not support the deletion of schema objects, so once they are installed, they cannot be deleted. Click Yes to continue.

FIGURE 2.2

Schema installation message.

The next screen, shown in Figure 2.3, will determine whether you want to use an enterprise policy, array policy, or mixed policy. In this screen, you also determine whether or not you will allow publishing rules or force packet filtering on the array.

To enable mixed policy, make sure that the Use This Enterprise Policy radio button is selected (along with the enterprise policy from the drop-down box,; the default policy is called

Enterprise Policy 1), and also that the Allow Array-Level Policy Rules That Restrict Enterprise Policy checkbox is checked. You can accept the defaults at this screen, and after the installation modify the enterprise policy settings for any array in an enterprise. Click OK to continue.

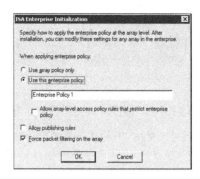

FIGURE 2.3

ISA Enterprise initialization.

Depending on your system, updating the schema in Active Directory can take a long time, but generally it takes only a few minutes. After this process is finished, a dialog box like the one seen in Figure 2.4 will appear to inform you that the schema has been successfully imported in the Active Directory. If you have more than one domain controller in your Active Directory domain, make sure that you wait for Active Directory replication before you install ISA Server as an array member. Instead of waiting for the Active Directory replication to occur, you can manually replicate the Active Directory database using Active Directory Sites and Services. Click OK to finish the schema installation.

FIGURE 2.4

Installation Successful message.

At this stage, the schema has been updated. Any future servers that will be added to this or any other array will not require you to go through the same steps.

> **TIP**
>
> You can run the ISA Server Enterprise Initialization Tool remotely, using Windows 2000 Terminal Services to update the schema. You can also install ISA Server 2000 remotely.

Installing ISA Server on a Windows 2000 Terminal Server

Most organizations will not install ISA Server and Terminal Server in Application mode on the same computer, especially when they are running the Enterprise Edition. However, if you are a small business and have a need to run them on the same computer, you should be aware of some points. On a Windows 2000 Server running Terminal Server in Application Server mode, you can't use the autorun option or ISA Server setup directly by executing `msisaent.exe`. In order to do an install such as this, the Terminal Server must be in Install mode to install applications. You can either use Add/Remove Programs in Control Panel to run the ISA Server setup, or you can use the following command at the command prompt:

`change user /install.`

After the installation is complete, make sure you put the Terminal Server back in Execute mode by using the following command:

`change user /execute`

For more information or help, enter this command at the command prompt:

`change user /?`

Updating the schema does not require rebooting your ISA Server computer.

Installing ISA Server Step-By-Step

It is now time to install ISA Server. Before you begin the ISA Server installation, you need to make sure that you have Windows 2000 Service Pack 1 or later installed on the computer. Otherwise, the setup will stop in the middle and prompt you to install the Service Pack and re-run the setup again. Service Pack 1 is available on the ISA Server CD under the `\Support\Windows2000_SP1` folder. Run the Service Pack 1 by double-clicking `sp1network.exe` to start the installation. After you're finished, you'll have to reboot the computer.

Assuming you have already installed Service Pack 1, you are ready to install the ISA Server Enterprise Edition. Use the ISA Server CD and select Install ISA Server from the autorun menu, or run %path%:\isa\setup.exe, where %path% is the path of the installation files. On the Microsoft ISA Server (Enterprise Edition) Setup screen, click Continue.

The CD KEY and EULA

Enter the 10-digit CD Key when prompted. The number is located on the sticker on the back of your CD case. On the next screen you are reminded to make a note of your Product ID, as shown in Figure 2.5. This is the number that Microsoft will ask you to give them if you call for technical support. If you forget to write down this number, you can find it listed in the About button on the Help menu.

FIGURE 2.5
Product ID notification.

At this point, the setup process searches your machine for any previously installed components. After this process is complete, the end user license agreement (EULA) appears. Read the agreement and if you agree, click I Agree to continue.

Installation Options

Figure 2.6 shows the main setup screen. You have the option of performing a typical, full, or custom installation. For the purposes of this book, we will perform a custom installation, so click on the Custom Installation box to continue. The custom installation defaults are what a typical installation would install. In addition, you have the option to change the installation folder where ISA Server will be installed.

FIGURE 2.6

ISA Server installation options.

Figure 2.7 shows the custom setup installation screen. There are three options to install: ISA Services, Add-in Services, and Administration Tools. ISA Services, which has no sub-options, is the option for installing the ISA Server "engine," and the caching, filtering, and publishing components. This option is checked by default.

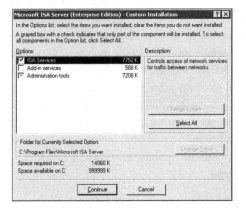

FIGURE 2.7

Custom setup installation options.

Highlight Add-in Services, and click the Change Option button. The screen that is shown in Figure 2.8 appears. You have two options that you can choose. The H.323 Gatekeeper service is selected by default. The H.323 service enables you to use NetMeeting or other multimedia services. The Message Screener is used to perform content filtering on incoming SMTP traffic. You can install the Message Screener only if SMTP service is installed on the ISA Server computer. If you choose not to install the Message Screener, you will still have some message filtering capabilities available to you. We will select both the H.323 and the Message Screener, as shown in Figure 2.8. The H.323 Gatekeeper service is discussed in more detail later in this chapter.

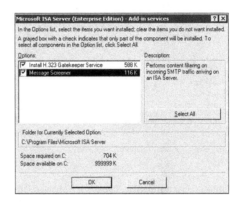

FIGURE 2.8
Add-in services options.

You should now be back to the main custom installation menu. Select Administration Tools, and click the Change Option button. The administration tools enable you to centrally manage ISA Server components and add-in services. In fact, you can install only the administration tools and manage another standalone ISA Server remotely. In that case, you don't need to have ISA Server running on the local computer that is being used to manage the remote server. You have two options when you click on Administration Tools and select Change Option. You can either select the ISA Management Administration Tool, which is selected by default, or you can select the H.323 Gatekeeper Administration Tool option. H.323 Gatekeeper Service offers registered clients the capability to use real-time multimedia conferencing over the Internet. Again, go ahead and select both the options, as shown in Figure 2.9, so you can have all the possible tools available to you.

At this point you are looking at Figure 2.10, which shows all the options that you've selected. Essentially, this screen shows the same results that you would have achieved if you were to select the Full Installation option in Figure 2.6.

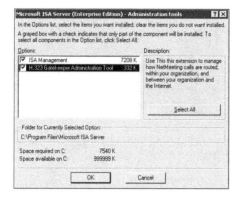

FIGURE 2.9

The H.323 Gatekeeper Administration Tool option.

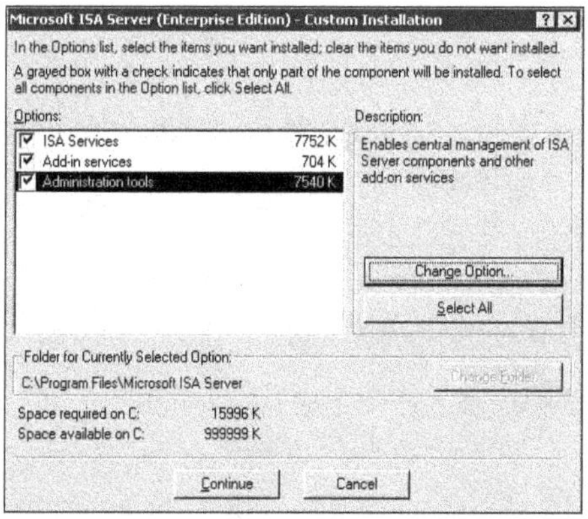

FIGURE 2.10

Adding Administration tools.

Array Selection

After you click Continue, ISA will search for the schema in Active Directory. When it is found, the screen shown in Figure 2.11 appears. Here you will determine whether the server will be a member of an array or a standalone server. Unless you are absolutely sure that your network will not grow, click Yes. For the purposes of this book, we will install ISA Server in an array.

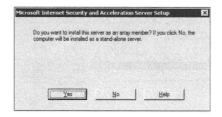

FIGURE 2.11
Choosing between an array and a standalone server.

Because you don't have an existing array to join, you will provide a name for the array. By default, the name provided is %servername% Array, where %servername% is the DNS name of your computer. After you have selected a name for the array, you will have the option to configure the enterprise policy settings and decide how they should be applied to the array, as shown in Figure 2.12. Enterprise policy consists of *site and content rules* and *protocol rules*. An enterprise administrator can apply an enterprise policy to all the arrays in the enterprise. Here are your options:

- Use Default Enterprise Policy Settings: The new array will use the default enterprise policy settings that were configured by the enterprise administrator. You must use this option if you are not the enterprise administrator.

- Use Custom Enterprise Policy Settings: The new array will use the custom enterprise policy settings, which you can only configure if you are an enterprise administrator.

If you choose the custom enterprise policy settings option, then the rest of the remaining options are available to you. Here are your options:

- Use Array Policy Only: If you select this option, the enterprise policy will not be applied to the array.

- Use This Enterprise Policy: The policy you select from the drop-down box will be applied to the array. You also have the option to select Allow Array-level Access Policy Rules That Restrict Enterprise Policy. Both the enterprise policy and the array policy will govern the array. The array policy may impose some additional limitations, but it won't be more permissive than the enterprise policy. In other words, the enterprise policy will always have the final say.

- Allow Publishing Rules: This option will let you publish servers by using Web publishing rules.

- Force Packet Filtering on This Array: Although packet filtering can't be enabled at the enterprise level, you can decide to force packet filtering at the array level.

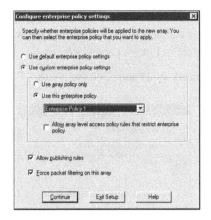

FIGURE 2.12
Configuring enterprise policy settings.

Installation Mode

Select an appropriate option and click Continue. This will take you to the screen seen in Figure 2.13, where you will select one of the three server modes. Here are your options:

Firewall Mode

This mode gives you enterprise firewall capabilities. You can secure your network by creating rules that enable you to control the traffic between your internal network and the Internet. This mode also enables you to publish internal servers, so people from the Internet can securely access your internally published servers.

Cache Mode

Cache mode will improve your network access by enabling you to quickly access objects from the cache instead of the Internet. You can control what objects are cached, and therefore save network bandwidth.

> **TIP**
>
> Cache mode is recommended only for ISA Server computers that are not directly connected to the Internet. If your ISA Server is directly connected to the Internet, then use the Integrated mode, which provides all the features of Firewall and Cache mode.

Integrated Mode

The Integrated mode gives you the best of both worlds. It enables you to use your ISA Server for all the Firewall and Cache features.

Not all features are available in all modes. The Integrated mode gives you all the features as mentioned previously, but the features that are available in Firewall and Cache modes vary. For a list of features that are available in Firewall and Cache mode, see Chapter 1.

Let's choose the default Integrated mode and click Continue.

FIGURE 2.13
Choosing the ISA Server installation mode.

Stopping IIS

ISA Server setup will stop all relevant services, including any services you might have if you are upgrading from Proxy Server, as well as any services from IIS if you have it installed on the same machine. IIS is installed by default in Windows 2000, so you should see the message shown in Figure 2.14 informing you that the IIS publishing service (W3SVC) will be stopped. Pay close attention to what else this box says. It is telling you that if you have IIS running on the ISA Server computer, you should either remove IIS or reconfigure your existing sites so they won't use port 80 or 8080, as these ports will be used by the ISA Server computer. Click OK to continue, and the setup process will continue stopping all relevant services.

FIGURE 2.14
Stopping IIS publishing services.

Cache Configuration

Next you will be prompted to configure the cache, as shown in Figure 2.15. This option is only applicable if you install ISA Server in Cache or Integrated mode. Here you need to configure an appropriate cache size. Cache can only be configured on drives that were formatted with NTFS. By default, ISA Server setup searches for a drive with the largest partition, then offers a 100MB cache configuration, as long as you have at least 150MB of free space available on that drive. Microsoft recommends that you allocate at least 100MB, plus 0.5MB for each additional Web Proxy client. For example, for 500 clients, you should allocate 350MB, as calculated below:

$$100 + (0.5 \times 500) = 350$$

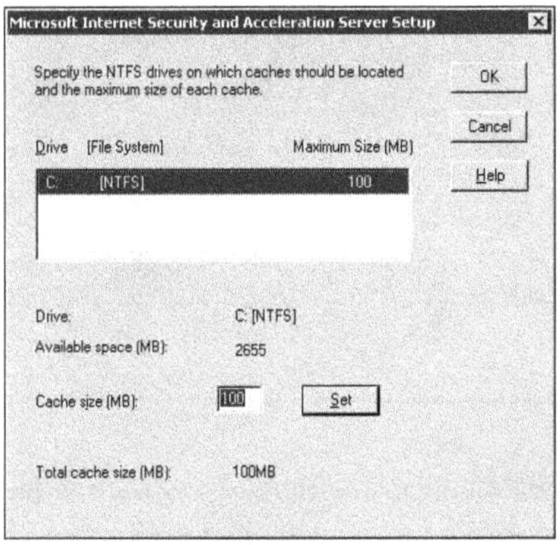

FIGURE 2.15
Configuring cache options.

Click OK to continue to the next screen.

> **TIP**
>
> When it comes to caching, you will achieve the best results when you use the fastest local drive with a low access time, a large memory buffer, and a high revolutions per minute (rpm) rate. Also, if possible, use a drive that does not contain the Windows 2000 or ISA Server system files.

LAT Configuration

If you have chosen to install ISA Server in Firewall or Integrated mode, you will see a screen asking you to construct a Local Address Table (LAT). The LAT is a table that contains all the internal IP address ranges on your private network, including the IP address of the internal interface of the ISA Server computer. The LAT is used by the internal clients to communicate with external networks. You can enter a range of IP addresses on the left-hand side, click Add, and they will be entered into the LAT, which is shown on the right-hand side. To remove a range from the LAT, click the entry on the right-hand side and click Remove. You can also let ISA Server construct a LAT automatically for you using the Windows 2000 routing table. To perform this function, click the Table button to get to Figure 2.16.

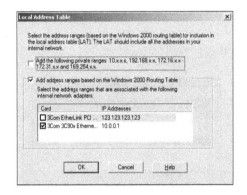

FIGURE 2.16
Constructing a LAT.

Let's take a closer look at what's happening here. Constructing an incorrect LAT can be disastrous, so be careful and make sure you understand the options for building a LAT.

If you don't feel comfortable building a LAT this way (with what's shown in Figure 2.16), then the simplest thing to do is to go back to the previous screen and manually add the range of IP addresses that belong to your internal network. For example, use the range from 10.0.0.0 to 10.255.255.255, and then click Add. That's it! You are done constructing a simple LAT entry.

If you want to add additional ranges, you can either add them manually or let the setup program build a LAT based on the routing table. The upper check box in Figure 2.16 permits you to include the private IP addresses reserved by the Internet Assigned Numbers Authority (IANA). These ranges cannot be used on the Internet, so they can be safely used on your private network.

TIP

For more information about IANA's Web site and TCP/IP address assignment, see Appendix C.

The lower half of Figure 2.16 permits you to add addresses from Windows 2000's routing table. In my case, I am using a 3COM EtherLink PCI adapter for my external network connected to the Internet, and a 3COM 3C90X Ethernet Adapter for my internal network. I will only select the second adapter, leave all other boxes unchecked, and let the routing table construct the LAT. A setup message, seen in Figure 2.17, warns you that the LAT has been constructed based on the routing table. Be aware that if the routing table is incorrect, then the LAT will be incorrect too.

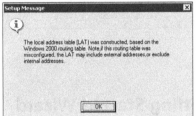

FIGURE 2.17

LAT warning message.

WARNING

LAT should only contain internal IP addresses. Make sure that there are no external addresses in the LAT. If the routing table was configured incorrectly, the LAT may contain incorrect information. For example, it might include some external addresses and exclude internal addresses.

Based on the options that I selected, Figure 2.18 shows the LAT entries on my ISA Server computer. This LAT includes only the IP address range used on the internal network. Notice that it doesn't include any valid IP address ranges that can be used on the Internet. If you made a mistake in constructing a LAT, don't worry; simply go back and reconstruct the LAT again by clicking on Construct Table as shown in Figure 2.18.

After you have constructed the LAT, the setup program will stop the relevant services and continue copying files to the hard disk. Finally, it will update your system, register the ISA Server COM objects, then start ISA Server services.

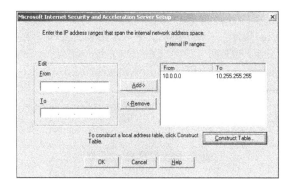

FIGURE 2.18
LAT entries on ISA Server computer.

The ISA Server Getting Started Wizard

When the services have been restarted, you have the option of starting the ISA Server Getting Started Wizard by launching the ISA Management Tool. If you are new to ISA Server, it is best to use the wizard to configure your server. Once you become familiar with the product, you can manually configure ISA Servers on other computers. You can always start this wizard in the ISA Server Management console after the product has been installed to configure the server.

If you decide to use the Getting Started Wizard, you are informed that the ISA Server setup has completed successfully. Congratulations! You have finished the ISA Server installation.

The next section covers the topic of uninstalling or reinstalling the ISA Server.

Uninstalling or Reinstalling ISA Server Step-By-Step

If you need to uninstall ISA Server, use the Add/Remove Programs option in the Control Panel. Highlight ISA Server and click the Remove button. You will be asked to confirm that you really want to uninstall the ISA Server. Click Yes.

The uninstall process will search for already installed components, and then stop all ISA Server and other relevant services. You will then be asked whether you want to remove the logs and configuration backup files generated by Microsoft ISA Server.

After you click Yes or No, the ISA Server removal process will remove all COM objects related to installation. If you selected Yes, all related files will be removed at this time.

Next, all relevant services are stopped and all files are removed. After the files are removed, your system is updated. This may take several minutes, so be patient. Finally, all services that were not removed are restarted. You will then receive a message that the removal of ISA Server was successful. Click OK to finish the uninstall process and close the Add/Remove Programs window.

The reinstallation process is very similar to the installation process, so we will not go through the complete routine. You will need to reinstall ISA Server if you had installed the server in one mode and now want to change the installation mode, or you installed the server in an array and now want to install it as a standalone server.

Running an Unattended Server Installation

You can install ISA Server unattended by using a file called MsISAund.ini. If the Setup program is unable to locate this file in the root directory of the first fixed drive, it searches for it in the path.

You can also uninstall and reinstall ISA Server using the unattended setup options at the command line. Here's the step-by-step procedure:

1. Create a file called MsISAund.ini in the root directory of the C drive on your computer where you want to install ISA Server.

2. Go to the command prompt and enter the following:

   %path%\isa\setup /qt /k"CD Key" [/Q [0|1|T] [/R] [/U]

   where %path% refers to the path to the ISA Server installation files. You may point to a local or a remote path on the network. The parameters seen previously are highlighted here.

- CD Key: The CD key which can be located on the back cover of the ISA Server CD-ROM.

- /Q [0|1|T]: Used to perform unattended setups. The 0 option will display the exit dialog box, 1 and T will not display the exit dialog boxes.

- /R: Used to perform unattended reinstallations.

- /U: Used to perform unattended uninstallations.

TIP

Before the unattended setup installs, verify that the LAT section of MsISAund.ini is correct. The unattended setup will fail if it doesn't find the IP address of at least one internal network adapter card in its LAT section of the MsISAund.ini file.

For information on creating the MsISAund.ini file, go to ISA Server Help and search for the word "MsISAund.ini." The Help file lists all the possible entries that can be used in this file.

Default ISA Server Settings

Table 2.5 lists some of the default settings used by ISA Server after the initial installation.

TABLE 2.5   ISA Server's Default Settings

ISA Server Feature	Default Setting
Access control	The default site and content rule called Allow Rule permits unlimited access to all clients all the time. However, because there are no protocol rules defined by default, access is prohibited. This is true unless you use an enterprise policy.
Alerts	All the alerts are active, except for the following: all port scan attack, dropped packets, protocol violation, and UDP bomb attack.
Caching	HTTP and FTP caching is enabled. Active caching is disabled. The cache size and the drive options are configured during the setup.
Client configuration	For Firewall and Web Proxy clients, automatic discovery is enabled.
LAT	Entries are configured during installation.
Packet filtering	Enabled in Firewall and Integrated mode, but disabled in Cache mode.
Publishing	All client requests are discarded. Internal servers do not publish to the outside world.
Routing	Web Proxy clients have direct access to the Internet addresses.

Migrating from Proxy Server 2.0

Microsoft provides a migration path from Proxy Server 2.0 to ISA Server 2000. This means that the migration will support Proxy Server's settings, cache configuration, monitoring settings, and the server rules in general. In addition, you can expect continued support for Winsock Proxy client.

Before you start the migration, make sure you back up the Proxy Server configuration. In fact, it's a good idea to back up the entire server, in case something goes wrong and you need to revert to the original configuration.

> **NOTE**
>
> There is no direct upgrade available from Proxy Server 1.0, Microsoft BackOffice 4.0, or Small Business Server 4.0 to ISA Server 2000.

Migrating Proxy Server 2.0 from Windows NT 4.0

Here's how you can upgrade from Proxy Server 2.0 if it is running on Windows NT 4.0:

1. Log on to Windows NT 4.0 as Administrator.
2. Disable all Proxy Server services. These services include the following:
   - wspsrv (Winsock Proxy service)
   - mspadmin (Proxy Server Administration)
   - mailalrt (Alert Notification Service)
   - w3svc (WWW Publishing Service)

   You can either use the GUI or the command prompt to stop the services. To stop the services at the command prompt, type the following:

   ```
   net stop service_name
   ```

   where *service_name* is the name of the service, for example, wspsrv, w3svc, and so on.
3. Start the Windows 2000 upgrade process.
4. When the upgrade is complete, install the latest Service Pack. At minimum, you'll need Service Pack 1.
5. Start the ISA Server installation. For details, see the beginning of this chapter. However, once you start the ISA Server upgrade, you can't go back to Proxy Server 2.0. That's why it is crucial that you back up your server before the upgrade.

> **TIP**
>
> During an upgrade from Windows NT 4.0 to Windows 2000, if you receive a message that Proxy Server is not supported on Windows 2000, simply ignore it.

The Effects of Migration

As mentioned earlier, most of the Proxy Server 2.0 configuration is migrated to ISA Server 2000. Here's a summary of how the configuration information is migrated:

- By default, Proxy Server 2.0 listens to HTTP requests on port 80, but ISA Server listens on port 8080. If you want to, you can also configure the ISA Server to listen on port 80.
- All cache configuration information is migrated to ISA Server, including the size of the cache and drive information. However, the cache contents are not migrated because of the difference in cache engines between the two products. Existing cache contents on Proxy Server 2.0 are deleted.
- Depending on the client browsers, users may not be able to access the Internet. By default, Proxy Server 2.0 uses Anonymous and Integrated authentication. For Web requests, ISA Server uses Windows Integrated authentication by default. Not all browsers support Windows Integrated authentication (Netscape is a good example). As a result, users may not get authenticated, and won't be able to access the Internet by default. You can simply enable the Basic authentication. For secure access, use Basic authentication with SSL.
- You can use mixed chains of Proxy Server 2.0 and ISA Server 2000 in your environment.
- Publishing servers in Proxy Server 2.0 must be configured as Winsock Proxy clients. In ISA Server, the publishing servers are configured as SecureNAT clients.
- Publishing properties in Proxy Server 2.0 are migrated to Web publishing rules.
- Web Proxy routing rules get migrated to routing rules in ISA Server.
- Domain filters in Proxy Server 2.0 get migrated to site and content rules.
- Proxy Server 2.0 SOCKS rules do not get migrated to ISA Server. In addition, Web Proxy service permissions are also migrated.
- Migrating a Proxy Server 2.0 to a standalone server migrates most of the rules and configuration information.
- If you migrate a Proxy Server 2.0 to a new ISA Server array, the default settings in the enterprise policy will determine how the rules are migrated to the ISA Server.

Migrating Proxy Server 2.0 from Windows 2000

To migrate Proxy Server 2.0 to ISA Server on a Windows 2000 computer, the choice you need to make is whether you want to upgrade ISA Server as a standalone server or install it in an array. As mentioned previously, migrating Proxy Server 2.0 to a standalone server will automatically migrate most of the settings. If you migrate it to an array, the default settings in the enterprise policy will determine how the Proxy Server rules are migrated to the ISA Server.

The steps for migrating are the same as the installation steps described earlier in this chapter.

How Proxy Server 2.0 Tasks are Performed in ISA Server

Table 2.6 shows how you can perform some of the common tasks in ISA Server as compared to Proxy Server 2.0.

TABLE 2.6 Comparing Proxy Server 2.0 Tasks to ISA Server 2000

Task Performed	Proxy Server 2.0 Method	ISA Server 2000 Method
Configuring LAT	Configure LAT from properties of any service	Construct LA. (You can also configure LDT)
Restricting access to sites or domains	Create domain filters	Create site and content rules
Configuring cache	Use Web Proxy Service properties to configure caching	Configure the cache properties for HTTP and FTP protocol
Restricting protocol usage	Configure Web Proxy or Winsock Proxy permissions to control access	Configure protocol rules
Configuring routing	Configure Routing on Web Proxy Service properties	Configure routing rules
Configuring packet filtering	Under Security, use the Packet filters tab	Configure IP packet filters
Publishing sites	Configure the properties of the Web Proxy service	Configure Web publishing rules

ISA Server Clients

There are three types of clients that are supported by ISA Server 2000. The clients are as follows:

- Firewall clients: These clients require the installation of firewall client software. They run Winsock applications that use ISA Server's firewall service.
- SecureNAT clients: These clients are network clients that do not have the firewall client software installed. They simply point to the ISA Server as their default gateway.
- Web Proxy clients: These are clients that have an HTTP 1.1-compliant browser application that is configured to use the ISA Server's Web Proxy service.

The Firewall and SecureNAT clients can potentially be the Web Proxy clients. If you configure the Web service on a client computer to use the ISA Server, then all Web-related requests are sent straight to the Web Proxy service. These requests include HTTP, HTTPS, FTP, and Gopher. All other requests will be handled by the firewall service.

Configuring Firewall Clients

Firewall clients can run on Windows 2000, Windows NT 4.0, Windows Me, Windows 98, and Windows 95 operating systems.

> **NOTE**
>
> 16-bit Winsock applications are supported only on Windows 2000 and Windows NT 4.0.

The Firewall client consists of the `mspclnt.ini` file, the `msplat.txt` file, and the Firewall client program itself. If you are familiar with Proxy Server 2.0, then you should recognize the `mspclnt.ini` and `msplat.txt` files. The `mspclnt.ini` file on the server is the master copy of the client configuration file. There is an `mspclnt.ini` file on the client computer as well. By default, this file is updated from the server every six hours. Here's a sample `mspclnt.ini` file:

```
; This file should not be edited.
; Changes to the client configuration should only be made using ISA Management.
;
[Common]
WWW-Proxy=SPARKLES
Set Browsers to use Proxy=1
Set Browsers to use Auto Config=0
Set Browsers to use Auto Detect=0
AutoDetect ISA Servers=0
WebProxyPort=8080
Configuration Url=http://SPARKLES:8080/array.dll?Get.Routing.Script
Port=1745
ServerVersion=11
Configuration Refresh Time (Hours)=6
Re-check Inaccessible Server Time (Minutes)=10
Refresh Give Up Time (Minutes)=15
Inaccessible Servers Give Up Time (Minutes)=2
[Servers Ip Addresses]
Name=SPARKLES
[Master Config]
Path1=\\SPARKLES\mspclnt\
[svchost]
```

The `msplat.txt` file on the client computer contains the local address table (LAT), which consists of the IP addresses of your internal network. This file is also updated from the server on a regular basis. The Winsock application on the client computer uses the LAT to determine whether the IP address is local or remote. If the IP address falls within the range of the internal network addresses listed in `msplat.txt`, the client makes a connection directly to the computer. If the address is not part of the internal network range, the client makes the connection through the ISA Server's Firewall service. Here's a sample from the `msplat.txt` file:

```
10.0.0.0      10.255.255.255
224.0.0.0     255.255.255.254
127.0.0.0     127.255.255.255
```

On the server, these files are located in the Clients folder, which is shared as `mspclnt`.

The `msplat.txt` file on the client is updated on a regular basis from the `msplat.txt` file on the server. What if you want a `msplat.txt` file on the client with custom entries in the LAT? Well, you can use an ASCII text editor such as Notepad to create a file and name it `LocalLAT.txt`. Place the file on the client in the Firewall Client folder. This LAT will have additional entries that you want to specify as internal IP addresses. Although your `msplat.txt` will still be updated regularly, the client will use both the `msplat.txt` and `LocalLAT.txt` files to determine whether the IP addresses are local or remote.

The `LocalLAT.txt` file may contain a single IP address that you want to include in the LAT, or it can contain a range of IP addresses. When you enter an IP address, you simply use the same IP address as the beginning and the end address of the range. Here's a sample `LocalLAT.txt` file:

```
10.2.13.125    10.2.13.125
```

Notice that the file only contains one entry that represents a single computer. The LAT on the ISA Server may not be aware of this address, so you can add this address to your `LocalLAT.txt` file.

Configuring ISA Server for Firewall Clients

To configure the ISA Server for Firewall clients, follow these steps. This configuration will be used by the Firewall clients when they refresh the settings from the ISA Server.

1. In the ISA Management console tree, click on Client Configuration.

2. Right-click the Firewall client in the right-hand window and click on Properties.

3. The Firewall client can be configured to connect to the ISA server computer either by DNS name (default), or by IP address, as shown in Figure 2.19.

4. You can also enable the clients to automatically discover the ISA Firewall by selecting the box Enable ISA Firewall Automatic Discovery in Firewall Client, also shown in Figure 2.19.

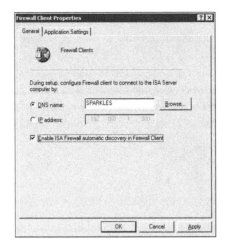

FIGURE 2.19
Configuring the Firewall client's properties on ISA Server.

NOTE

The Firewall client can automatically detect the connectivity to the ISA Server. If the connection is not there, it disables itself. This enables users to easily travel between locations, such as home and work, without reconfiguring the Firewall client.

Configuring Firewall Client's Web Browser Settings on ISA Server Computer

1. In the ISA Management console tree, click on Client Configuration.

2. Right-click the Web Browser in the right-hand window and click on Properties.

3. On the General tab, ensure that the Configure Web Browser During Firewall Client Setup check box is checked, as shown in Figure 2.20. This is the default setting.

4. You can use an automatic configuration script by choosing one of the two options shown in Figure 2.21.

5. On the Direct Access tab, you can configure the servers and domains that the client can access directly without going through the ISA Server. By default, the Bypass Proxy for Local Servers and the Directly Access Computers Specified in the Local Domain Table (LDT) boxes are already checked, as shown in Figure 2.21.

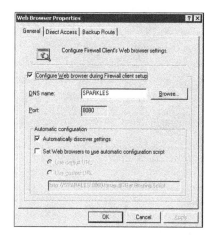

FIGURE 2.20

Configuring the Firewall client's browser settings.

2

ISA SERVER
INSTALLATION AND
CONFIGURATION

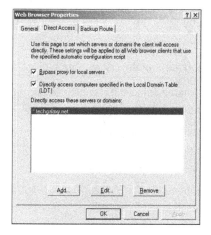

FIGURE 2.21

Configuring direct access for the Firewall client's browser settings.

6. Click on Add and add the servers or domains that should be accessed directly. You can include a range of computers or domains. If you want to add an entire domain, simply enter *.domain_name, as shown in Figure 2.22. Simply typing an asterisk (*) will include all the domains. These settings apply to clients that use automatic configuration scripts.

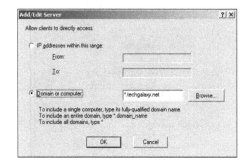

FIGURE 2.22

Configuring direct access for the clients.

7. On the Backup Route tab, you can configure a backup route that clients can use if the server becomes unavailable.

8. Check the If ISA Server Is Unavailable, Use This Backup Route to Connect to the Internet box and specify either Direct Access (default), or an Alternate ISA Server. These settings apply to clients that use automatic configuration scripts.

Configuring Firewall Client on the Client Computer

To install the Firewall client software on the client computer, follow these steps:

1. Connect to the mspclnt shared folder on the ISA Server computer and run setup.exe. For example, \\sparkles\mspclnt\setup.exe.

2. When the setup is complete, the Firewall client is enabled automatically.

3. To disable the Firewall client, go to Control Panel, double-click Firewall Client and uncheck the Enable Firewall Client box. You can also use the icon in the system tray to disable the Firewall client.

> **NOTE**
>
> The Firewall Client should not be installed on the ISA Server computer.

Configuring SecureNAT Clients

SecureNAT clients are easy to implement. All you have to do is configure a default gateway on the client (statically or dynamically using DHCP) that will route the traffic through the ISA Server. Typically, you will point the client to the ISA Server as a default gateway. However, you could route the traffic through the routers so it will go out to the Internet via the ISA Server.

Although NAT in Windows 2000 doesn't really have an authentication mechanism, you can apply ISA Server rules on the SecureNAT clients to implement security policies. For example, you can configure server publishing rules to publish servers, such as FTP servers, as SecureNAT clients.

SecureNAT clients don't keep a copy of the LAT. Therefore, when they request an object, the request is sent to the ISA Server, which decides where to send the packets. If the request is for objects on the Internet, the ISA Server computer translates the packets on behalf of the client and forwards the request to the Internet.

To configure a SecureNAT client on a simple network that doesn't contain any routers, simply point the default gateway to the ISA Server computer's internal network interface. Here is the procedure for Windows 2000 computers.

1. Right-click My Network Places and click on Properties.
2. Double-click Local Area Connection (I usually rename my Local Area Connection to the network card that I am using, such as INTEL, or 3COM) and click on Properties.
3. Double-click Internet Protocol (TCP/IP) and configure the client either to obtain an IP address and DNS server address automatically, or configure the client with a static IP address, subnet mask, default gateway, and preferred DNS server, as shown in Figure 2.23.

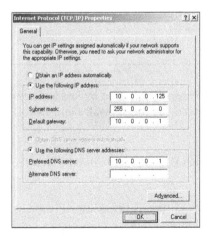

FIGURE 2.23

Configuring a SecureNAT client.

On a more complex network that includes several routers between the SecureNAT client and the ISA Server, configure the SecureNAT client's gateway to point to the last router in the chain.

> **TIP**
>
> If the SecureNAT client's default gateway is a router other than the ISA Server, make sure that it doesn't discard packets destined for the Internet. Let the ISA Server decide what packets to discard.

On a typical network, the SecureNAT clients will require access to objects on the internal network as well as the Internet. You need to ensure that the clients are configured to use an internal DNS server. The internal DNS server must have the capability to resolve both internal and external IP addresses. One way to achieve this objective is to forward requests from internal DNS server to your ISP so that external addresses on the Internet can also be resolved.

Configuring Web Proxy Clients

Similar to the SecureNAT clients, Web Proxy clients do not require any software installation. However, you need to configure the Web browser applications on the clients. You can automate the process so that the clients can automatically download a script from the ISA Server computer whenever the client opens the browser. The default location of the URL is:

```
http://array_name/array.dll?Get.Routing.Script
```

where *array_name* is the name of the ISA Server array. For example, `http://SPARKLES:8080/array.dll?Get.Routing.Script`.

> **TIP**
>
> If the clients use the RealPlayer application by RealNetworks, Inc., do not configure it as a Web Proxy client. Instead, let the firewall client handle it.

Here's how to configure Internet Explorer 5.0 to use the Web Proxy service:

1. Start Internet Explorer.
2. Click on Tools, then click on Internet Options.
3. Click on the Connections tab, then click LAN Settings at the bottom of the screen.
4. Click the Use a Proxy Server check box, as shown in Figure 2.24.

FIGURE 2.24
Configuring IE 5.0 for Web Proxy Service.

5. In the Address box, type the name of the ISA Server computer, or the name of an array.

6. In the Port box, type the port number. Generally it is port number 8080.

7. Optionally, check the box Bypass Proxy Server for Local Addresses, so the browser won't bother going through the Proxy Server for addresses that are local to the internal network.

Configuring Direct Access

Figure 2.22 shows how the client's browser can be configured for direct access by using an exception list. You can specify that local servers or domains included in the Local Domain Table (LDT) should be accessed directly by the client by bypassing the Web Proxy service. As previously mentioned, these settings are applied to clients that use the automatic configuration script specified on the General tab, as shown in Figure 2.25. The figure shows that the default URL is used. You can also use a custom URL pointing to a different location.

NOTE

The Local Domain Table is a listing of domain names that are internal to your network. When Firewall clients need to resolve a domain name, they first check their copy of the LDT. If the domain exists in the LDT, it is resolved directly. Otherwise, the request is sent to the ISA Server, so it can resolve the request from a DNS server on the client's behalf. An LDT is configured from the ISA Management console under Servers and Arrays, *<your server name>*, Network Configuration, and finally Local Domain Table (LDT).

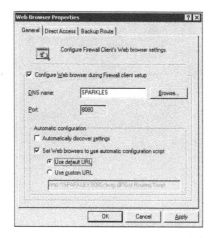

FIGURE 2.25
Configuring the automatic configuration script.

Accessing the Internet from the ISA Server Computer

When you configure the browser on the ISA Server computer, make sure that you use the IP address of the internal interface of the ISA Server computer. Avoid using the NetBIOS or DNS name of the server. If you were to use the DNS or NetBIOS name to configure the browser, the name would be resolved to the IP address of the external interface of the ISA Server computer. Obviously, the LAT doesn't include the IP address of the external interface of the server (and it better not!). As a result, you wouldn't be able to access the Internet. Therefore, you need to configure the browser to connect to the Internet through the Web Proxy service.

Additional Tips

Here are some additional tips that will help you determine what type of clients you should be deploying on your network.

- Implement the Firewall client if you want to use user-based authentication. SecureNAT doesn't support this feature. Web Proxy clients can use user-based authentication, but only if the Web application that they are using will pass the authentication credentials.
- Configure published servers as SecureNAT clients. Instead of messing with the configuration on the publishing servers, all you have to do is create a server publishing rule on the ISA Server. Avoid configuring publishing servers as Firewall clients, because the configuration will be too complicated.
- If you simply want to avoid installing software and messing with client configuration, then use the SecureNAT client. SecureNAT clients only require that you configure a default gateway that sends the traffic to the Internet through the ISA Server, either

directly or indirectly via routers. In comparison, Web Proxy clients require that you configure the Web applications on the clients, and Firewall clients require that you install client software on each computer.

> **NOTE**
>
> Neither SecureNAT nor Firewall clients are supported in Cache mode.

Configuring the H.323 Gatekeeper Service

H.323 Gatekeeper protocol is an International Telecommunication Union (ITU) standard that defines how multimedia equipment and services that lack Quality of Service (QoS) can communicate across networks. The H.323 Gatekeeper consists of several components, and enables you to configure incoming connections for applications that use H.323 protocol, such as NetMeeting 3.0. Applications that use H.323 protocol offer communication services to H.323 registered clients. The standard also defines how calls can be made between a local area network (LAN) and a public switched telephone network (PSTN).

> **NOTE**
>
> The H.323 Gatekeeper service does not offer any security.

H.323 Overview

H.323 transactions have two endpoints:

- Origination endpoint (for example, H.323-registered clients, such as Microsoft NetMeeting clients)
- Destination endpoints (the ISA Server computer)

The gatekeepers serve many purposes. They can control access to your network by not only permitting or denying incoming calls; they can also control the bandwidth. In addition, they can also provide address resolution. For example, they can convert e-mail addresses into network addresses. With the H.323 Gatekeeper service, you can place calls using e-mail addresses, phone numbers, or IP addresses.

All inbound calls that come into your network through the ISA Server computer require the H.323 Gatekeeper service. If the clients want to receive communications from the Internet, they must register with the H.323 Gatekeeper service. As far as outbound calls are concerned, they may or may not require you to register, depending on whether they require translation services or not.

Let's take a scenario where you want to contact a user named Stefanie from your home or work over the Internet. Stefanie is registered with the H.323 Gatekeeper service as `Stefanie@techgalaxy.net` on TechGalaxy network. Even though Stefanie doesn't have her name registered on the Internet, you will still be able to contact her because she has registered with the H.323 Gatekeeper service. You can use NetMeeting 3.0 or later to contact her at `Stefanie@techgalaxy.net`, even across firewalls and routers.

Adding H.323 Gatekeeper to ISA

Here's how you can add and configure H.323 Gatekeeper service on your ISA Server computer.

1. Right-click H.323 Gatekeepers in the ISA Management console and click on Add Gatekeeper.

2. In the Add Gatekeeper screen, select This Computer to add the service to the local computer. To add the service to a remote computer, select Another Computer and type its *fully qualified domain name* (FQDN).

3. Selecting This Computer will add several entries to the ISA Management console, as shown in Figure 2.26.

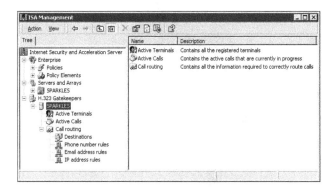

FIGURE 2.26

Adding H.323 Gatekeepers to ISA Server.

4. Right-click on the server name under H.323 Gatekeepers and select Properties. On the Network tab, you can specify the network adapter that you want to the Gatekeeper to use, as shown in Figure 2.27.

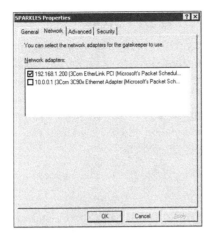

FIGURE 2.27
Configuring a network adapter for Gatekeeper.

2
ISA SERVER
INSTALLATION AND
CONFIGURATION

5. The Advanced tab (see Figure 2.28) enables you to specify the registration time in seconds (the default period is 6 minutes, or 360 seconds). You can also configure the time in seconds before an active call will expire. The default period for this is 35 seconds.

6. You can click on Compact Database to compact (defrag) the database. However, be aware that the database defragmentation will temporarily disable the Gatekeeper service and will cause the administrative connection to be dropped.

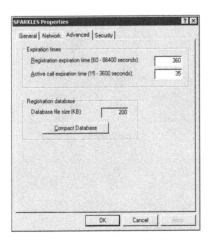

FIGURE 2.28
Configuring advanced options for the Gatekeeper service.

Working with the H.323 Protocol

The H.323 Gatekeeper service consists of several components, including H.323 Proxy and H.323 Protocol. It's an ITU standard that was developed because the quality of voice over the Internet has been less than perfect. The proposed improvements will split the messages, so some of them can be carried over the Internet, and the rest on the standard telephone line (PSTN). This standard permits you to connect a client using a phone line to an IP-based client using a computer. For more information on H.323, go to http://www.itu.int/ and do a search on H.323.

To control incoming and outgoing H.323 traffic, you can configure H.323 protocol rules. Here's how you configure the rules:

1. In the ISA Management console, first go to Servers and Arrays, then go to your server, Extensions, and click on Application Filters.

2. In the details pane on the right-hand side, right-click on H.323 Filter, then click on Properties.

3. On the General tab, check the Enable This Filter box as shown in Figure 2.29.

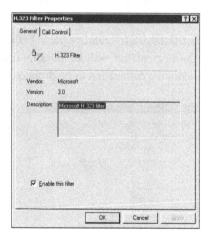

FIGURE 2.29
Enabling the H.323 filter.

4. On the Call Control tab, you can use a different Gatekeeper and specify Call Direction and Media Control options, as shown in Figure 2.30. The options are rather self explanatory. The option Use DNS Gatekeeper Lookup and LRQs for Alias Resolution is used to specify that DNS should not query for H.323 Gatekeepers on the Internet.

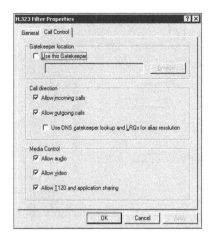

FIGURE 2.30
Enabling call control options for the Gatekeeper service.

Configuring H.323 Permissions

To configure the H.323 Gatekeeper permissions use the following procedure.

1. Right-click on the H.323 Gatekeeper server under H.323 Gatekeepers and select Properties.

2. Click Add and select the users or group that you want to add. Select the appropriate permissions so that the users will have either Read, Modify, or Full Control permissions.

3. For more granular control, click Advanced on the Security tab, and then click on View/Edit. As Figure 2.31 shows, you can configure Allow or Deny for a dozen different options.

Working with Clients and H.323

As previously mentioned, every H.323 transaction has two endpoints—origination and destination. You register the endpoints with the H.323 Gatekeeper using H.323 Registration, Admission, and Status—also known as H.323 RAS.

TIP

When discussing H.323, the RAS protocol refers to H.323 Registration, Admission, and Status (H.323 RAS). Do not confuse this with the Remote Access Service (RAS) that is typically used for making dial-up connections over a standard telephone line.

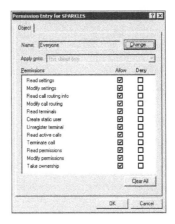

FIGURE 2.31
Configuring permissions for the Gatekeeper service.

H.323 protocol has a couple of versions. Version 1 uses a type E164 phone number and type H.323 ID addressing. Version 2 of the protocol uses e-mail ID-type addressing.

Summary

Chapter 2 discussed the steps needed to install ISA Server. First, the hardware requirements to install ISA Server Enterprise Edition were discussed. You were introduced to both the minimum and recommended hardware requirements. Then the steps required to add the schema in Active Directory were covered, followed by the step-by-step processes to install, uninstall, and reinstall the ISA Server product. In addition, the unattended installation process using the MsISAund.ini file was discussed.

In the client section, the Firewall, Web Proxy, and SecureNAT clients were explored. You also learned the steps involved in configuring these clients.

Businesses currently running Proxy Server 2.0 will benefit from the section on migrating from Proxy Server. This section looks at the effects of migrating, and there is also a section on how the Proxy Server 2.0 tasks are performed in ISA Server 2000. This should assist you in a smoother transition to the ISA Server.

The final section covered the H.323 Gatekeeper service in detail. You learned how to add H.323 Gatekeeper service, configure permissions, and work with the clients.

Now that you are familiar with the ISA Server product and architecture from Chapter 1, and have learned how to install ISA Server in this Chapter, in the next two chapters we will cover the security and acceleration aspects of the ISA Server.

Chapter 3 will cover ISA Server's security concepts, including packet filtering, intrusion detection, and virtual private networks (VPNs). In Chapter 4, we will discuss the acceleration concepts that will cover all the caching features of ISA Server.

ISA Security Concepts Part I

IN THIS CHAPTER

- Emphasizing Network Security   70
- Running the Security Wizard   71
- ISA Server Rules   74
- VPN Support   87
- Setting Up a Local ISA VPN Server   89
- Comparison of Existing Security Solutions   93
- DMZ Overview   94
- Summary   96

As one might expect, security concepts will get a lot of coverage in an ISA Server book. Because we have a large number of important items to cover, the ISA Server security concepts are broken down into two chapters in this book: Chapter 3, "ISA Security Concepts Part I," and Chapter 4, "ISA Security Concepts Part II."

ISA Server can be implemented as a dedicated firewall to protect your local area network from potential intruders on external networks. You can configure rules and filters that prevent unauthorized users from entering your network, and you can limit the access of authorized users to only the contents that they should be accessing, thus securing your valuable corporate resources.

In this first of two security chapters, we will focus on topics such as the ISA Server Security Configuration wizard. This wizard enables you to tighten your security considerably. We will explore site and content rules in detail. Rules enable you to control the flow of traffic to meet your security needs. In other words, they determine which computers, users, or applications should be able to access resources on your network. Rules can be configured for both inbound and outbound traffic. We will also discuss the support for Virtual Private Networks (VPNs) in ISA Server. You will learn how to configure both ends of a VPN tunnel using the ISA Server wizards. Later in this chapter, you will also find a comparison of existing security solutions.

When discussing security and firewalls, it's hard not to talk about *demilitarized zones (DMZs)*. A DMZ provides an extra layer of protection against outside attacks. In this chapter, first you will be presented with an overview of DMZs, followed by an explanation of a couple of common DMZ scenarios in use today.

After exploring the security items found in this chapter, move on to Chapter 4, "ISA Security Concepts II." The primary focus of this chapter will be on packet filtering. You will learn the fundamentals of packet filtering, including the creation and application of filters. You will also be presented with the application filter concepts.

Emphasizing Network Security

As a person responsible for securing your network, it is probably no surprise that you have to be security conscious from the get go. Some administrators leave their system unprotected in the beginning while they slowly work on different aspects of their system. Needless to say, this could be a huge security risk.

Let's take a real-world scenario that's more common than a lot of folks realize. As you may know, businesses that have standardized on Compaq's servers can use Compaq's Web-enabled management software to manage their systems. The wide range of components that can be managed includes RAID configurations and free hard disk space to IP addresses and serial numbers. You can even restart the server remotely and get into the management tools.

Well, you say, that sounds pretty cool. So what's the problem? Well, the problem is that some newbie administrator may not realize that Compaq's management software running any Web-based management tool on port 2301 can act as a proxy server. This could potentially leave the server wide open to folks on the Internet, unless the administrator changes the default configuration before connecting the server to the Internet. With the default username (administrator) and password (administrator) known to everyone, hackers can have anonymous access to the server. By the way, Compaq has a security patch available for Windows NT 4.0 and Windows 2000 to fix the problem with the Web-enabled management software. The patch is available at http://www.compaq.com/support/files/server/us/download/9608.html.

If you don't take precautionary measures to secure your network devices, you are taking a risk. Change the default passwords on systems before you put them in production; don't enable services unless you have properly configured them; don't share folders unless you've set the permissions; don't enable Web sites unless you've configured proper authentication—you get the point. Take security seriously, go through the security checklists, and be overly cautious. Now, let's explore the security options ISA Server offers you as you plan and implement a security system to protect personal and/or corporate data and servers.

Running the Security Wizard

To begin, you need to be aware of the ISA Server Security Wizard. With this handy wizard you can tighten your security on all the servers in an array. Keep in mind that running this security wizard is one way to secure your network—it is not the only way. The ISA Server Security Wizard is a good place to start securing your network, but we will cover other methods that can be used with this wizard to help lock down your network infrastructure effectively.

There are three levels of security that are available using the wizard, as explained here:

- *Dedicated*—Use this setting when your ISA Server is installed as a dedicated standalone Firewall server. When you use this security level, there should be no other servers or applications running on the ISA Server computer. The security templates used by this option offer the highest level of protection. The template tightens the security by configuring stricter password, account lockout, and local policies. It also makes numerous registry changes, such as disallowing server shutdown without a logon, and clearing the pagefile at shutdown.

- *Limited Services*—This is the setting that you should use when your ISA Server is installed as a combined Firewall and Cache server. This is also the setting you should use for ISA Servers that are domain controllers. The templates used by this option offer a medium level of protection. For example, the template on a domain controller will force users to logoff when their logon hours expire. On a Windows 2000 server, it will remove users from the Power Users group.

- *Secure*—You should use this level of security when additional servers are installed on the ISA Server, such as application or database servers. For example, if you are running Exchange or IIS server on the same computer as ISA Server, this is the setting you should use. The templates used by this option offer a relatively lower level of protection. For example, it removes most password restrictions and essentially removes restrictions on account lockout policy. Use this option with care, because it may lessen your security considerably compared to your existing level.Depending on whether there is a Windows 2000 domain controller or a standalone server, the Security Wizard can use one of three security templates to increase security for Windows 2000 components. The security templates are located in the `winnt\security\templates` folder. Table 3.1 lists the security levels and the templates associated with each level.

TIP

I have seen some administrators use this wizard and then complain about their ISA Server getting "messed up." The wizard makes literally dozens of changes to the registry, file permissions, and user rights. My recommendation is that you read and understand the information in the security templates before you implement them.

TABLE 3.1   ISA Server Security Configuration

Security Level	Windows 2000 Server Security Templates	Windows 2000 Domain Controller Security Templates
Dedicated (highest level)	hisecws.inf	hisecdc.inf
Limited Services (medium level)	securews.inf	securedc.inf
Secure (lowest level)	basicsv.inf	basicdc.inf

Now that you have been given some background and specific warnings, let me tell you about my general philosophy about such wizards. Frankly, security wizards make me nervous and I don't always trust them. I am not convinced that the wizards will *only* make the changes that they are supposed to make. Why is it that a wizard can make the configuration changes one way, but won't let you undo those changes? I don't mind using wizards for certain tasks, but using wizards to secure my server is not my cup of tea.

CAUTION

The ISA Server Security Configuration Wizard doesn't have an "undo" feature. Before you run the wizard, make sure you've backed up your operating system and ISA Server configuration. The Security Wizard, among other things, modifies numerous operating system registry settings, which makes reverting back to the original configuration a very time consuming and difficult task. ISA Server lists the configuration changes to a file called securwiz.log in the ISA Server installation folder, but the log only tells you that it changed the setting, it doesn't tell you what exactly the change was.

To configure the appropriate security level, use the following procedure:

- In the ISA Server Management console, click on Servers and Arrays, the name of the array or server, and select Computers.
- In the right-hand pane, right-click the ISA Server computer that you want to secure and click on Secure to start the wizard. You will receive the first page of the ISA Server Security Wizard.
- Read the warning carefully on the first screen of the ISA Server Security Configuration Wizard.
- On the next screen of the wizard, select an appropriate system security level. Use the aforementioned descriptions to decide which level to choose. Secure level is the default.
- Click Finish on the next screen to finish the security configuration.

WARNING

If you just go by the name, it may seem that the Secure level is the most secure of the three choices, but in fact it is the least secure level. The Dedicated level offers the highest security, the Limited Services offers a medium-level security, and the Secure level offers the lowest level of security among the three.

Once you are satisfied with the level of protection that is appropriate for your servers (for instance, by running the ISA Server Security Configuration Wizard), you can then configure additional security options by establishing ISA Server rules. This provides even greater control at a more detailed level over your network traffic.

ISA Server rules are generally used to control outgoing traffic from the internal network to the Internet. In the next chapter we will explore IP packet filters, application filters, and intrusion detection filters, all of which are used to control incoming traffic. Now let's examine the ISA Server rules.

ISA Server Rules

The ISA Server rules determine what network resources client machines are permitted to access. You configure rules to control incoming traffic from the Internet to your internal network, and outgoing traffic from your internal network to the Internet. However, the rules are primarily used for managing inbound traffic.

There are several types of rules supported by the ISA Server. These rules include access policy, bandwidth, protocol, routing and chaining, scheduling, server publishing, site and contents, and Web publishing rules. The following sections will explore the site and content, protocol, bandwidth, and publishing rules.

Site and Content Rules

Site and content rules are used to allow or deny clients access to certain contents on the Internet. This rule works in conjunction with the protocol rules. In other words, clients are allowed access if the site and content rule specifically allows access. However, even if the site and content rule allows the client to access the contents, you still need to create a protocol rule, as you will learn more about in a moment, that allows the client to communicate using that protocol.

If you configure two conflicting rules, one that allows access and the other that denies access, the "deny rule" takes precedence and is processed first. Let's say as an IT manager you configure a couple of site and content rules. Rule #1 allows only the managers to access certain contents. Rule #2 denies all employees access to the same contents. As a manager, you will not be able to access the contents because the "deny rule" will be processed first.

When dealing with arrays, you can create site and content rules both at the enterprise level and at the array level. When you enable the array-level rules, they add additional restrictions to the existing enterprise-level site and content rules. For example, let's say that you are using an enterprise policy that permits all employees to use ICQ Chat at all times. You can configure a site and content rule at the array level that permits temporary employees to use ICQ Chat only during lunch hours, which will further restrict the existing enterprise policy. When you apply an enterprise policy to an array, you can only add deny rules at the array level, which simply gives you the capability to apply additional restrictions at a lower level.

Site and content rules are useful in applying various kinds of restrictions or granting different levels of permissions to the clients. For example, you can decide whether a site and content rule applies to all destinations, all internal destinations, all external destinations, to a certain destination set; or you can configure an exception rule so that it can apply to all destinations except the one you list. The rules either "allow" or "deny" access to destinations.

You can also decide at what times the rule should be in affect by using a predefined schedule. For example, you can apply the rule only to weekend or weekday hours. In addition, the rules can be applied to certain client address sets, to specific users or groups, or to any request. If that's not enough, you can even control the content groups to which the rules are applied. For example, the rules can be applied to only certain types of contents, such as macro documents or applications.

With this level of control, you can come up with all kinds of options to either deny or permit only certain users to access specific objects, at specific times, from specific locations. For example, you can restrict a group of contractors from downloading videos and images from external Web sites during 8:00 a.m. and 9:00 a.m. when the traffic is heavy on your network. As another example, you can create a rule that permits only employees in the IT department to download applications, but limit them from downloading the files only after hours or weekends. You could create an exception that enables the IT manager or the network administrator to download the files at any time.

Now that you have a better understanding of what the rules are used for, you will learn how to configure them.

Let's say you want to configure a rule that will enable your internal clients to access all contents on the Internet at all times. To configure such a site and content rule for the enterprise policy, use the following procedure:

1. In the ISA Server Management console, click on Enterprise, Policies, *<your enterprise policy>*, Site and Content Rules.

2. Right-click the Site and Content Rules and select New, then click on Rule to start the New Site and Content Rule Wizard.

3. Enter a name for the rule, for example Internet Access, as shown in Figure 3.1. Notice that there is a note warning you to create new policy elements that may be required by the rule before using the wizard. You might have to create a destination set, a client address set, a schedule, and a content group.

FIGURE 3.1
The New Site and Content Rule Wizard.

4. On the Rule Action screen, select Allow.

5. On the Rule Configuration screen, you will use the default selection Allow Access Based On Destination, as shown in Figure 3.2. If you don't specify clients or a schedule on this screen, the rule you create will be applicable to all the clients.

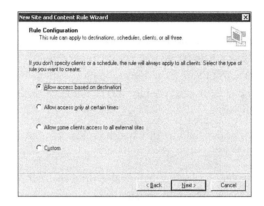

FIGURE 3.2

Rule configuration for the site and content rule.

6. On the Destination Sets screen, decide how you want to apply this rule. Select All Destinations (the default option), but notice the other options listed in the drop-down box.

7. Click Finish on the final screen to complete the wizard.

Figure 3.3 shows the rule you just created inside the ISA Management console. Notice in the right-hand pane that the rule applies to the enterprise and allows any request to access all contents at all the destinations all the time.

FIGURE 3.3

The site and content rule at the enterprise level.

To configure a site and content rule at the array level, you will go through the same process as described previously.

Protocol Rules

Protocol rules are used to control clients' access to the Internet. They can allow or deny use of protocol definitions and can apply to either all or selected IP traffic. ISA Server comes with several common protocol definitions. You can add additional protocols to customize your environment.

As mentioned earlier, the protocol rules and the site and content rule work hand in hand. Remember from our earlier discussion that even if the site and content rule enables the client to access the contents, you still need to create a protocol rule that enables the client to communicate using that protocol.

TIP

When you disable an application filter, its protocol definition is no longer available to the client. In other words, clients using that protocol definition will be denied access.

Similar to the site and content rules, the rules that deny protocols are processed before the rules that allow access.

Let's say you want to create a protocol rule for a group of temporary employees that denies them access to ICQ 2000 chat during business hours. Here's how you will configure the rule.

1. In the ISA Server Management console, click on Enterprise, Policies, *<your enterprise policy>*, Protocol Rules. For an array policy, you will go to Servers and Arrays, *<your server name>*, Access Policy, Protocol Rules.

2. Right-click Protocol Rules and select New, then click on Rule to start the New Protocol Rule Wizard.

3. Enter a name for the rule on the first screen; for example ICQ 2000.

4. On the Rule Action screen, choose Deny.

5. On the Protocols screen, select an option from the drop-down box to apply the rule. We will select Selected Protocols, as shown in Figure 3.4, because we only want to deny the TEMPS Group from accessing the ICQ 2000 protocol during work hours. Check the ICQ 2000 box. (Also note in Figure 3.4 the list of protocols to choose from.) If you need something other than Selected Protocols, some of the other options you can choose from are as follows:

3

ISA SECURITY
CONCEPTS PART I

- All IP Traffic
- Selected Protocols
- All IP Traffic Except Selected

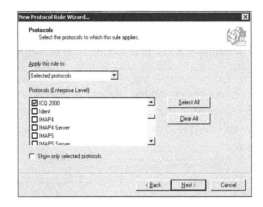

FIGURE 3.4

Configuring the protocol to which the rule applies.

6. On the Schedule screen, select Work Hours from the drop-down box. The other options are Always and Weekend.

7. On the Client Type screen, select Specific Users and Groups.

8. In the Users and Groups screen, add the TEMPS group.

9. Click Finish on the final screen to complete the wizard.

After you have created the rule, you can double-click the rule to access its properties. On the Schedule tab, you can customize the hours for the TEMPS group. The default hours are Monday through Friday 9 a.m. to 5 p.m.

You can create additional schedules by clicking on the New button. This brings up the new schedule window that shows the TEMPS group's work schedule, which is Monday through Friday from 9 a.m. to 12 p.m. Figure 3.5 shows the new custom hours that you've configured for the TEMPS group.

TIP

At first sight, it might not be obvious what the selected scheduled hours are for a particular protocol. Depending on the area of the window that you've selected, the hours shown at the bottom are not necessarily the hours that are active. Highlight the dark (active) area with the mouse and you'll notice the exact hours at the bottom of the screen, as shown in Figure 3.5.

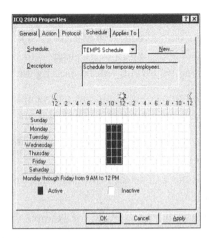

FIGURE 3.5

Applying a custom schedule to a protocol rule.

> **TIP**
>
> You can define new schedules; however, after the new entries are added, there is no delete option to get rid of them. To delete the entry, go to ISA Server Management console, Enterprise, Policy Elements, Schedules. You'll see the schedules you've created in the right-hand pane. When you try to delete the entry you'll be warned that if this policy element is used by any rule, ISA Server will not start.

Bandwidth Rules

Bandwidth rules are available in all ISA Server installation modes. The bandwidth rule works with the Quality of Service (QoS) scheduling service in Windows 2000 to prioritize network connections. The connections have a default scheduling for priority. If there is a bandwidth rule associated with a connection, its priority is changed accordingly. The bandwidth rule itself is not responsible for controlling the bandwidth of the connections; it simply communicates with the QoS to let it know how the priority should be set on a connection. It is the responsibility of the QoS service to control the bandwidth.

There's a default bandwidth rule that is guaranteed a minimum bandwidth by the QoS in Windows 2000. This rule can't be deleted or modified. You can create your own bandwidth rules to overwrite the default configuration. The range can be anywhere between 1 and 200 for both inbound and outbound traffic. For example, if you want Microsoft SQL Server to have more bandwidth on the network than other services, you can create a bandwidth rule for SQL

Server and set the priority to a higher number; for example 200 (the maximum priority). On a busy network, when five clients send a request to Microsoft SQL Server and two send it to Microsoft Exchange Server, the bandwidth from five users will be evenly split among the five SQL Server users. The remaining bandwidth will be used by the two Exchange users.

Let's take a look at a bandwidth rule configuration as an example of this process. The following procedure describes how you can configure a bandwidth rule for Microsoft SQL Server.

1. In the ISA Server Management console, click on Server and Arrays, *<your server name>*, Bandwidth Rules.

2. Right-click Bandwidth Rules and select New, then click on Rule to start the New Bandwidth Rule Wizard.

3. Enter a name for the rule on the first screen; for example `Microsoft SQL Server`.

4. On the Protocols screen, select an option from the drop-down box to apply the rule. For our example we will select Selected Protocols, as shown in Figure 3.6, and check the Microsoft SQL Server box. All the options available are listed here:

   - All IP Traffic
   - Selected Protocols
   - All IP Traffic Except Selected

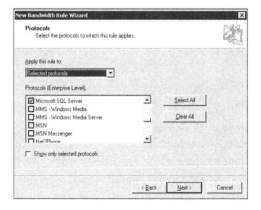

FIGURE 3.6
Configuring a bandwidth rule.

5. On the Schedule screen, select Always.

6. On the Client Type screen, select Any Request.

7. On Destination Sets screen, select All Destinations.

8. On the Content Groups screen, select All Content Groups.

9. On the Bandwidth Priority screen, select Use Default Scheduling Priority. (You will create a new priority in a moment).

10. Click Finish on the final screen to complete the wizard.

11. Right-click the new rule you just created and select Properties.

12. On the General tab, ensure that the Enable box is checked.

13. On the Bandwidth tab, check the Specified Priority Box and click on New.

14. Enter the information shown in Figure 3.7 in the New Bandwidth Priority box and click OK to close the window.

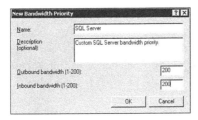

FIGURE 3.7

Creating a new bandwidth priority.

15. On the Bandwidth tab, select your new SQL Server entry from the drop-down box, as shown in Figure 3.8.

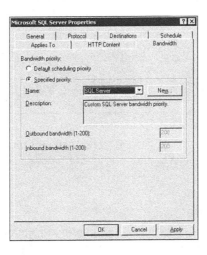

FIGURE 3.8

Specifying a new bandwidth priority.

16. Click OK to apply the settings.

> **TIP**
>
> After you close the Window shown in Figure 3.7 and the entry is created, you won't see a Delete option. Even if you cancel out and don't click the Apply or OK button, the entry will still be saved. To delete the entry, go to ISA Server Management console, Enterprise, Policy Elements, Schedules. You'll see the schedules you created in the right-hand pane. When you try to delete the entry you'll be warned that if this policy element is used by any rule, ISA Server will not start.

Publishing Policy Rules

Publishing policy rules consist of two rules that allow information on servers in the internal network to be securely published to the external Internet clients. The two rules are known as:

- Server publishing rule
- Web publishing rule

The internal published servers are actually SecureNAT clients, so they don't need any special configuration. All you have to do is point them to the ISA Server computer as a default gateway. The external users communicate with the ISA Server computer, and in fact can't tell that they are really talking to a server inside the corporate network. The ISA Server acts as an intermediary and translates packets back and forth. The only IP address visible to the external clients is the IP address of the ISA Server computer.

Let's first take a closer look at the server publishing rules; we will then look at the Web publishing rules.

> **NOTE**
>
> The server publishing rules are available in Firewall and Integrated ISA Server mode—not in the Cache mode. The Web publishing rules are available in all three modes.

Server Publishing Rule

By default, ISA Server blocks all incoming traffic from the Internet. To allow an internal server to be accessible to the external clients, you create a server publishing rule. For example, to publish your FTP server to folks on the Internet, you'll create a server publishing rule on your ISA Server.

Server publishing rules can be limited to certain clients by using client address sets, which include the IP addresses of internal and possibly external clients.

When IP packet filtering is enabled on the ISA Server computer, the server publishing rules are applied to the client address sets. When IP packet filtering is disabled, the server publishing rule is applied to all the clients. This may not seem like a big deal, but let's look at an example so you can better understand what the consequences may be.

As an example, let's say you publish an FTP server only for the finance department so no one else can access their files. When IP filtering is enabled, only the finance department can access the files; however, if you disable IP filtering, the rule is applied to all the clients. Depending on how all the rules are configured and whether they are allow or deny rules, there is a possibility that you may end up giving access to more than just the finance department.

Let's say you want to publish an Exchange server located on the internal network inside the ISA Server computer. To configure a server publishing rule to publish this server, use the following procedure:

1. In the ISA Server Management console, click on Server and Arrays, *<your server name>*, Publishing, Server Publishing Rules.

2. If the enterprise policy settings are not configured to allow publishing, you won't be able to create a server publishing rule at the array level. See the following tip.

3. Right-click Server Publishing Rules and select New, then click on Rule to start the New Server Publishing Rule Wizard.

4. Type a name for the server publishing rule. Be sure to read the note that states that you may have to create new policy elements required by the rule before you use the wizard.

5. On the Address Mapping screen, type the IP address of the internal Exchange server that you want to publish under the IP address of the internal server. Under External IP Address on ISA Server, type the IP address of the external interface on your ISA Server that is connected to the Internet.

6. On the Protocol Settings tab, apply the rule to the Exchange RPC Server. Figure 3.9 shows the built-in list of protocols that are available to you.

7. On the Client Type screen, select Any Request.

8. Click Finish to complete the wizard.

> **TIP**
>
> If you don't see the options to create a new server publishing rule or a Web publishing rule on the array members, it is probably because the enterprise policy settings are not configured to allow publishing. To enable this option, go to the properties of your server and on the Policies tab, check the Allow Publishing Rules option. The missing options should become available to you immediately. You must be a member of the Enterprise Admins group to allow publishing rules.

FIGURE 3.9
Configuring a server publishing rule.

Web Publishing Rule

The Web publishing rule is used for publishing Web servers only. To publish all other servers, you need to use the server publishing rule.

Using the Web publishing rule, you make your internal servers available to external clients so they can access HTTP contents on the Web server. The ISA Server works as the intermediary and forwards HTTP requests to the internal Web server. If the contents are available in the ISA Server cache, it will respond on behalf of the Web server and return the contents to the client from the cache. The published Web server doesn't support digest or Basic authentication—and it better not, or else it will expose its IP address to the clients on the Internet.

You will notice a default Web publishing rule in the ISA Management console. This rule applies to all requests to all the destinations and is configured to discard all requests. This rule cannot be modified or deleted; and if you have additional rules, this rule will be applied last.

When the requests come in, ISA Server checks to see whether there are rules and if the request matches the rule. If it does, the request is processed accordingly; if it doesn't, the default rule is applied (processed last in order) and the request is discarded.

Let's work through an example of a Web publishing rule. Say you want to publish a Web server called WEB1 to the external clients. To create a Web publishing rule, use the following procedure:

1. In the ISA Server Management console, click on Server and Arrays, <*your server name*>, Publishing, Web Publishing Rules.

2. If the enterprise policy settings are not configured to allow publishing, you won't be able to create a Web publishing rule at the array level. See the preceding tip.

3. Right-click Web Publishing Rules and select New, then click on Rule to start the New Web Publishing Rule Wizard.

4. Type a name for the Web publishing rule. Be sure to read the note that states that you may have to create new policy elements required by the rule before you use the wizard.

5. On the Destination Sets screen, choose an appropriate option. The options are listed here:

   - All Destinations
   - All Internal Destinations
   - All External Destinations
   - Specified Destination Set
   - All Destinations Except Selected Set

   We will apply this rule to All Destinations.

6. On the Client Type screen, select Any Request. You can also select specific computers, users, or groups.

7. On the Rule Action screen, check the option Redirect the Request To This Internal Web Server (Name or IP Address), as shown in Figure 3.10, and type the IP address of the internal server that you want to publish. You can also use the fully qualified domain name of the server.

8. On the next screen, click Finish to complete the wizard.

After the rule has been created, you can modify it by right-clicking the rule and selecting Properties. On the Bridging tab (see Figure 3.11), you can redirect the HTTP or SSL requests as HTTP, SSL, or FTP. For SSL, you can require that the site be published using SSL and 128-bit encryption. In addition, you can use a certificate to authenticate to the SSL Web server.

3

ISA SECURITY CONCEPTS PART I

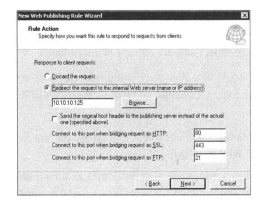

FIGURE 3.10
Redirecting a Web request to an internal published server.

TIP

The default port numbers for HTTP (80), SSL (443), and FTP (21) shown in Figure 3.10 are used only if you select to bridge the specific protocol. The bridging option is available on the Bridging tab, as shown in Figure 3.11.

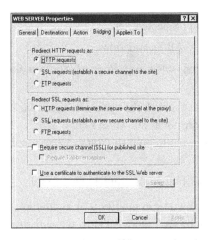

FIGURE 3.11
Configuring the bridging option for a Web publishing rule.

VPN Support

A Virtual Private Network (VPN) enables you to extend the functionality of your private network to a remote network by using the Internet as the backbone. VPNs can be used in several different scenarios. ISA Server uses Windows 2000's Routing and Remote Access service to manage VPNs and offers wizards to configure VPNs in two of the most popular scenarios:

- A branch office connecting to another branch office
- Employees connecting to the corporate network remotely

A VPN enables users to exchange information between two computers as if they were connected via a point-to-point link. Even though these computers can be located in remote sites, the information exchanged is encrypted and therefore secure. For example, let's assume that your Human Resources (HR) director, Shannon, wants to be able to work from home. With a VPN, you could allow her to access your corporate network via her Internet connection at home by creating a virtual "tunnel," as shown in Figure 3.12. First Shannon will use her modem to connect to her ISP. Then she will make a second connection to create a VPN tunnel to the corporate network. Once connected to the network, Shannon will be able to perform most of the tasks that she normally does while she is on the corporate network at work. She will be able to access the HR database, print to the network printers, access files in her home folder, and surf the Internet. Because Shannon handles confidential employee information, it is imperative that the data traveling between her home computer and the corporate network is secure. Creating a virtual tunnel encrypts data traveling inside the tunnel and offers the level of security that she needs.

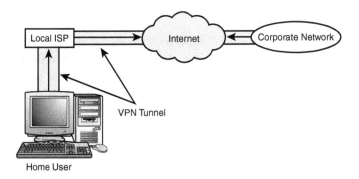

FIGURE 3.12

A VPN tunnel from home to corporate network through an ISP.

In addition to the users, entire networks, such as branch offices, can access your corporate network via a VPN. Again, data is encrypted between both ends of the VPN tunnel; therefore all communication is secure. For example, if you have offices in Seattle and San Francisco and you want to use the Internet as a secure tunnel between the two offices, you can set up an ISA Server in both cities and create a virtual tunnel between them, as shown in Figure 3.13.

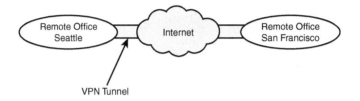

FIGURE 3.13
VPN tunnel between two offices across the Internet.

> **NOTE**
>
> For additional reading, check out my article "VPN Deployment Using Windows 2000" on the Microsoft TechNet CD, or online at http://www.microsoft.com/technet/tree-view/default.asp?url=/technet/columns/profwin/pw0201.asp. The article covers configuring a VPN server, levels of encryption supported by VPNs, and the PPTP and L2TP packet structure.

PPTP, L2TP, and IPSec

In order to create VPNs that are secure, ISA Server supports the use of several protocols that will help you develop your VPN infrastructure. ISA server uses Point-to-Point Tunneling Protocol (PPTP) and Layer 2 Tunneling Protocol (L2TP) to create VPNs across TCP/IP-based networks. The use of IP Security protocol (IPSec) is also supported to help ensure secure data transfer across the Internet, or between computers within a local area network. Let's look at these protocols in more depth.

PPTP

PPTP is an extension to the Point-to-Point Protocol (PPP) and supports multiple protocols that will communicate over the Internet. A PPTP tunnel encapsulates IP, IPX/SPX and NetBEUI protocols inside PPP datagrams. This means that you can use a NetBEUI application on a server across the Internet, even though NetBEUI is not a routable protocol and therefore cannot be used to communicate directly on the Internet. PPTP doesn't require any dial-up connections. For example, if you already have a T1 or DSL connection to the Internet, you simply create a

PPTP tunnel. In a typical scenario, a home user can dial into the ISP's server with a modem, which will connect the user to the Internet, and then create a second connection using PPTP and establish a VPN.

As mentioned earlier, PPTP can encrypt data passing through the VPN tunnel. It uses Microsoft Point-to-Point Encryption (MPPE) to encrypt data either with the default 40-bit encryption, or the stronger 128-bit encryption. Installing Windows 2000 Service Pack 2 on Windows 2000 computers will automatically upgrade the encryption level to 128-bit.

TIP

If you want MPPE to encrypt data, use MS-CHAP, MS-CHAP v2, or EAP/TLS authentication. MS-CHAP v2 and EAP/TLS support mutual authentication; therefore, if these protocols are the only protocols configured, make sure that both the server and the clients support them. The connection will be disconnected if, for example, the server doesn't identify itself to the client.

L2TP

L2TP is a combination of Layer 2 Forwarding (L2F) and PPTP. It provides similar functionality as PPTP to establish VPN connections. Although configuring PPTP on the server is much simpler, L2TP offers a higher level of security. With PPTP, you can use MPPE to encrypt data. With L2TP, you use IPSec to encrypt data. When using L2TP, you need to ensure that both the VPN client and the VPN server support L2TP and IPSec. In addition, keep in mind that only Windows 2000 and Windows XP support L2TP and IPSec; Windows NT and Windows 9x don't.

Setting Up a Local ISA VPN Server

In the section VPN Support, I mentioned that the ISA Server offers wizards to configure VPNs in two common scenarios: a branch office connecting to another branch office, and an employee connecting to the corporate network. To create a VPN tunnel between two branch offices across the Internet, you will use the Local ISA Server VPN Wizard and the Remote ISA Server VPN Wizard. Later, you will learn how to configure your server for the second scenario so that the users can create a VPN tunnel to access resources on your corporate network.

To create a VPN tunnel between two networks across the Internet, you need to run the Local ISA Server VPN Wizard on one end of the tunnel and the Remote ISA Server VPN Wizard on the other end. For example, if you want to connect two branch offices in Denver and Miami, run the Local ISA Server Wizard first on the ISA Server in Denver, create a .vpc file, and then use this .vpc file when you run the Remote ISA Server Wizard in Miami. Here's the step-by-step procedure to create the first end of the tunnel.

1. In the ISA Server Management console, click on Server and Arrays, *<your server name>*, Network Configuration.

2. Right-click Network Configuration and select Set Up Local ISA VPN Server to start the Local ISA VPN Wizard.

3. If Routing and Remote Access service is not running on the ISA Server, you will see a message telling you that the Routing and Remote Access service must be started before the VPN setup wizard can continue. Click Yes to start the service.

4. On the ISA VPN identification screen, type a short name to identify the local network, such as DENVER. Also, type a name for the remote network, such as MIAMI. Notice that the connection will be identified as DENVER_MIAMI.

5. On the ISA VPN Protocol screen, select a tunneling protocol that will be used for establishing a VPN. You can use L2TP, PPTP, or both. For our example, we will use PPTP.

6. On the Two-way Communication screen, select the box Both the Local and Remote ISA VPN Computers Can Initiate Communication, as shown in Figure 3.14, if you want either end to be able to initiate connection. Otherwise, leave the box unchecked so only the remote computer can initiate communication. Also, in this screen enter an IP address and the name of the remote VPN computer or domain. If you use the domain name, make sure you use the NT-style name; for example, TechGalaxy instead of TechGalaxy.net.

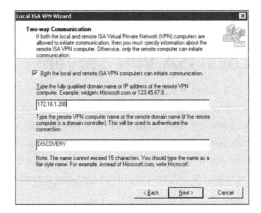

FIGURE 3.14

Enabling two-way communication.

7. On the Remote VPN Network screen, enter the range of IP addresses on the remote VPN network that can be accessed by the local VPN computer. This will be the range of computers in Miami that can be accessed by the local VPN in Denver. The figure shows one range of IP addresses. You could add additional ranges of addresses if necessary.

8. On the Local VPN Network screen, select the IP address of the external interface of the local VPN computer and then specify the range of IP addresses on the local VPN that can be accessed by the remote VPN computer, as shown in Figure 3.15. The remote VPN computer in Miami will use the IP address of the local VPN computer in Denver to create the tunnel. Once connected, it will be able to access computers in Denver that fall within the range of IP addresses that you have specified here. These IP address ranges are also used to create static routes that are managed through the Routing and Remote Access console.

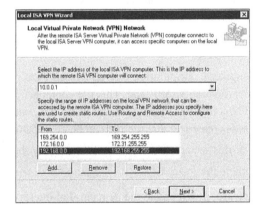

FIGURE 3.15

Configuring local VPN options.

9. On the ISA VPN Computer Configuration File screen, provide the name of the configuration file that will be used to configure the remote VPN computer. The file will be saved with a .vpc extension, for example denver_miami.vpc. Also provide a password to encrypt this file so that only the administrator of the remote VPN computer will be able to access it.

10. On the final screen of this wizard click on Details and verify that everything looks right.

11. Click Finish to complete the wizard.

This will create a Routing and Remote Access demand-dial interface. To verify that the interface was created properly, go to the Routing and Remote Access console in Administrative Tools on the ISA Server computer. Click on the server name and then click Routing Interfaces. In the right-hand pane, verify that a demand-dial interface called DENVER_MIAMI exists. Although you created this interface in ISA Management console, any changes to this interface must be made in Routing and Remote Access.

Remember, now you need to run the Remote ISA VPN Wizard on the remote VPN computer to create the other end of the tunnel.

Setting Up a Remote ISA VPN Server

The procedure for setting up a remote ISA Server VPN is somewhat different to the one discussed previously. At the remote location in Miami, you will use the .vpc file that was created in Denver to create the second end of the tunnel. Here's the step-by-step procedure:

1. In the ISA Server Management console, click on Server and Arrays, <*your server name*>, Network Configuration.
2. Right-click Network Configuration and select Set Up Remote ISA VPN Server to start the Remote ISA VPN Wizard.
3. In the ISA VPN Computer Configuration File screen enter the path to the file in the File Name box, such as A:\denver_miami.vpc. This file contains configuration information about the remote VPN computer. Also, in the Password box, enter the password that was used when this file was created so that the file can be decrypted.
4. On the final screen of this wizard click on Details and verify that everything looks right.
5. Click Finish to complete the wizard.

When you complete the wizard, it will create the demand-dial interface, configure packet filtering for security, and configure static routes so that traffic from the local network can be forwarded to the remote network. Again, as in the previous section, the interface is created and can now be managed from the Routing and Remote Access console instead of the ISA Management console.

At this point, you have created both ends of the VPN tunnel, and users in Denver and Miami will be able to communicate using it.

Setting Up ISA Server to Accept Client VPN Requests

So far we've talked about the scenario where two branch offices can be connected through a VPN tunnel. Let's look at the second scenario that is used for clients to connect to your corporate network.

ISA server offers this additional wizard that configures your server to accept connections from remote clients. This enables users to create VPN connections from their home computers to the corporate network so they can access resources on the network. Typically, mobile users benefit from this type of connectivity because they can dial-in to their local ISP and then create a VPN tunnel to their company network. This saves money on long distance charges and offers users secure connectivity to the company resources.

Here's how you set up ISA Server to accept VPN requests from the clients:

1. In the ISA Server Management console, click on Server and Arrays, <*your server name*>, Network Configuration.

2. Right-click Network Configuration and select Allow VPN Client Connections to start the ISA VPN Configuration Wizard.

3. Click Details to see configuration information and then click Finish to complete the wizard. Congratulations! You just completed the world's shortest wizard with only two steps—start and finish.

4. If you are prompted to restart the Routing and Remote Access service, click Yes to continue.

What did this wizard do in the background? It configured your Routing and Remote Access server as a VPN server so clients can be properly authenticated. It also automatically configured IP packet filters for you. There is one thing that the wizard doesn't do, and you need to take care of that business manually. You need to give the appropriate rights to the user to dial in to your network. This can be achieved either by configuring user account properties in Active Directory Users and Computers, or through Remote Access Policies.

Allowing Outbound PPTP Access

The previous situation applied to external users coming into your network through the Internet. If your internal clients have a need to create VPN tunnels from the internal network to a server on the Internet, you can enable outbound PPTP on the ISA Server computer. For example, you have some consultants working at your site that require access to their e-mail on their corporate network server. You can allow PPTP through the ISA Server so they can securely access their corporate server and read their e-mail. Here's how to enable the PPTP option:

1. In the ISA Server Management console, click on Server and Arrays, <*your server name*>, Access Policy, IP Packet Filters.

2. Right-click IP Packet Filters and click on Properties.

3. On the PPTP tab, check the box PPTP Through ISA Firewall.

Comparison of Existing Security Solutions

The main purpose of a firewall is to isolate your network from external threats, just like a firewall in a house prevents fire from spreading through the rest of the house. In order to implement a solution that protects a network from Internet attacks, there are a number of methods that are currently in use. Some of these solutions include implementation of a Proxy server, NAT server, bastion host, a firewall, a demilitarized zone, and so on. Some of these solutions are meant for a small office or home network (such as a NAT server); others are used in large enterprises (such as firewalls).

Both Proxy and NAT servers more or less have similar capabilities. They translate clients' requests so that the external hosts see the requests coming from only one IP address—the server's IP address. You can even run message and Web servers inside your Proxy or NAT server. To the outside world, it looks like they are directly communicating with these servers, although in reality the server is acting as an intermediary.

> **NOTE**
>
> For more details on Proxy Server 2.0, check out my article "Proxy Server 2.0" at `http://www.win2000mag.com/Articles/Print.cfm?Action=Print&ArticleID=3848`. For more information on NAT Server, check out "Windows 2000's Network Address Translation" at `http://www.win2000mag.com/Articles/Print.cfm?Action=Print&ArticleID=7882`. The article also compares Proxy server to NAT server.

A *bastion host* is a single computer that isolates the internal network from the Internet. With a single point of defense against outside intruders, if a bastion host is not secured properly, you run the risk of compromising resources on your internal network. A lot of people that connect to the Internet using Digital Subscriber Lines (DSL) or cable modems use this type of configuration. A bastion host configuration is similar to a Proxy or a NAT server configuration.

All of these solutions offer some type of firewall functionality. To enhance security, organizations that require a higher level of protection implement various types of *demilitarized zones* (DMZs).

Let's look at how you can use DMZs to protect your network.

DMZ Overview

A demilitarized zone is also referred to as a *screened subnet*, or a *perimeter network*. In this book I will refer to it as a DMZ, as it's a common terminology that has been around for a long time.

While a bastion host separates your internal computers from the Internet by using a single computer, a DMZ isolates your network with a small separate network that is in addition to your internal network and separate from the Internet, as shown in Figure 3.16. A DMZ is sort of a neutral zone where clients from the Internet can access resources such as Web servers, but can't access the internal network. Two common implementation of DMZs, three-homed fire-walls and back-to back firewalls, are covered later in this chapter.

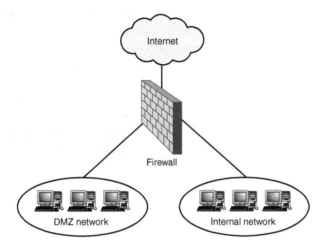

FIGURE 3.16
A sample DMZ configuration.

A DMZ provides an extra layer of defense against attacks, because if security is compromised, hackers will only gain access to your DMZ, not your internal network. For example, you can place your Web servers, DNS servers, and e-mail servers in the DMZ and allow both the internal and external clients access to these servers.

DMZ Scenarios

As I mentioned previously, there are a couple of common ways that you can incorporate a DMZ in your network configuration. The first implementation is known as a three-homed fire-wall configuration, and the second way is known as a back-to-back firewall configuration. Both of these implementations offer better security than a bastion host. There are some other possible scenarios, but we will limit our discussions to the two scenarios I just mentioned.

Three-Homed Firewall Configuration

In a three-homed firewall configuration, you install three network adapters in your ISA Server computer that will act as a firewall. Each network card will route traffic to one of these three networks.

- Network adapter 1 is connected to the internal network.

- Network adapter 2 is connected to the DMZ network.
- Network adapter 3 is connected to the Internet.

The sample DMZ configuration in Figure 3.16 shows a three-homed firewall configuration. This configuration provides better security than the bastion host configuration, and you have the added benefit of managing both the DMZ and the internal network from one location. However, one disadvantage of this configuration is that if hackers are able to penetrate your firewall, they will have access to both the DMZ and the internal network.

> **TIP**
>
> When working with ISA Server, use IP packet filtering, application filtering, and intrusion detection filtering to secure inbound traffic. Use site and content rules and protocol rules to control outbound traffic.

Back-to-Back Firewall Configuration

A three-homed configuration is a simpler way to add a DMZ to your network, but is not as secure as a back-to-back configuration. A back-to-back firewall configuration is shown in Figure 3.17. In this scenario, two ISA Server computers are used as back-to-back firewalls with a DMZ network sandwiched in between.

As you can see, one ISA Server (the external firewall) is connected to the Internet and the DMZ network, whereas the other ISA server (the internal firewall) is connected to your internal network and the DMZ network. With this approach, a potential hacker would need to pass through two ISA Server computers to gain access to your internal network.

Another advantage of a back-to-back configuration is that you can better manage your security by configuring rules that are more restrictive, compared to the three-homed configuration. One disadvantage of back-to-back configuration is that your enterprise security picture can get more complicated, as now you have to manage two firewalls.

Summary

This chapter covered the security aspects of ISA Server 2000. We started off by discussing site and content rules concepts. We covered protocol rules, bandwidth rules, and publishing policy rules. The discussion on rules was followed by a comparison of existing security solutions. We compared various security solutions in practice today, such as Proxy servers, NAT servers, bastion hosts, firewalls, and DMZs.

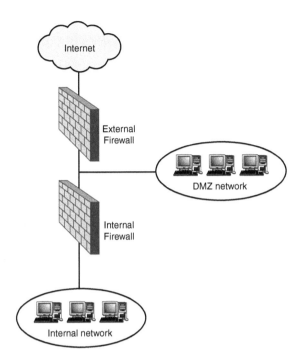

FIGURE 3.17

A back-to-back firewall configuration.

The VPN section included an explanation of VPN tunneling concepts, as well as the procedures for setting up local and remote ISA VPN servers. You also learned how to configure your Routing and Remote Access server as a VPN server, so that the server can accept client VPN requests.

In the DMZ section we covered the two most common types of DMZ implementations, the three-homed firewall and back-to-back firewall configurations.

In the next chapter, we will cover the important concepts of packet filtering. First we will introduce the creation and application of packet filtering. Then we will focus on application filters. Application filters have the capability to redirect, block, or even change the data when it reaches the ISA Server. Finally, you will learn the ins and outs of the built-in application filters that are provided with the ISA Server.

3

ISA SECURITY
CONCEPTS PART I

ISA Security Concepts Part II

IN THIS CHAPTER

- **Packet Filtering**   100
- **Application Filtering**   107
- **Summary**   119

This second chapter on ISA Security Concepts introduces the concepts associated with IP packet filtering. With filtering, you can manage IP packets traveling to and from your ISA Server computer. Filtering is an important part of ISA Server security because it gives you enormous control over the inbound and outbound traffic. In fact, there are some situations where the use of packet filtering is mandatory.

You will also learn about application filter concepts. Application filtering works in a different way compared to packet filtering. With packet filtering, only the header of the packet is examined. With application filtering, the entire message is examined for potential problems. We will also explore the built-in application filters that are provided with ISA Server.

Let's first talk about the fundamentals of packet filtering, including the creation and application of filters. Later we will compare static and dynamic filters, and examine application filters in great detail.

Packet Filtering

IP packet filtering is available on ISA Server computers in either Integrated or Firewall mode. It enables you to manage IP packets traveling to and from the ISA Server computer. Packet filtering is not something that you are required to enable, because even if you don't configure filtering, traffic is not allowed between your internal network and the Internet unless you create explicit rules that allow access. However, there are some situations that require the use of IP packet filters. Here are at least three scenarios that require the use of packet filters.

- You are running services on the ISA Server computer that need to communicate with the Internet. For example, you have some applications that talk to the Internet.
- You are publishing servers that reside in a three-homed DMZ.
- You need to run protocols other than TCP or UDP protocols.

With ISA Server, you can use packet filtering to grant or deny access by the following characteristics:

- Protocol
- Direction
- Port
- Type
- Local computer
- Remote computer

You create filters in ISA Server to either allow or block traffic, although all traffic is blocked by default unless you explicitly allow it. There are two types of static IP packet filters—Allow and Block. Allow filters are primarily used to define which packets will be allowed to come in to the internal network on the external interface of the ISA Server. Block filters define which packets will be blocked. They are the exceptions to the Allow filters.

All filters that meet the conditions of Allow filters are permitted to come in. All filters that meet the conditions of Block filters are blocked access. If a packet meets the condition of both an Allow and Block filter, it will be denied access. In other words, if you apply conflicting packet filters, the request will be blocked. For example, if you are hosting a Web site and have a filter that allows incoming traffic, the inbound request might still be denied if you are located on an IP address where a Block filter has denied incoming Web requests.

TIP

Packet filtering requires that ISA Server is installed in either Firewall mode or Integrated mode. You can't configure packet filtering if you've installed ISA Server in Cache mode.

Creating an IP Packet Filter

Let's say you want to create an IP packet filter for Terminal Services, which uses port 3389. To create the filter, use the following procedure:

1. In the ISA Server Management console, click on Servers and Arrays, the name of your server (or array), Access Policy, IP Packet Filters.

2. On the View menu, click Advanced. You could also use the Taskpad view, but this example will use the Advanced view.

3. Right-click on IP Packet Filters and select New, Filter.

4. On the New IP Packet Filter Wizard screen, enter a name for the filter, such as Terminal Services.

5. On the next screen, set this filter for All ISA Server Computers In the Array, or choose a specific server by clicking Only This Server and then select the server from the drop-down box.

6. On the Filter Mode screen select Allow Packet Transmission.

7. On the Filter Type screen, select Custom.

8. On the Filter settings screen, choose TCP as the IP Protocol; select Both under Direction; enter Fixed Port under Local Port; type 3389 under Port Number, and select All Ports under Remote Port, as shown in Figure 4.1.

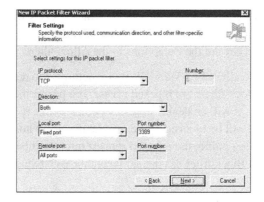

FIGURE 4.1

Filter settings options for packet filtering.

9. On the Local Computer screen, accept the default setting.

10. On the Remote Computers screen, accept the default setting.

11. Click Finish to complete the New IP Packet Filter Wizard.

12. You will have a custom filter added to the ISA Server Management console, as shown in Figure 4.2. The filter is created in the right-hand pane under Access Policy, IP Packet Filters, and it's automatically enabled.

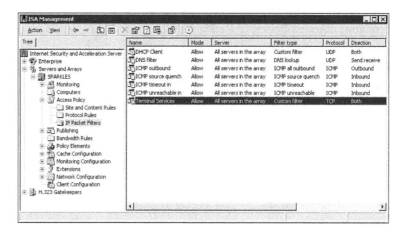

FIGURE 4.2

Adding a custom IP packet filter.

CAUTION

By default, when you create an IP packet filter it only applies to the first bound IP address on the external interface. If you have multiple IP addresses bound to the external interface and you create a "deny all" packet filter, some traffic might still go through the ISA Server because the filter won't apply to the other IP addresses. So the moral of the story is this—when you create packet filters, ensure that you are creating filters for each IP address that is bound to the external network interface, or else you will have just created a potential security hole.

Applying an IP Packet Filter to a Server

When you create an IP filter using the wizard, as described in the previous section, the filter is automatically enabled. You could go back into the Properties of the filter and modify its properties. For example, you can disable a filter that was enabled by default. You could also decide whether to apply the filter to a specific server, or to apply it to all the servers in an array.

To apply a static IP filter to a server, use the following procedure:

1. In the ISA Server Management console, click on Servers and Arrays, the name of your server (or array), Access Policy, IP Packet Filters.
2. On the View menu, click Advanced. You could also use the Taskpad view, but this example will use the Advanced view.
3. In the right-hand pane, double-click the filter that you want to apply; for example, the DNS filter, and you will receive that filter's property box.
4. On the General tab, verify that the Enable This Filter option is checked. It is easy to tell whether a filter is enabled or disabled in the ISA Server Management console. The filters that are disabled are distinguished by a red arrow next to their name. For example, the DHCP Client filter in Figure 4.2 is disabled.
5. As Figure 4.3 shows, you can apply this filter to either All Servers In the Array (the default), or Only This Server, in which case you can select a specific server.
6. Click OK to close the window.

4

ISA SECURITY
CONCEPTS
PART II

FIGURE 4.3

Applying a packet filter to a server.

Configuring a Protocol for an IP Filter

With IP packet filters, you can control traffic destined for individual computers on your internal network. Furthermore, you can allow or block traffic on certain ports using specific protocols. For example, you may create an IP filter that allows traffic on port 110 for POP3. Then create a block filter that limits access to port 110 for a set of external computers. There are more than a dozen predefined filters provided by ISA Server. You can either use one of these predefined filters, or create your own custom filters. However, keep in mind that the predefined filters cannot be modified.

When you create an IP filter, you specify a protocol that will be used by the filter to control the type of network traffic that will be allowed or blocked by the filter. To configure a protocol for an IP filter, use the following procedure:

1. In the ISA Server Management console, click on Servers and Arrays, the name of your server (or array), Access Policy, IP Packet Filters.

2. On the View menu, click Advanced. You could also use the Taskpad view, but this example will use the Advanced view.

3. In the right-hand pane, double-click the filter that you want to apply; for example, the DNS filter, and you will receive that filter's property box.

4. On the Filter Type tab, select a Predefined filter from the drop down box, as shown in Figure 4.4, or select Custom to create a custom filter. If you select Custom, you will need to specify a protocol, port, and direction.

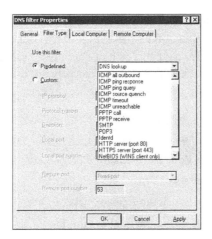

FIGURE 4.4
Adding a predefined packet filter.

5. Using the dialog box seen in Figure 4.4, click on the Local Computer tab. You have four options as to how the filter is applied. The options you will see are as follows:

Default IP Address(es) On the External Interface(s)—The ports will be opened and blocked only on the default IP address for each external interface on the ISA Server. This is the default option.

This ISA Server's External IP Address—The packet filter applies only to this specific external IP address on the ISA Server.

This Computer (On the Perimeter Network)—The packet filter applies only to this specific IP address in the demilitarized (DMZ) zone.

These Computers (On the Perimeter Network)—The packet filter applies only to this range of IP addresses in the DMZ zone.

6. Click on the Remote Computer tab. You will have three options as to how the filter is applied:

All Remote Computers—The packet filter applies to all external computers.

This Remote Computer—The packet filter applies to this specific external computer.

This Range Of Computers—The packet filter applies only to this range of IP addresses on the external network.

Configuring IP Fragment Filtering

IP Packets traveling across a wire can be broken down into smaller fragments. When the packets arrive at the destination, they are reassembled. Hackers can potentially grab these "fragmented"

IP packets and reassemble them in a way that can be harmful to the receiving computer or the network. If you enable the option to filter these fragmented packets, the Firewall and Web Proxy service on the ISA Server computer will discard these packets. For security purposes, it is a good idea to filter these packets and protect your network from some well-known attacks that can cause denial of service, degradation of service, or disable the targeted computers.

To enable IP fragment filtering, use the following procedure:

1. In the ISA Server Management console, click on Servers and Arrays, the name of your server (or array), Access Policy, IP Packet Filters.
2. Right-click IP Packet Filters and then select Properties.
3. On the General box, verify that the Enable Packet Filtering option is checked.
4. On the Packet Filters tab, check the Enable Filtering Of IP Fragments box, as shown in Figure 4.5.

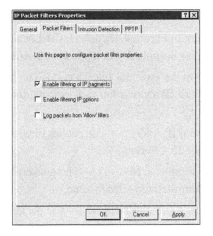

FIGURE 4.5

Enabling filtering of IP fragments.

NOTE

Do not enable IP fragment filtering if you want to permit audio and video streaming through the ISA Server computer.

Static Versus Dynamic Packet Filtering

Packets can be permitted to come into your network either *statically* by configuring packet filters, or *dynamically* by configuring publishing rules or access policy rules. By enabling packet filtering, you are instructing the ISA Server to drop all packets, unless you explicitly allow them to enter your network.

How do you decide whether to use a publishing or access policy rule, or to use IP packet filtering? The answer lies in the way the ports are opened. Ports can be opened dynamically, as in the case of access policy rules and publishing rules, or statically, as in the case of packet filtering. Opening ports dynamically is preferred; therefore, you don't want to create an IP packet filter to allow your network clients to access Web sites on the Internet. Instead, create an access policy rule that allows outbound HTTP traffic.

Dynamic packet filtering opens a port when a request is made by the client, and then shuts it down when the communication is over. For example, if you are viewing a Real Media stream, ISA Server can open the port (and multiple ports if necessary) when the connection is established, stay open as long as the stream is playing, and close the connection when the stream is finished.

Application Filtering

Application filtering works under a different concept than packet filtering. With packet filtering, only the header of the packet is examined. With application filtering, the entire message is examined for potential problems. ISA Server provides support for application filters developed by third parties to extend its security capabilities. There are many third party vendors writing application filters for ISA Server. For a listing of third party tools that work with ISA Server, visit http://www.techgalaxy.net/ISAServer.htm.

> **NOTE**
>
> Like packet filters, application filters only work if the ISA Server was installed in either Firewall or Integrated mode.

Application filters have the capability to analyze streams (series of packets) instead of packets. In addition, they have the capability to redirect, block, or even change the data when it reaches the ISA Server. Application filters are also specific to individual ISA Server computers. Therefore, if you want to have similar security control on all the servers, you need to install the filters on all the ISA Server computers in an array. Adding a new application filter to the server requires restarting the Firewall service. There are several filters that are already installed on ISA Server computer, seen in the following list.

- HTTP redirector filter
- FTP filter
- SOCKS filter
- RPC filter
- SMTP filter
- H.323 protocol filter
- Streaming media filter
- Intrusion detection filters

Let's explore these built-in application filters more closely in the next section.

Exploring Built-in Application Filters

As was noted previously, ISA Server comes with many predefined application filters. The following section describes the filters already installed on your system when you install ISA Server.

> **NOTE**
>
> As previously mentioned, you can install third party filters if you want. For a listing of third-party filters that work with ISA Server, visit http://www.techgalaxy.net/ISAServer.htm.

Application filters only work on the machine they are installed on. Therefore, if you are installing an application filter on an array, you must install the filter on every machine in the array. Figure 4.6 shows a listing of the built-in application filters available in ISA Server.

HTTP Redirector Filter

The built-in HTTP redirector filter is responsible for forwarding (redirecting) the HTTP requests from Firewall and SecureNAT clients to the Web Proxy service. The Firewall client's browser doesn't need to be configured to use ISA Server. Let's take a look at a familiar figure that depicts ISA Server architecture in Figure 4.7. This is also Figure 1.1 in Chapter 1. The ISA Server architecture gives you a good idea of the relation of HTTP redirector in the entire scheme of things.

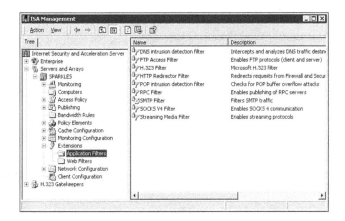

FIGURE 4.6

ISA Server's built-in application filters.

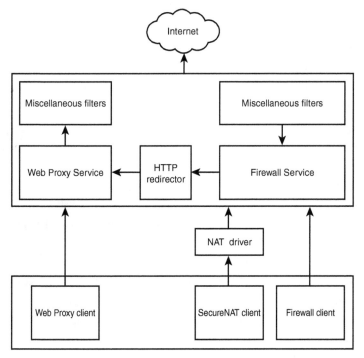

Internal Network

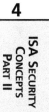

4

ISA SECURITY
CONCEPTS
PART II

FIGURE 4.7

Microsoft ISA Server architecture.

The HTTP redirector can either redirect HTTP requests from Firewall and SecureNAT clients to the Web Proxy service, or it can directly send requests to the Web server. When it bypasses the Web Proxy service and the requests are sent directly to the Web server, the requests are obviously not cached, because the Web Proxy service was not involved in the process.

> **NOTE**
>
> When the HTTP redirector is enabled and the requests from Firewall clients are redirected to the Web Proxy service, the client's authentication information is lost, so the requests are considered unauthenticated. If you are not allowing unauthenticated requests, these requests will be denied.

To configure the HTTP redirector filter, use the following procedure:

1. In the ISA Server Management console, click on Servers and Arrays, the name of your server (or array), Extensions, Application Filters.
2. Right-click HTTP Redirector Filter in the right- hand pane and click on Properties. You will receive the HTTP Redirector Filter Properties dialog box.
3. On the General tab, verify that the Enable This Filter box is checked.
4. On the Options tab, decide how you want ISA Server to respond to the HTTP requests from the clients. Here are your options:

   - Redirect To Local Web Proxy Service—Use this option if you prefer that the Web Proxy service on the local ISA Server handle the requests. This is the default option. You will also see the following choice as a subset to this option:
   - If the Local Service Is Unavailable, Redirect Requests To Requested Web Server—When the Web Proxy is not available, you can redirect requests to another Web server.
   - Send To Requested Web Server—Select this option if you want the client's request to be forwarded to the Web server that the client has specified.
   - Reject HTTP Requests From Firewall and SecureNAT Clients—This option will simply discard all HTTP requests from both Firewall and the SecureNAT clients.

FTP Access Filter

The FTP filter's job is to forward FTP requests from the SecureNAT clients to the Firewall service. You have the option to use a user-defined protocol definition for FTP, but you are better off using the FTP access filter instead, because it offers several advantages over the protocol definition.

The FTP filter is more than just a filter for ports 20 and 21. With the FTP filter, ports are opened and closed dynamically. In addition, the filter provides security for SecureNAT clients by performing address translation for the secondary connection. The FTP filter can also determine read and write permissions on the fly. If you were to create a protocol definition for FTP, none of these capabilities would be available to you.

Unlike most filters, the FTP filter doesn't offer any additional configuration parameters. The only option on the Properties box is a check box that enables or disables the filter.

SOCKS filter

If you have clients that use SOCKS applications, such as Macintosh or UNIX clients, the built-in SOCKS application filter will allow communication with the Internet, with the Firewall service acting as an intermediary.

By default, ISA Server uses port 1080 for SOCKS and supports SOCKS version 4.3. However, you can change the default port by following the procedure described below:

- In the ISA Server Management console, click on Servers and Arrays, the name of your server (or array), Extensions, Application Filters.
- Right-click SOCKS V4 Filter in the right-hand pane and click on Properties.
- On the General tab, ensure that the Enable This Filter option is checked.
- On the Options tab, change the default port 1080 to the new desired port number.

RPC Filter

If you are publishing internal RPC servers that are located inside your network to the clients outside your network, RPC filter can provide that functionality. What you need to do is create a publishing rule for the RPC protocol to publish an RPC server. By using a publishing rule, you will be able to securely publish RPC server without compromising security. To the outside world, it looks like they are directly communicating with the ISA Server because they can only see the IP address of the ISA Server computer. In the background, the ISA Server facilitates the communication between external clients and the publishing RPC server without requiring any special configuration on the RPC server.

Similar to the FTP filter, the RPC filter doesn't offer any additional configuration parameters. The only option on the Properties box is a check box that enables or disables the filter.

SMTP Filter

With the SMTP application filter, ISA Server can examine inbound or outbound traffic on port 25, and filter contents based on a sender's name, domains, keywords, and SMTP commands. For example, if your company is receiving a large amount of unsolicited e-mails from a specific domain, you can block all messages from that domain. Furthermore, the SMTP filter provides filtering via keywords. For example, you can set a filter that automatically deletes any messages with "I LOVE YOU" in the message header or body. Obviously, in this example, network users do take the risk of losing messages from loved ones but as an administrator, you are probably more concerned about the network security. Luckily you do have the option to either put these messages on hold or to forward it to someone for further investigation.

And that's not it. You can enable an attachment rule and decide how to manage e-mail attachments. This is great news for network administrators, because e-mail attachments are a big source for spreading harmful viruses across the Internet. Now they have the capability to filter harmful messages based on the keywords, in addition to filtering e-mail attachments. Similar to the keyword filtering, the attachments can be configured to be automatically deleted, forwarded to a user (for example, the administrator), or placed on hold.

Furthermore, you can generate alerts and automatically check for SMTP buffer overrun attacks with this filter. Buffer overruns occur when an SMTP command is sent with a length that exceeds a certain value.

TIP

According to Microsoft, to take advantage of advanced content screening you need to configure an optional ISA Server component known as Message Screener. This component doesn't necessarily need to be installed on the ISA Server computer. It is recommended that you install it on a separate computer that is also running IIS and SMTP Server. For more information, check out the document `smtpfilter.htm` in the `\support\docs` folder on the ISA Server CD.

Configuring the SMTP Filter

Now that you understand how you can utilize the SMTP filter, let's look at the configuration steps. You must have the proper rights to configure the enterprise policy in order to modify SMTP filter properties. To configure the SMTP filter, use the following procedure:

1. In the ISA Server Management console, click on Servers and Arrays, the name of your server (or array), Extensions, Application Filters.
2. Right-click SMTP Filter in the right-hand pane and click on Properties to get the SMTP Filter Properties dialog box.
3. On the General tab, check the Enable This Filter box, seen near the bottom. Note that the built-in SMTP Filter is disabled by default.
4. On the Attachments tab, click on Add to configure a Mail Attachment Rule.
5. On the Mail Attachment Rule screen, apply an action to messages that contain an attachment with one of the three properties: Attachment Name, Attachment Extension, or Attachment Size Limit (In Bytes), as shown in Figure 4.8. The three actions that you can

take are: Delete Message, Hold Message, and Forward Message To. Figure 4.9 shows a list of attachments that the SMTP filter will be processing. You can change the priority order by using the up or down arrow.

FIGURE 4.8

Enabling the attachment rule for the SMTP filter.

FIGURE 4.9

Adding attachments that should be filtered.

6. On the Users/Domains tab, add the sender's name or domains that you want to filter out. The SMTP filter will reject messages from the senders and domains that you will add on this tab.

7. On the Keywords tab, add the keywords that will be used by the SMTP filter to determine whether the incoming messages should be discarded, as shown in Figure 4.10.

These are the keywords used in the e-mail messages that you would like to filter out. A keyword may be part of the message header, the message body, or either the header or the message body. For example, Figure 4.10 shows that messages that contain the word "Lottery" in the header will be automatically deleted. However, messages that contain the words "I love you" in the header will be forwarded to someone for inspection of the common I Love You virus.

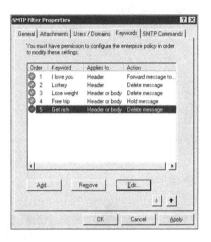

FIGURE 4.10
Filtering messages based on keywords.

8. On the SMTP Commands tab, you can add additional SMTP commands, edit the existing commands, or remove them. This screen shows the SMTP commands, whether they are enabled or not, and the maximum length in bytes. To disable a command, highlight the command, click Edit, and uncheck the Enable An SMTP Command box.

H.323 Filter

As network bandwidth An increases exponentially, the popularity of conferencing applications, such as Microsoft NetMeeting, will continue to grow. The H.323 specification provides multimedia products such as NetMeeting 3.0 the capability to communicate across the Internet. With ISA Server, the H.323 filter can provide users video, audio, and data connectivity.

There are several protocol definitions that are installed when you install the H.323 Gatekeeper service. You use protocol rules in conjunction with the protocol definitions to control clients' access. There are protocol definitions for allowing incoming and outgoing calls, allowing audio and video, allowing T120, and application sharing that are predefined with H.323 Gatekeeper. You could, for example, limit your clients' access to only audio or only incoming calls by configuring protocol rules. Protocol definitions are covered in more detail in Chapter 6, "Configuring Policy Elements."

To configure the H.323 filter, use the following procedure:

1. In the ISA Server Management console, click on Servers and Arrays, the name of your server (or array), Extensions, Application Filters.
2. Right-click H.323 Filter on the right-hand pane and click Properties.
3. On the General tab, ensure that the Enable TThis Filter box is checked.
4. On the Call Control tab, check the Use This Gatekeeper box and enter the FQDN of the H.323 Gatekeeper that will be used by the ISA Server, as shown in Figure 4.11.
5. Check or uncheck the appropriate actions for Call Direction and Media Control.

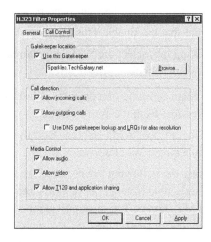

FIGURE 4.11
Configuring the H.323 filter.

Streaming Media Filters

Another aspect of the increasing bandwidth of the Internet is the popularity of streaming media products, such as Windows Media Player, Real Player, and QuickTime. ISA Server provides a built-in filter for these media types.

The streaming media filter is used to allow Firewall and SecureNAT clients the capability to use streaming media protocols to access streaming media servers, such as Windows Media Technology (WMT) servers.

An added benefit of the streaming media filter is the fact that *live stream splitting* can be used. For example, if you have 100 users listening to a Webcast simultaneously on the Internet, you can set up a local WMT server to receive the Webcast, and then forward it to all the clients. This saves your Internet bandwidth.

> **TIP**
>
> To take advantage of live stream splitting, you must first install Windows Media Services on your Windows 2000 computer.

To configure the streaming media fact filter, use the following procedure:

1. In the ISA Server Management console, click on Servers and Arrays, the name of your server (or array), Extensions, Application Filters.
2. Right-click Streaming Media Filter on the right-hand pane and click Properties.
3. On the General tab, ensure that the Enable This Filter box is checked.
4. On the Live Stream Splitting tab, select the WMT Live Stream Splitting mode, as shown in Figure 4.12. Here are your options:

   - Disable WMT Live Stream Splitting (the default option)—Use this option if the media stream will not be accessible from the WMT server.
   - Split Live Streams Using a Local WMT Server—Use this option if the media stream will be accessible from a single WMT server.
   - Split Live Streams Using the Following WMT Server Pool—Use this option if the media stream will be accessible from a pool of WMT servers. Click on Add and add the IP addresses for the WMT servers. You must provide the IP addresses of internal WMT servers. ISA Server will check against the LAT to ensure that you don't add external addresses here. You also need to provide the WMT administrator's account credentials.

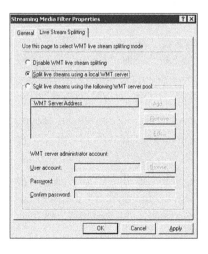

FIGURE 4.12

Configuring the streaming media filter.

TIP

When you configure live stream splitting and select the option to use a WMT server pool, you need to enter the user account of the WMT server administrator. Make sure that this user account is a member of the Netshow Administrators group on every WMT server in the pool.

Intrusion Detection Filters

The intrusion detection filters analyze inbound traffic looking for any possible intrusions from the outside world. ISA Server comes with Domain Name System (DNS) and Post Office Protocol (POP) intrusion filters. Let's look at what type of intrusions these filters can detect.

DNS Intrusion

The DNS intrusion filter has the capability to check for the following intrusions:

- DNS Hostname Overflow—Hostname overflow occurs when a hostname exceeds a certain predefined length.
- DNS Length Overflow—Length overflow occurs when DNS responses contain an IP address that is more than the standard four bytes in length.
- DNS Zone Transfer from Privileged Ports (1-1024)—This occurs when a client application transfers a DNS zone from a local DNS server on a privileged port. Privileged port numbers 1-1024 are used by a client process.
- DNS Zone Transfer from High Ports (above 1024)—This occurs when a client application transfers a DNS zone from a local DNS server on a high port.

To configure the DNS intrusion filter, use the following procedure:

1. In the ISA Server Management console, click on Servers and Arrays, the name of your server (or array), Extensions, Application Filters.
2. Right-click DNS Intrusion Detection Filter on the right-hand pane and click Properties.
3. On the General tab, ensure that the Enable This Filter box is checked.
4. On the Attacks tab, you can filter the inbound traffic for one of the following four filters, as shown in Figure 4.13:
   - DNS host name overflow
   - DNS length overflow
   - DNS zone transfer from privileged ports (1-1024)
   - DNS zone transfer from high ports (above 1024)

4

ISA SECURITY
CONCEPTS
PART II

Microsoft ISA Server 2000

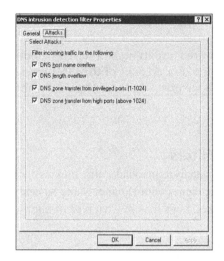

FIGURE 4.13
Configuring the DNS intrusion detection filter.

POP Intrusion

Similar to DNS host name overflow and DNS length overflow, the POP intrusion detection filter analyzes inbound traffic and looks for any possible buffer overflows. Hackers can attempt to cause a buffer overflow on the POP server so they can execute commands and possibly gain root-level access.

To configure the POP intrusion filter, use the following procedure:

1. In the ISA Server Management console, click on Servers and Arrays, the name of your server (or array), Extensions, Application Filters.

2. Right-click POP Intrusion Detection Filter on the right-hand pane and click Properties.

3. On the General tab, ensure that the Enable This Filter box is checked, as shown in Figure 4.14.

4. The POP intrusion detection filter doesn't offer any additional configurable parameters.

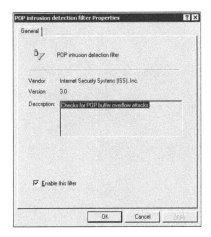

FIGURE 4.14
Configuring the POP intrusion detection filter.

Summary

This second chapter on security was focused on IP packet filtering. We started off by discussing what IP packet filters are used for. Filters are created in ISA Server to either allow or block traffic, although all traffic is blocked by default unless you explicitly allow it. You were introduced to two types of static IP packet filters: Allow and Block. You also learned about the situations where the use of packet filtering is mandatory.

This chapter also introduced the application filter concepts in detail. Application filtering works in a different way compared to packet filtering. With packet filtering, only the header of the packet is examined. With application filtering, the entire message is examined for potential problems. In this chapter, we explored the built-in application filters in great detail.

The next chapter will explore ISA Server's caching concepts. You will learn about the caching features such as distributed caching, hierarchical caching, scheduled caching, forward caching, and reverse caching. In addition to configuring these caching features, you will also learn how to optimize the cache performance.

4

ISA SECURITY
CONCEPTS
PART II

ISA Acceleration Concepts

IN THIS CHAPTER

- Forward Caching   122
- Reverse Caching   127
- Scheduled Caching   128
- Active Caching   131
- Negative Caching   133
- Distributed Caching   135
- Hierarchical Caching   136
- Introduction to CARP   137
- Cache Drives   140
- .cdat Files   141
- Summary   142

When ISA Server is installed in Integrated or Cache mode, it can keep frequently accessed objects on the Web in its cache. ISA Server can cache both HTTP objects (such as Web pages, graphics, and videos) as well as FTP objects (such as text files or programs). Retrieving objects locally from the server's cache improves performance and reduces bandwidth utilization. Because the cached Web objects accelerate the process, this feature is the *acceleration* component of Internet Security and Acceleration Server.

In this chapter we will explore ISA Server's caching concepts. We will look at the caching features such as distributed caching, hierarchical caching, scheduled caching, forward caching, and reverse caching. We will learn how to configure them and talk about the functions used to optimize caching performance.

Where you get the contents, from the Internet or from cache, is determined by the cache policy. We will cover the details of configuring cache policy for HTTP and FTP objects. In addition, we will look at the Cache Array Routing Protocol (CARP), how caching works in an array, the files that are used by the cache, and how to configure the cache drives.

Forward Caching

When one talks about caching in ISA Server, they usually are referring to *forward caching*. This is the type of caching that ISA Server performs when the internal clients access contents on the Internet. In other words, when a client accesses external resources on the Internet, the ISA Server caches the objects, so that next time the client can access the objects quickly from the local cache.

The next few sections discuss several important caching concepts. First you will be introduced to the requirements for forward caching. Then you will be presented with the advantages of caching in general. A sidebar discusses a useful tool that Microsoft provides with ISA Server to view the cached contents. Web and FTP objects have a limited lifespan, and the section on understanding TTL will explain this concept. Finally, you will learn how ISA Server cache works behind the scenes.

Forward Caching Requirements

Depending on the number of clients that will be accessing the servers on the Internet, you will need to meet different hardware requirements so that the ISA Server can properly fulfill clients' requests. For example, if the number of users accessing objects on the Internet is up to 500, the requirements can be significantly different when you double the clients to 1000. In larger enterprises where you may have several ISA Servers, you should consider setting up arrays. For details on my hardware recommendations for forward caching, see Chapter 2, "ISA Server Installation and Configuration."

Advantages of Caching

Whether you implement forward or reverse caching, the benefits are the same. Clients can access contents from the ISA Server's cache quickly instead of waiting for ISA Server to retrieve the contents. When one user connects to a Web site and downloads certain contents, the rest of the users will be able to quickly get to the same contents if ISA Server is configured to cache the contents. For these users, the performance enhancement becomes even more obvious as they retrieve more and more contents and don't have to wait for the usual download times as they did without the objects being cached.

Caching also saves valuable network bandwidth because the lines don't have to be tied to retrieve the same contents over and over again. As we will discuss later, you can even schedule the content downloads, which enhances the performance even further.

Another advantage that caching can provide, especially if your network has an unreliable connection to the Internet, is that it can store frequently accessed Web objects locally when the Internet is not accessible. If this occurs, your network users will be able to see Internet contents even if the Internet connection is unavailable. Furthermore, cache additions are initially stored in RAM, allowing for faster access. Periodically, when system usage is low, the Web Proxy service copies several objects at a time to the hard disk cache. This is known as a *batch update*. In addition, it creates a backup of its cache folder. The backup folder can be helpful in recovering cached contents. Sometimes the Web Proxy service may terminate abnormally; for example, it may hang. When the service is restarted, the backup folder is used to recover the cached contents that otherwise may have been lost.

ISA Server Cache Directory Tool

ISA Server comes with a tool known as Cache Directory Tool (CacheDir.exe), which is located on the ISA Server CD under the \Support\Tools\TroubleShooting folder. You must execute this tool from the location where you've installed ISA Server. Simply copy the CacheDir.exe file from the CD to your ISA Server installation folder, which is located by default in \Program Files\Microsoft ISA Server, and execute it.

This graphical tool can be used to display the cache contents in real-time on the ISA Server hard disk. One thing to keep in mind is that the tool doesn't display the contents in RAM; it only lists contents located in the disk cache. To display as much cache contents as possible, first copy the contents from RAM to the hard disk by restarting the Web Proxy service, and then start the Cache Directory Tool. To view the cache contents in real-time, simply execute `CacheDir.exe` to start the graphical user inter-face. To save cache content information to a file, type the following at the command prompt:

```
CacheDir.exe -dump > filename.txt
```

where `filename.txt` is the name of the text file that will contain the cache information.

The tool allows you to mark certain contents as obsolete, which means that the ISA Server won't return these objects to the client from its cache, although they may still be residing in the servers' cache. To mark objects as obsolete, right-click a URL in the details pane and select Mark As Obsolete. You can also right-click and select Show Headers to see additional information about the objects.

Understanding TTL

ISA Server caches the objects for a certain *Time-To-Live (TTL)* value. Each object is marked with a TTL and when it expires, the object expires. The client contacts the ISA Server and requests the objects. The server checks to see whether there are objects in the cache with a valid TTL value. If the objects exist, they are returned to the client. Otherwise, depending on how you've configured your cache policy, the server goes to the Internet and retrieves the objects for the client.

For HTTP objects, the TTL can be configured as a percentage of the time of the content's existence. For example, unless the source specifies expiration, objects with a TTL value set to 40% will be updated less frequently than the objects that have a TTL value set to 20%.

Configuring TTL Values for HTTP Objects

To configure a TTL value for HTTP objects, use the following procedure:

1. In the ISA Management console, click on Servers and Arrays, *<your server name>*, Cache Configuration.
2. Right-click Cache Configuration, then click Properties.
3. On the HTTP tab, ensure that the Enable HTTP Caching box is checked.
4. As Figure 5.1 shows, you can configure one of the following three options. The objects in the cache can be updated

   Frequently (Expire Immediately)—This will keep the contents fresh for the users (shorter TTLs), but will affect network performance because the contents are downloaded more frequently from the Internet.

   Normally—This option is the default and offers a happy medium. Objects will be cached frequently, but not enough to affect the network performance too much.

Less Frequently (Reduced Network Traffic Is More Important)—This option will improve network performance as the cache is updated less frequently (longer TTLs), but the contents may be somewhat outdated.

Set Time To Live (TTL) of Object in Cache To—This option is used when you want to customize the TTL and have more control over how the contents should be updated. Figure 5.1 shows custom TTL values. This Percentage of Content Age (Time Since Creation or Modification) specifies how long before the contents should expire. The value is expressed in percentage. Lower values mean the cache will be updated more frequently. You can also specify a minimum and maximum time that the HTTP objects should be cached by entering a value in the No Less Than and No More Than boxes.

5. To reset the values to default, click on the Restore Defaults button. This will reset all the custom TTL values to the default and switch you to the Normally option for cache updates.

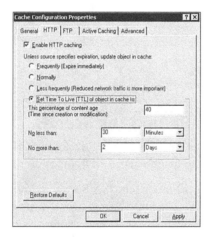

FIGURE 5.1
Configuring TTL values for HTTP objects.

Configuring TTL Values for FTP Objects

To configure a TTL value for FTP objects, use the following procedure:

1. In the ISA Management console, click on Servers and Arrays, *<your server name>*, Cache Configuration.

2. Right-click Cache Configuration and then click Properties.

3. On the FTP tab, ensure that the Enable FTP Caching box is checked.

4. As Figure 5.2 shows, you only have one option to configure TTL for all FTP objects. You can specify time in seconds, minutes, hours, days, and weeks. The default setting updates the FTP cache every 1440 minutes (24 hours).

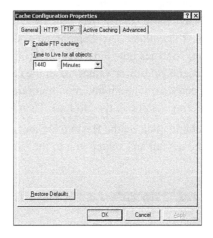

FIGURE 5.2
Configuring TTL values for FTP objects.

ISA Server Cache—Behind the Scenes

As we've discussed, ISA Server can cache frequently accessed HTTP and FTP objects for the clients so that the objects can be quickly retrieved from the cache instead of the Internet.

To illustrate a step-by-step procedure on how ISA Server performs forward caching, let's use the following scenario. Rose, a user in the IT department, accesses the Microsoft.com Web site every morning after she gets to work at 8 a.m. Sam, another user in IT, does the same thing, except that he has different hours and gets into the office at 9 a.m. Both Rose and Sam access the same ISA Server. The following steps occur at 8 a.m.:

1. Rose's browser requests contents from Microsoft.com.

2. ISA Server checks to see whether it contains Microsoft.com in its cache. For the sake of argument, Microsoft.com is not in the cache, so ISA Server will request it from the Internet.

3. Microsoft.com contents are returned to the ISA Server.

4. ISA Server puts the contents of Microsoft.com into its cache, and then also sends the contents to Rose's Web browser.

When Sam arrives at the office at 9 a.m., the following steps will occur:

1. Sam's browser requests Microsoft.com.

2. ISA Server checks to see whether it contains Microsoft.com in its cache.

3. The contents of Microsoft.com are in the cache, and the cache contents are sent to Sam's browser.

Obviously, Sam benefits from the availability of contents in the cache, as he doesn't have to wait for the contents to be downloaded from the Internet. All other users that request the same objects will also benefit from the cached contents. Needless to say, even Rose will get to the objects quicker the next time she requests the same objects.

> **NOTE**
>
> By default, smaller objects (fewer than 12,800 bytes) are kept in memory as well as on the hard disk. Larger objects are only cached on the hard disk. You can change the maximum size of objects in RAM by configuring the option Maximum Size of URL Cached in Memory (bytes). See the section Configuring Negative Caching later in this chapter for more details.

Reverse Caching

If you recall from our earlier discussions, forward caching is used to cache objects for the internal clients accessing contents on the Internet. *Reverse caching* is the exact opposite. It is used to provide caching for external Internet clients that are accessing your internal servers. The published servers (Web servers) that the external clients access are located behind the ISA Server computer, and are therefore invisible to the clients. The ISA Server simply impersonates the published servers and caches the contents for the external clients.

Reverse Caching Requirements

According to Microsoft, a single 450MHz Pentium III ISA Server can easily handle about 250 hits per second from Internet users. For a larger number of hits, you might want to consider faster computers. As a guideline, for each additional 250 hits per second, Microsoft recommends you add an additional ISA Server computer. Microsoft's guidelines are usually conservative. I recommend you don't use anything less than a Pentium III 1GHZ processor and 512MB of RAM for an ISA Server. Keep in mind, this is a *recommendation*, not a *requirement*.

You can configure the amount of free memory that ISA Server should use for caching. By default, ISA Server will use 50% of free memory for caching. Depending on the amount of objects that you will be caching, make sure that you have enough memory to serve all your caching needs with still enough RAM left for other services and processes. If your ISA Server is primarily used for Web caching, you can set this to a higher percentage, such as 80%. However, if you are running additional services or applications on the ISA Server, then use a lower percentage.

Advantages of Reverse Caching

Like forward caching, reverse caching provides speed advantages to your external clients. In addition, because there is limited traffic from your ISA Server to the Web server, less network bandwidth is used.

Let's say Microsoft TechNet wants to make certain articles on its online Web site available to Internet users. Microsoft knows that these articles are very popular and will be accessed by a large number of people. With reverse caching, these popular articles can be retrieved from the server's cache. Because the contents are coming from cache, more people will be able to access the articles in a shorter period.

Scheduled Caching

If you are a busy network administrator, the last thing you need is to be tied up on the phone all day long just to get price updates from your hardware vendor. It would be much easier if the vendor would just fax you the updated prices overnight, so when you arrive at the office they would be waiting for you. *Scheduled caching* works in the same fashion. You can provide ISA Server with a schedule to automatically download Internet objects during a specific day, time, or repeating schedule.

The scheduled cache content download service can be used when you install ISA Server in Cache or Integrated mode. To use this service, you create jobs in ISA Management console, and Windows 2000's scheduled cache content download service (w3prefch) uses those jobs to fetch contents from the Web servers on the Internet. You can schedule downloads of a single URL, multiple URLs, or a complete Web site.

NOTE

You can configure scheduled cache content downloads for both inbound and outbound traffic. However, do not configure scheduled cache content download jobs from a Web server that requires user authentication. If you do, the scheduled content download will fail.

Creating a Scheduled Cache Download Job

To create a scheduled cache content download job, use the following procedure:

1. In the ISA Management console, click on Servers and Arrays, *<your server name>*, Cache Configuration, Scheduled Content Download Jobs.

2. Right-click Scheduled Content Download Jobs, click New, then click Job to start the Scheduled Content Download Job Wizard.

3. Enter a name for the job, such as ISA Server on Microsoft.com.

4. On the Start Time screen, select the date and time to start the downloads, as shown in Figure 5.3.

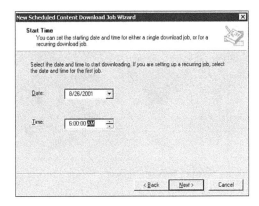

FIGURE 5.3

Specifying date and time for downloading cache contents.

5. On the Frequency screen, specify how often you want the contents to be downloaded, as shown in Figure 5.4.

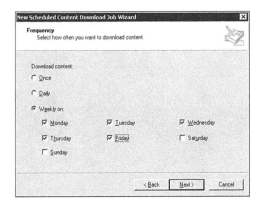

FIGURE 5.4

Specifying the frequency for downloading contents.

6. On the Content screen, specify the URL, as shown in Figure 5.5. Notice that the URL can point to any page, not just the home page of a Web site. You can limit the download to the URL domain and avoid downloading from the sites to which the URL links. In addition, you can also cache the dynamic content.

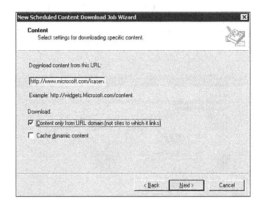

FIGURE 5.5

Specifying the downloading of specific Web contents.

7. On the Links and Downloaded Objects screen, shown in Figure 5.6, you can specify whether to always override the object's TTL or only to override TTL if it is not defined. Under Links Depth, you can decide how deep you want to travel into the links, or configure the ISA Server to have no limit on maximum depth. You can even limit the maximum number of objects that are cached. The default is 99,999, but you can go as high as 999,999,999.

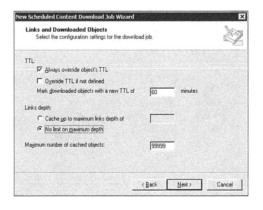

FIGURE 5.6

Configuring the TTL and links for downloaded objects.

8. On the final screen, click Finish to complete the wizard.

After you have created a scheduled job, you can change the location from which you want to download the contents by going to the properties of the job and clicking on the Parameters tab. Type a different URL under Begin Downloading From URL, as shown in Figure 5.7.

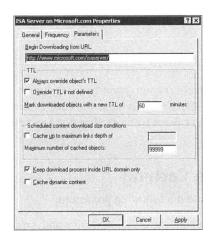

FIGURE 5.7
Customizing URLs that are downloaded.

Advantages of Scheduled Caching

Scheduled content download jobs enable you to download objects that you believe will be heavily used during peak hours of operation. For example, if you notice in your log files that 20% of your outbound Web traffic is going to Amazon.com, you may want to create a download job to download the Amazon.com Web site during off-peak hours. Therefore, when users access Amazon.com during the peak hours, you will have a cached copy available for them.

As I mentioned earlier, you can create a scheduled content download job to download a single URL, an entire Web site, or even multiple domains. Optionally, you can specify to cache objects that are under normal circumstances not cacheable as noted in their HTTP headers.

Another advantage of scheduled caching is that not only can you request download jobs that are outbound to the Internet, but you can also request inbound jobs that go to internal Web servers located behind your ISA Server.

Active Caching

When you enable *active caching*, ISA Server examines the objects in the cache to determine how popular they are. Objects that are accessed frequently are refreshed before they expire. As an administrator, you can configure the frequency with which the objects are updated.

Active caching actively retrieves Web objects and stores them in the cache on the ISA Server computer. In general, active caching will affect the bandwidth usage, because in order to keep the objects fresh in the cache, ISA Server has to make more trips to the Internet to actively update the objects.

The next section describes how you can configure active caching, followed by the section that explains how active caching works.

> **NOTE**
>
> Don't worry if you use a dial-up connection to the Internet. Active caching will auto-matically dial out to your ISP, and then close the connection after it has updated the cache. However, if you don't want to be dialing out too often, disable active caching.

Configuring Active Caching

To configure active caching, use the following procedure:

1. In the ISA Management console, click on Servers and Arrays, *<your server name>*, Cache Configuration.

2. Right-click Cache Configuration and then click Properties.

3. On the Active Caching tab, ensure that the Enable Active Caching box is checked.

4. As Figure 5.8 shows, the objects in the cache can be automatically retrieved using one of the following three options:

   Frequently (Client Performance Is More Important)—This will keep the cached contents fresh for the users, but will affect network performance because the contents are down-loaded more frequently from the Internet.

   Normally (Client Performance and Reduced Network Traffic Are Equally Important)—This option is the default and offers a happy medium. Objects will be cached frequently, but not enough to affect the network performance too much.

   Less Frequently (Reduced Network Traffic Is More Important)—This option will improve network performance as the cache is updated less frequently, but there is less likelihood that the objects will be fresh in the cache.

5. To reset the values to default, click the Restore Defaults button. This will reset the value to the default Normally option for cache updates.

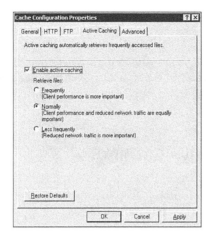

FIGURE 5.8
Configuring active caching options.

How Active Caching Works

When active caching is enabled on an ISA Server, the following steps occur with a cached object:

1. If an object is already in the cache and another client requests the object before its TTL has expired, the object is placed on an "active list."

2. The object will remain on the active list if a client continues to request the object within the specified TTL.

3. As long as the object remains on the active list, it will be actively downloaded before the TTL expires. Depending on how busy ISA Server is (and ISA Server takes that into consideration when using active caching), the download can occur anywhere from half of the TTL remaining, up to just before the TTL expires.

4. If a client does not request the object within the specified TTL, the object is removed from the active list, and will not be an object that is downloaded with active caching until it is put on the list again.

Negative Caching

Negative caching is a rather interesting concept. Even if the TTL for an object has expired, the ISA Server can be configured to retrieve it from the cache when the object is unavailable on the Internet. In other words, when ISA Server can't retrieve contents from the Internet, you can cache the response to the clients' requests. This is known as *negative caching*. Because the error messages are cached, the clients see the messages very quickly.

> **CAUTION**
>
> One thing to keep in mind when you configure negative caching is that the results are cached even if the Web site is not available. When the Web site becomes available again, the clients may still continue to receive error messages until the TTL for the objects expires.

Configuring Negative Caching

Configuring negative caching causes HTTP objects with the following codes to be cached: 203 (partial information), 300 (redirection), 301 (object has moved permanently), and 410 (object is gone).

Here's how you can configure negative caching:

1. In the ISA Management console, click on Servers and Arrays, *<your server name>*, Cache Configuration.
2. Right-click Cache Configuration and then click Properties.
3. On the Advanced tab, check the box Cache Objects Even If They Do Not Have an HTTP Status Code of 200, as shown in Figure 5.9. This will cause ISA Server to cache objects that do not include an OK response (HTTP code 200).

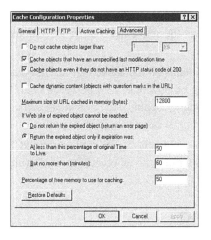

FIGURE 5.9
Configuring negative caching options.

You can configure ISA Server to return expired objects when a Web server is not available. Here's the procedure:

1. In the ISA Management console, click on Servers and Arrays, *<your server name>*, Cache Configuration.

2. Right-click Cache Configuration and then click Properties.

3. On the Advanced tab, as shown in Figure 5.9, select the option Return The Expired Object Only If Expiration Was and configure the TTL values as follows:

   At Less Than This Percentage of Original Time To Live—Enter the maximum period in percentage format of the original TTL setting that the ISA Server will return expired objects. The default is 50%.

   But No More Than (Minutes)—Specify the maximum time, in minutes, for which the ISA Server will return objects even after the object's TTL has expired. The default is 60 minutes.

TIP

The ISA Server installation folder contains a folder called ErrorHtmls. The default location is C:\Program Files\Microsoft ISA Server\ErrorHtmls. This folder contains the error messages that the Web server returns to the client. Customize the error messages by editing the HTML pages so they are more relevant and useful to the clients.

Distributed Caching

Up until now, we have assumed that all of the caching has been taking place on one computer. However, you might be wondering what happens when you have an array. This is where distributed caching (and hierarchical caching) plays a role in your network.

Furthermore, if you have a larger network, routing may play a significant role in how your ISA Servers are set up. A cache is no good if your users cannot access it properly, so knowing these types of caching is important for making ISA Server useful in your network.

Distributed caching enables a cache to be spread out among all ISA Server computers in an array. An *array* is a group of ISA Server computers that is configured to provide load balancing and distributed caching. The array is managed as a single logical entity and provides fault tolerance.

ISA Server uses Cache Array Routing Protocol (discussed later in this chapter) to make the group of computers in an array look like a single logical entity. For example, although you might have five computers in an array, each with 20GB cache drives, ISA Server will recognize them as one logical cache that's 100GB in size.

Hierarchical Caching

Hierarchical caching simply extends the distributed caching functionality by chaining arrays of ISA Server computers to form a hierarchy. Hierarchical caching is also referred to as *chained caching*, because in essence the arrays are chained together. The main advantage of hierarchical caching is that in addition to improving cache performance, by moving the cache closer to the users, it provides fault tolerance and distributes the server load to several computers.

In hierarchical caching, servers can be chained individually or as arrays. When the clients request an object from the array, the request is sent upstream until the object is located. Let's say the object was located upstream on the third server. After the object is found, it is returned to the client and is cached at every server on its way back to the client.

Typical Hierarchical Caching Scenario

In a typical scenario, branch offices are configured so that the cache requests are routed upstream to the corporate headquarters before ending up on the Internet. Figure 5.10 shows how hierarchical caching works. Let's walk through a step-by-step procedure in this scenario.

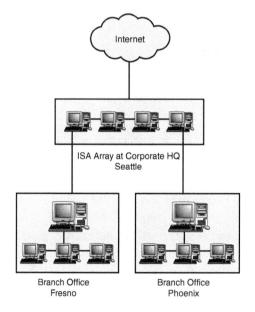

FIGURE 5.10

A typical hierarchical caching scenario.

The corporate headquarters is located in Seattle. The branch offices are located in Fresno and Phoenix. Each branch office has its own ISA Server for the local clients. The corporate headquarters in Seattle has an array of ISA Servers. The clients go through the Seattle array to get to the Internet.

1. Chris requests a URL from the local ISA Server in Fresno. Let's assume that the page is not available in the cache.

2. The ISA Server forwards the request to the ISA Server array in Seattle. The page is not located in the cache, so it is retrieved from the Internet.

3. The server in the array that retrieves the page adds it to its cache and then forwards it to the ISA Server in Fresno.

4. The server in Fresno caches the page and then sends it to Chris. He has to wait a little while for the page to load, because it has to be retrieved from the Web.

5. His co-worker Shawn requests the same page a little bit later.

6. The local ISA Server in Fresno already contains the page, so Shawn gets to see it right away. Shawn wants to share the cool information on the page with his boss in Seattle, so he sends the URL to her in an e-mail.

7. Brenda clicks on the URL and gets the information quickly from the server in Seattle because it was already cached before it was sent to Chris in the first place.

8. Steve in Phoenix happens to access the same page. The ISA server in Phoenix doesn't have the page, so it forwards the request to Seattle.

9. The page is already cached in the array in Seattle, so it is sent to the server in Phoenix.

10. The server in Phoenix caches the page locally and then sends the page to Steve. Although Steve has to wait for the page to load, it's not as long as Chris had to wait in Fresno when he requested the page. This time the request didn't go all the way to the Internet, so the access time was relatively shorter.

Introduction to CARP

The *Cache Array Routing Protocol* (CARP), a protocol that Microsoft used in Proxy Server 2.0, is used in ISA Server for enhancing routing and cache requests within ISA Server arrays. By using hash-based routing, CARP determines an ideal path to locate the cached objects in an array. This section will take an in-depth look at CARP and discuss how this protocol can be implemented in your network.

Understanding CARP

In 1995, an industry standard emerged known as Internet Cache Protocol (ICP). The purpose of ICP was to enable communication among multiple proxy servers on a network. Microsoft developed CARP to overcome the limitations in ICP and used it to implement distributed caching in Proxy Server 2.0.

In large networks that consist of several ICP-based servers, there are several network bandwidth issues that need to be addressed. Also, when you are dealing with large arrays with several servers, you may encounter duplicated cached objects. Instead of using queries for distributed caching, CARP uses hash-based routing that is smart in the sense that for any given URL request, the browser will know exactly where the request is located in an array. CARP treats all members of an array as one unit and avoids duplication of cached contents. This not only reduces network traffic, it enhances performance for end users.

CARP is the protocol that ISA Server uses to determine the fastest path from the workstation to the server that is holding the requested object. Using CARP provides the following advantages:

- CARP automatically adjusts to the addition or removal of servers in an ISA Server array.
- Instead of using queries, CARP uses hash-based routing techniques, which offers efficient routing, and therefore improved performance.
- CARP prevents all ISA Servers from containing mirrored data.
- Unlike ICP arrays, where addition of servers in an array degrades performance, CARP's performance increases as more servers are added to the array.
- CARP runs on top of the HTTP protocol.

Difference Between ICP and CARP

Some Proxy servers use ICP as their protocol for determining the location of the cached objects. However, Microsoft created CARP to try to circumvent some of the issues with ICP.

One of the biggest issues with ICP is that it performs queries to determine the proxy server that contains the cached object. This can result in increased network traffic, especially if you have a large number of proxy servers in your array.

Another issue with ICP is the fact that performance is seriously affected as more servers are added to an array. According to Microsoft tests, performance actually increases as additional servers are added to an ISA Server array.

Another potential issue with ICP is the fact that over time, all computers in an array can have redundant data. CARP prevents this common occurrence from happening. For example, if your ISA array is comprised of help desk analysts providing support for Microsoft products, the following situation can occur. If a common help desk problem leads the help desk analysts to the same Web objects at support.microsoft.com, the cache on each array member can be filled with those specific objects if ICP is used. With CARP however, Microsoft uses special routing algorithms to ensure that this does not happen.

CARP's Use in ISA Server

As mentioned previously, with CARP no queries are performed on your network. CARP uses a hash-based algorithm. Using a hash-based algorithm to locate an object with CARP is done using the following steps:

1. Each ISA Server in the array is located in the Active Directory schema. When servers are added or removed, all members are notified.

2. A hash is computed for each server and each URL that a user requests. The computation takes place both on the client and on the server side.

3. Using these hashes, an algorithm is used to produce a *score*. Therefore, the ISA Server computer that has the highest score becomes the owner of the information.

4. The server receives the client's request and if it can't handle the request, it forwards it to another member of the array.

One advantage of CARP in ISA Server is that CARP automatically provides support when a computer is added or deleted from the array. If one of the ISA Servers goes down, the requests are simply rerouted to the ISA Server that has the next highest score.

Enabling CARP in ISA Server

To enable CARP in ISA Server, use the following procedure:

1. In the ISA Management console, go to Servers and Arrays, right-click the name of the array and then click Properties.

2. On the Incoming Web requests tab, check the box Resolve Requests Within Array Before Routing, as shown in Figure 5.11.

FIGURE 5.11

Enabling CARP for incoming Web requests.

NOTE

By default, CARP is only enabled for outgoing Web requests. If you want to enable CARP for incoming Web requests, check the box Resolve Requests Within Array Before Routing, as shown in Figure 5.11.

CARP's Use in Distributed and Hierarchical Caching

In distributed caching, CARP takes the ISA Server computer with the highest score and returns the Web object to the end user. However, there might be situations where the client doesn't support CARP. Because each ISA Server in an array is aware of all the other members in the array, it can forward the request to another member in the array. Note, however, that the original ISA Server will not cache the object; thus resulting in less potential for a cache to become filled with the same objects.

In hierarchical caching, the request is sent downstream to the same ISA Server that originated the request. This also prevents the potential of having all machines in the array having the same objects.

NOTE

For more information on CARP, check out Microsoft's white paper "Cache Array Routing Protocol and MS Proxy Server version 2.0" at http://www.microsoft.com/technet/archive/proxy/prxcarp.asp.

Cache Drives

Now that you have an understanding of caching theory, it is also important to know about the physical aspects of caching. This section will discuss the cache drives themselves, what their requirements are, and the files they use.

Cache Requirements

ISA Server stores cache information on a drive that you specify during installation. This location must be a local NTFS drive that has a drive letter assigned to it. If you are using FAT partitions, you will need to convert to NTFS before configuring the cache.

For best results, use a drive other than the one that has the ISA Server or the Windows 2000
operating system installed on it. In addition, ensure that the partition is defragmented. If not,
format the partition before using it for caching. Another factor that will affect the performance
of caching on your ISA Server is the speed of the hard disk. For improved performance, use a
hard disk with a higher spin rate, lower seek time, and larger buffer.

As long as you have at least 150MB of free disk space on an NTFS partition, the ISA Server
will configure a cache size of 100MB. Just for the record, the minimum size allowed for the
cache is 5MB.

.cdat Files

ISA Server stores cached information in a .cdat file that is located in the \urlcache subdirec-
tory of the drive where the cache is installed. During installation, ISA Server creates the .cdat
file with the same size of the requested cache. However, if you have requested a cache that is
larger than 10GB, ISA Server will create one .cdat file for each 10GB of drive space you specify for the cache. For example, if you specify a cache size of 36GB, a total of four .cdat files
will be created; three .cdat files with each containing 10GB, and one that contains 6GB.

As Web objects are continually added to the cache, ISA Server automatically adds them to the
.cdat file. When the .cdat file becomes full, it removes the older objects as it writes newer
objects to the file.

NOTE

Don't try to modify the .cdat files. You could possibly corrupt your cache. If your
cache files somehow become corrupted, try using the following procedure to fix the
problem. Stop the Web Proxy service, delete the \urlcache folder(s), and then restart
the Web Proxy service. Obviously, you will lose any existing cache but will be able to
slowly rebuild the cache contents.

You can adjust the size of the cache by using the following procedure:

1. In the ISA Management console, go to Servers and Arrays, *<your server name>*, Cache Configuration, Drives.
2. In the right-hand pane, double-click the server.
3. In the Maximum Cache Size (MB) box, type the desired size of the cache in megabytes and then click Set, as shown in Figure 5.12.
4. If you have multiple drives, repeat the same procedure for each drive.

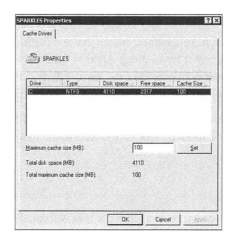

FIGURE 5.12
Adjusting the cache size.

Summary

Caching is known as the *acceleration* portion of Internet Security and Acceleration Server. Chapter 5 introduced ISA Server's acceleration concepts. The many types of caching, such as forward, reverse, active, scheduled, and negative caching were explained. In addition, distributed and hierarchical caching were introduced for administrators who will be using ISA Server in larger networks.

You also discovered CARP, the cache array routing protocol used by distributed and hierarchical caching routing requests . Finally, Chapter 5 also showed information on cache drives and their requirements.

In Chapter 6, "Configuring Policy Elements," you will explore the various components of the policy elements in ISA Server. You will look at the client address sets, destination sets, content groups, bandwidth priorities, protocol definitions, and a whole lot more.

Configuring Policy Elements

IN THIS CHAPTER

- Policy Elements Overview   144
- Bandwidth Priorities   145
- Client Address Sets   149
- Content Groups   152
- Destination Sets   156
- Dial-up Entries   158
- Protocol Definitions   159
- Schedules   170
- Using Array and Enterprise Policy Elements Together   172
- Summary   172

In this chapter, we will first define policy elements and then take a look at each policy element that ISA Server provides, as well as how to use enterprise and array policy elements together.

ISA Server policy elements include the following:

- Bandwidth priorities
- Client address sets
- Content groups
- Destination sets
- Dial-up entries
- Protocol definitions
- Schedules

Policy Elements Overview

If you are an avid e-mail user, you know the frustration of sending out an e-mail to a whole group of users only to find out that you missed a few users who needed to see it. A few users changed their e-mail addresses and never received the e-mail, and a few more users didn't even need your e-mail because it didn't apply to them. That's why many e-mail programs come with the functionality of distribution lists.

Distribution lists enable you to specify one e-mail address for a whole group of e-mail users. If a user needs to be added, you simply add the name to the distribution list. If a user changes his or her e-mail address, you simply modify the address within the distribution list. If the user doesn't need to be on the list, you can simply remove them from the distribution list. Management of distribution lists is much easier than managing multiple e-mail accounts.

In much the same way distribution lists are used by e-mail applications, ISA Server provides what are known as *policy elements*. You can group common elements together (e-mail addresses within an e-mail program) and give them a specified name (a distribution list), making ISA management much less cumbersome.

Policy elements can be created either for each array policy or for an enterprise policy.

Enterprise-level policies, which apply to enterprise-level rules, can only be created by members of the Enterprise Admins group. For standalone ISA Servers, you can only create array-level policy elements, because those computers are not part of the domain. In a large enterprise, you might have a combination of array- and enterprise-level policies. If so, you can apply enterprise-level policy elements to your array-level rules.

Bandwidth Priorities

The first policy element we will discuss is *bandwidth priorities*. Bandwidth priorities determine the priority level that a connection has to ISA Server. For example, if you have a frequent flyer gold card with a major airline, chances are that you will have the opportunity to board the airplane before other members of coach class. Likewise, if you are flying first class, most airlines will have you board before those of you flying in coach class, and, in most cases, even before they board the gold card members. Therefore, the priorities of boarding an airplane are first class, gold card members, and then coach class, usually from the back of the plane to the front of the plane.

Connections through ISA Server are treated in a similar respect. If there are multiple requests for the ISA Server (passengers), network connections with the greater bandwidth priority (first class tickets or gold card members) will be processed first (board the plane).

A default bandwidth priority is installed when ISA Server is installed, and it guarantees a minimum bandwidth. A connection that has a bandwidth priority, no matter how low, will still take precedence over a connection with the default bandwidth priority. Similarly, a passenger with a boarding pass will take precedence over someone who is flying on standby.

Bandwidth priorities can be used for internal users accessing the Internet and for external clients accessing your internal resources. The priority for both is set on a numerical scale between 1 and 200, with 200 being the highest priority.

If you are a member of the help desk team at your company, you probably hear from the same users time after time complaining about the slow Internet access. You can create a bandwidth priority called "complainers," add these users to a bandwidth rule that uses this policy element, and give it a priority of 200.

> **NOTE**
>
> Although you can specify bandwidth priorities, you cannot specify bandwidth quotas. For example, you cannot specify that users can only download 10MB worth of Internet contents per day. In addition, you cannot assign specific bandwidth, such as 20kb/s.

Windows 2000 QoS

Windows 2000 supports Quality of Service (QoS), a mechanism that enables administrators to control the quality of service to end users. This includes access to network resources and applications across disparate networks. ISA Server builds on QoS by informing QoS how to prioritize network connections. In reality, ISA Server doesn't even know how bandwidth priority works. The configuration of the bandwidth rules is only a fancy way to configure QoS on the ISA Server computer itself. For more information, check out Microsoft's white paper on QoS at `http://www.microsoft.com/windows2000/techinfo/howitworks/communications/trafficmgmt/enablingqos.asp`.

Creating a Bandwidth Priority

There's a default bandwidth rule that can't be modified or deleted. This rule applies to all IP traffic, at all destinations, all the time, for all content groups, and has an inbound and outbound bandwidth set to 100. This rule is applied last in order and ensures that if you don't have a bandwidth rule, at least you will be guaranteed a minimum bandwidth priority assigned by the default Windows 2000 scheduling. However, if you want to control how much bandwidth should be allocated to specific clients' requests, you first create new policy elements that can be applied to the rule, then you create a new bandwidth priority.

It will be helpful to understand that even though the default bandwidth rule (under Publishing) cannot be modified, the default bandwidth priority (under Policy Elements, Bandwidth Priorities) can be modified. As previously mentioned, its default value is 100. So the point to understand here is that even though the default bandwidth rule can't be modified and everything in its properties is grayed out, it is quite possible to modify the default bandwidth priority which is used by the default rule.

Let's say you want to reserve higher bandwidth for all network administrators that use Terminal Services for remote administration. First, create a policy element under Bandwidth Priorities, then create a bandwidth rule. Here's how you will create a new bandwidth priority policy element:

1. In the ISA Management console, go to Servers and Arrays, *<your server name>*, Policy Elements, Bandwidth Priorities.
2. Right-click Bandwidth Priorities and click on New; then click Bandwidth Priority.
3. In the Name box enter a name, such as `Remote Administration`.
4. In the Description box enter an optional description.
5. In the Outbound Bandwidth (1-200) box type a number between 1 and 200 (for example, `150`). Also enter a value in the Inbound Bandwidth (1-200) box. The inbound bandwidth priority is used by ISA Server to allocate the bandwidth for requests from external clients for resources on the internal network. The outbound bandwidth priority is used to allocate the bandwidth for requests from internal clients for objects on the Internet.
6. Click OK to create the bandwidth priority policy element.

After you have created a bandwidth priority policy element, you need to create a bandwidth priority rule. Here's how you will create a new bandwidth priority rule.

1. In the ISA Management console, go to Servers and Arrays, *<your server name>*, Bandwidth Rules.

2. Right-click Bandwidth Rules and click on New; then click Rule to start the New Bandwidth Rule Wizard.

3. Enter a name for the bandwidth rule, such as `Terminal Services`.

4. On the Protocols screen, you can choose to apply the rule to All IP Traffic, Selected Protocols, or All IP Traffic Except Selected. Because you want to enable IT Administrators to use Terminal Services, you will select Selected Protocols and then check the RDP (Terminal Services) box, as shown in Figure 6.1.

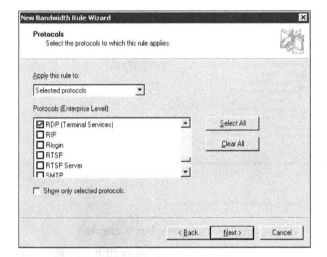

FIGURE 6.1

Selecting a protocol for a new bandwidth rule.

5. On the Schedule screen, select the default schedule of Always.

6. On the Client Type screen, select Specific Users and Groups.

7. On the Users and Groups screen, click Add and select IT Administrators Group. This will limit the rule so it is only applied to the IT Administrators group.

8. On the Destination Sets screen, select All Destinations.

9. On the Content Groups screen, select All Content Groups.

10. On the Bandwidth Priority screen, you will select the Custom Priority radio button. If you had previously configured bandwidth priorities, you could have selected them in the drop-down box. Don't worry if you didn't. You can always modify the priorities after the wizard is complete.

11. On the final screen, click Finish to complete the wizard.

Figure 6.2 shows your new bandwidth rule. To change the priority level, double-click the Terminal Services rule and follow these steps:

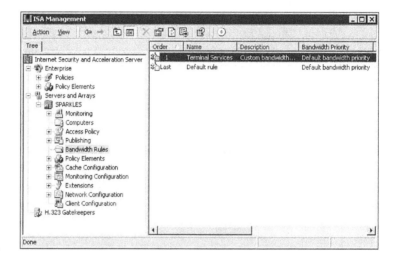

FIGURE 6.2

The bandwidth rule order in ISA Management console.

1. On the General tab, ensure that the Enable box is checked.

2. On the Bandwidth tab, click on Specified Priority (if it isn't already selected) and then click New.

3. On the New Bandwidth Priority screen, enter a name for the priority such as Terminal Services, an optional description, and an inbound and an outbound bandwidth value (for example 150).

4. On the Bandwidth tab, select the custom priority you just created from the drop-down box, as shown in Figure 6.3.

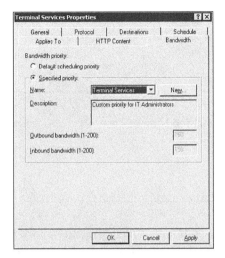

FIGURE 6.3
Configuring the Bandwidth tab for a custom bandwidth priority.

TIP

You can change the order of the rule in the right-hand pane (see Figure 6.2) of the ISA Management console. To change the order, right-click a rule and then select Move Up or Move Down. The option is only available when you have more than one rule (excluding the default rule). The default rule cannot be modified, deleted, or renamed. In addition, its order cannot be changed by moving it up or down.

Modifying and Deleting a Bandwidth Priority

Modifying a bandwidth priority is simple. To do so, right-click the specified bandwidth priority located in the results pane, and select Properties. You can configure any of the seven tabs, as shown in Figure 6.3.

To delete a bandwidth priority, right-click the bandwidth priority you want to delete and select Delete. Click Yes when asked for confirmation.

Client Address Sets

Client address sets are a popular policy element. They enable you to group your network users into elements. When you publish servers to external clients, you can limit the rules by applying them to certain client address sets. For example, if you have remote offices in Toronto, Chicago, and Boston, you could create three client address sets—one for each location, with the server publishing rules applied to all three. Obviously, the IP addresses that you specify in the client address sets are not limited to the internal network clients; they can include Internet clients.

> **NOTE**
>
> Client address sets are specified by IP address only. You cannot create a client address set using computer or user names.

> **CAUTION**
>
> You might apply a server publishing rule to a client address set thinking that the rule will only apply to IP addresses that you've specified in the client address set. However, this is only true if the IP packet filtering is enabled. If IP packet filtering is disabled, the server publishing rule will apply to all clients.

Creating a Client Address Set

To create a client address set, use the following procedure. You can create a client address set for both an array and for enterprise setups.

To begin creating a client address set for an array, go to the ISA Management console, select Servers and Arrays, *<your array name>*, Policy Elements, and Client Address Sets. If you are creating a client address set for the enterprise, begin in the ISA Management console, go to Enterprise, Policy Elements, and Client Address Sets. After you have arrived in the proper array or enterprise configuration box, the following steps will help you complete the creation of the client address set:

1. Right-click Client Address Sets, New, then click Set.
2. Enter a name for the Client Set, for example Toronto Users, as shown in Figure 6.4. Enter an optional description if you so desire.
3. Under the Members section, click Add and type the range of IP addresses that belong to the Toronto users.

Modifying and Deleting a Client Address Set

To modify a client address set, right-click on the set you want to modify in the results pane and select Properties. On the General tab, you can modify the name or the optional description. On the Address tab, you can add, edit, or remove the IP address sets, as shown in Figure 6.5.

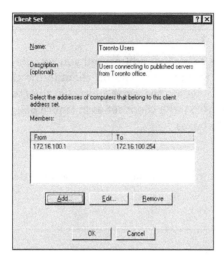

FIGURE 6.4

Creating a client address set.

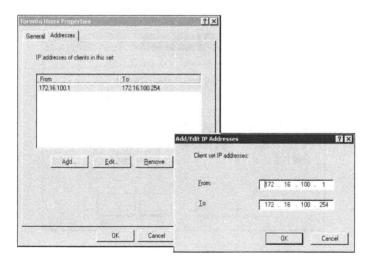

FIGURE 6.5

Modifying a client address set.

> **TIP**
>
> You cannot add domains to a client address set; you can only add IP address ranges. However, if you wanted to add only a specific client in the client address set, you can add a single IP address by typing the same address in the From and To boxes. For example, to add 172.20.10.64 as a client set as in Figure 6.5, you'll type 172.20.10.64 in both the From and To boxes.

To delete a client address set, right-click on the set you want to delete and select Delete. Click Yes to confirm deletion.

> **CAUTION**
>
> When you delete a client address set, pay close attention to the dialog box, as shown in Figure 6.6. If you delete a client address set and a rule is configured to use the set, ISA Server will not start.

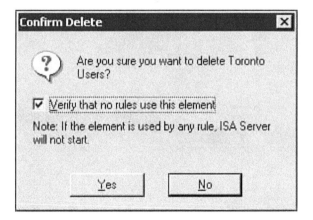

FIGURE 6.6
Confirmation dialog box for deleting a client address set.

Content Groups

Content groups are a listing of built-in file extensions and Multipurpose Internet Mail Extensions (MIME) types. If you create site and content rules, or bandwidth rules, you can limit these rules to certain content groups. Needless to say, this gives you a lot more control over your security and access management, because not only are you controlling access to specific destinations, you are also able to control access to certain contents.

As a client, when you request HTTP contents, the ISA Server looks at the MIME types or the file name extensions to determine whether a rule applies to a content group with the filename extension that you requested. If it does, ISA Server processes the rule.

As a client, when you request FTP objects, ISA Server handles it in a similar fashion by looking at the filename extension. If the rule applies to a content group, ISA Server proceeds by processing the rule.

> **NOTE**
>
> You can use content groups with HTTP and FTP traffic only. HTTPS traffic is not supported.

Content groups can be used to control the types of files that can be downloaded from the Internet. This is accomplished by using the file's MIME type. For example, if you don't want your users downloading QuickTime movie files, you would add a content rule for the .mov extension.

ISA Server has built-in content groups that are pre-configured for specific file types. To view a list of the content groups that were installed with ISA Server, click on an array or select Enterprise, Policy Elements, and then select Content Groups. The list of built-in content groups is located in the right-hand pane, as shown in Figure 6.7.

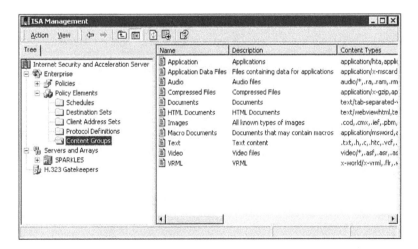

FIGURE 6.7
ISA Server's built-in content groups for common file types.

> **NOTE**
>
> By default, Microsoft's Internet Information Server (IIS) 5.0 comes with a number of pre-configured associations. Non-Microsoft Web servers may use their own default associations. See Appendix D for a table of the common MIME types found in IIS 5.0.

Adding a Content Group

First, to add a content group in an array, navigate to the ISA Management console, go to Servers and Arrays, *<your array name>*, Policy Elements, Content Groups. To add a content group to an enterprise setup, navigate to the ISA Management console and go to Enterprise, Policy Elements, Content Groups. To create a new content group, use the following procedure:

1. Right-click Content Groups and click on New, then click Content Group.

2. Enter a name for the New Content Group, for example QuickTime, as shown in Figure 6.8.

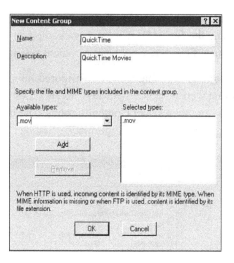

FIGURE 6.8

Creating a new content group.

3. Enter an optional description.

4. Under Available Types, select .mov from the drop-down box, and then click Add. Click OK to close the window.

Modifying and Deleting a Content Group

To modify a content group, right-click on the group you want to modify in the results pane and select Properties. On the General tab, you can modify the name or the optional description. On the Content Types tab, you can add or remove the MIME type, as shown in Figure 6.9.

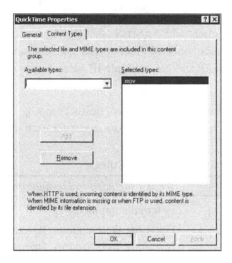

FIGURE 6.9
Modifying a content group.

To delete a content group, right-click on the group you want to delete, and select Delete. Click Yes to confirm deletion.

CAUTION

When you delete a content group, pay close attention to the dialog box, as it will tell you that if you delete a content group and a rule is configured to use the group, ISA Server will not start.

TIP

When configuring content groups, you can use asterisks as wildcards if you are working with MIME types. However, wildcards are not supported with file extensions. If you want to configure all text types (text/html, text/plain, text/rich text, and so on) simply use text/* in the Available Types field.

Destination Sets

ISA Server also provides you with the capability to limit what addresses clients can access by using *destination sets*. A destination set can include IP ranges, computer names, and paths. There are internal destination sets, which include computers inside your internal network, and external destination sets, which include computers outside your internal network.

Destination sets differ from client address sets in that the client address sets can be specified only by a range of IP addresses, while destination sets can be specified by a computer name, multiple computer names, an IP address, multiple IP addresses, or even sub-directories on a computer.

There are several rules that can take advantage of destination sets. Table 6.1 shows what types of computers are usually included in the destination sets for each of these rules.

TABLE 6.1 Computers Included in Various Rules

Type of Rule	What's Included in Destination Sets?
Bandwidth Rule	External computers
Routing Rule	Outgoing Web requests: External computers Incoming Web requests: Internal computers
Site and Content Rule	External computers
Web Publishing Rule	Internal computers

Let's verify some terminology you just encountered in the previous table. *Internal* refers to computers on your internal private network. *External* refers to the computers on the Internet.

Creating a Destination Set

This section will show you how to create a new destination set. To start, if you are creating a destination set in an array, begin in the ISA Management console. Next, go to Servers and Arrays, *<your array name>*, Policy Elements, Destination Sets. For an enterprise destination set within the ISA Management console, navigate to Enterprise, Policy Elements, Destination Sets. After you have arrived in the proper starting place, use the following procedure:

1. Right-click Destination Sets and click on New, then click Set.

2. Enter a name for the New Destination Set, for example `Microsoft Corporation`.

3. Enter an optional description.

4. In the Include These Destinations section, click Add.

5. In the Add/Edit Destination screen, either select a domain or specify a range of IP addresses. To add a specific computer, make sure the Destination button is selected and enter the computer's fully qualified domain name in the box provided. To add an IP address, enter an IP address in the box labeled From. To select a range of IP addresses, also enter an ending IP address in the box labeled To. You can also type the path to a specific folder or file in the Path box. We will use a wildcard to specify all the computers in the Microsoft.com domain, as shown in Figure 6.10.

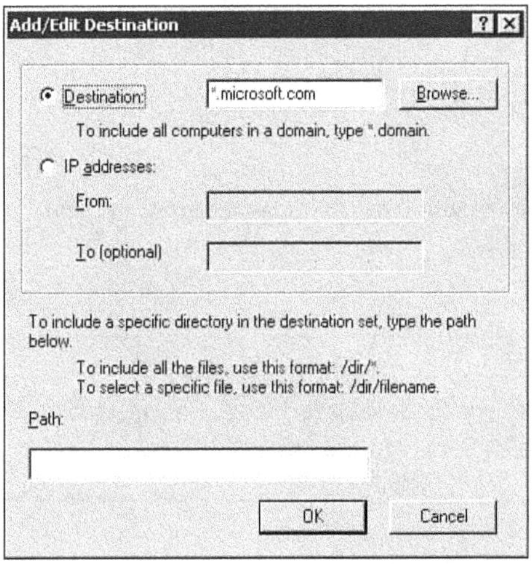

FIGURE 6.10
Creating a destination set.

6. Add additional domains or a range of IP addresses if desired.

7. Click OK to close the window.

TIP

You must enter the path in a UNIX-style format, using the forward slash (/) instead of the backslash (\). The entries are not case sensitive.

Modifying and Deleting a Destination Set

To modify a destination set, right-click on the destination set you want to modify in the results pane, and select Properties. On the General tab, you can modify the name or the optional description. On the Destinations tab, you can add, edit, or remove the entries.

To delete a destination set, right-click on the destination set you want to delete, and select Delete. Click Yes to confirm deletion.

> **CAUTION**
>
> When you delete a destination set, pay close attention to the dialog box. If you delete a destination set and a rule is configured to use the set, ISA Server will not start.

Dial-up Entries

Dial-up entries specify the method used to connect an ISA Server computer to the Internet. Only one dial-up entry can be active for an array at any time, and it specifies how the array itself can connect to the Internet.

> **NOTE**
>
> In order for a dial-up entry to be created, the dial-up connection must be established and created on every ISA Server in the array.

Creating a Dial-up Entry

To create a new dial-up entry, use the following procedure.

1. In the ISA Management console, go to Servers and Arrays, *<your server name>*, Policy Elements, Dial-up Entries.
2. Right-click Dial-up Entries and click on New, then click Dial-up Entry.
3. Enter a name for the new dial-up entry, for example `Connect to Internet`, as shown in Figure 6.11.
4. Enter an optional description.
5. In the Network Dial-up section, click Select and choose a network dial-up connection. This connection has to exist beforehand. If it doesn't, create a new connection using Network and Dial-Up Connections and then get back to this screen.
6. In the Network Dial-up Account section, click Set Account to add an account that has a dial-up access to the Internet.
7. Click OK to create the dial-up entry.

FIGURE 6.11

Creating a dial-up entry.

Modifying and Deleting a Dial-up Entry

To modify a dial-up entry, right-click on the entry that you want to modify in the results pane and select Properties. On the General tab, you can modify the name or the optional description. On the Dial-up Entry tab, you can select a different dial-up entry or change the network dial-up account.

To delete a dial-up entry, right-click on the entry you want to delete and select Delete. Click Yes to confirm deletion.

Setting an Active Dial-up Entry

By default, the first dial-up entry you create is set to be the active dial-up entry. To make a specific dial-up entry the active entry, right-click on the appropriate entry, and select Set As Active Entry. Your change will take place immediately. Note that if you change an active dial-up entry while an active connection to the Internet is taking place, that connection will be immediately disconnected. Also, you cannot delete an active dial-up entry.

Protocol Definitions

Protocol definitions ease your work as an administrator, because they give you control over the protocols that can be used by the clients. There are several Web protocol definitions that come pre-configured with ISA Server, such as FTP, Gopher, HTTP, and HTTPS. If you apply rules using these protocol definitions, you in effect create dynamic filtering, as opposed to static filtering. In addition to the Web protocol definitions, there are dozens of additional protocols that are available to you after installing ISA Server. If that's not enough, you can even add your own protocol definitions, should you have an unusual protocol that you need to manage. Furthermore, third party vendors can create application filters that contain protocol definitions.

Protocol definitions can be used in different places. For example, you can use them with protocol rules, server publishing rules, and even application filters.

> **NOTE**
>
> When working with protocol definitions, there's a limit to what you can and cannot modify or delete. Although built-in protocol definitions cannot be modified or deleted, any definitions that you create as an administrator can be modified or deleted. But you cannot change the primary connection information; you can only add information about secondary connections. Any protocol definitions that are installed with the application filters cannot be deleted either, but they can be modified.

Built-in Protocol Definitions

A list of built-in protocol definitions installed by ISA Server can be viewed by clicking on any array or, if you are using an enterprise policy, by selecting Enterprise. For example, to view the list for an Enterprise, go to Policy Elements, Protocol Definitions. The definitions are listed in the right-hand pane, as shown in Figure 6.12.

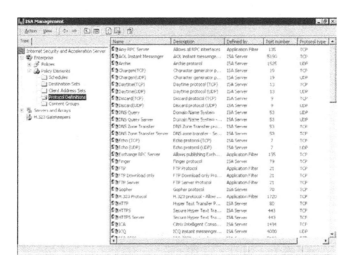

FIGURE 6.12
Built-in protocol definitions.

Although the list of built-in protocol definitions is available in the ISA Management console, you will find the list in Table 6.2 handy as a quick reference guide. It lists the port number, the type of protocol (TCP or UDP) and the direction.

TABLE 6.2 ISA Server's Built-in Protocol Definitions

Built-in Protocol	Description	Defined by	Port No.	Protocol Type	Direction
Any RPC Server	Allows all RPC interfaces	App. filter	135	TCP	Inbound
AOL Instant Messenger	AOL Instant Messenger	ISA Server	5190	TCP	Outbound
Archie	Archie Protocol	ISA Server	1525	UDP	Send/Receive
Chargen (TCP)	Character generator (TCP)	ISA Server	19	TCP	Outbound
Chargen (UDP)	Character generator (UDP)	ISA Server	19	UDP	Send/Receive
Daytime (TCP)	Daytime protocol (TCP)	ISA Server	13	TCP	Outbound
Daytime (UDP)	Daytime protocol (UDP)	ISA Server	13	UDP	Send/Receive
Discard (TCP)	Discard Protocol (TCP)	ISA Server	9	TCP	Outbound
Discard (UDP)	Discard Protocol (UDP)	ISA Server	9	UDP	Send/Receive
DNS Query	Domain Name System	ISA Server	53	UDP	Send/Receive
DNS Query Server	Domain Name System – Server	ISA Server	53	UDP	Receive/Send
DNS Zone Transfer	DNS Zone Transfer	ISA Server	53	TCP	Outbound
DNS Zone Transfer (Server)	DNS Zone Transfer - Server	ISA Server	53	TCP	Inbound

TABLE 6.2 Continued

Built-in Protocol	Description	Defined by	Port No.	Protocol Type	Direction
Echo (TCP)	Echo protocol (TCP)	ISA Server	7	TCP	Outbound
Echo (UDP)	Echo protocol (UDP)	ISA Server	7	UDP	Send/Receive
Exchange RPC Server	Allows publishing Exchange Server	App. filter	135	TCP	Inbound
Finger	Finger protocol	ISA Server	79	TCP	Outbound
FTP	File Transfer Protocol	App. filter	21	TCP	Outbound
FTP Download only	FTP Download only protocol	App. Filter	21	TCP	Outbound
FTP Server	FTP Server protocol	App. Filter	21	TCP	Inbound
Gopher	Gopher protocol	ISA Server	70	TCP	Outbound
H.323 protocol	H.323 Protocol	App. filter	1720	TCP	Outbound
HTTP	Hyper Text Transfer Protocol (HTTP)	ISA Server	80	TCP	Outbound
HTTPS	Secure Hyper Text Transfer Protocol	ISA Server	443	TCP	Outbound
HTTPS Server	Secure Hyper Text Transfer Protocol - Server	ISA Server	443	TCP	Inbound
ICA	Citrix Intelligent Console Architecture	ISA Server	1494	TCP	Outbound

TABLE 6.2 Continued

Built-in Protocol	Description	Defined by	Port No.	Protocol Type	Direction
ICQ	ICQ instant messenger protocol (legacy)	ISA Server	4000	UDP	Send
ICQ 2000	ICQ 2000 protocol	ISA Server	5190	TCP	Outbound
Ident	Ident protocol	ISA Server	113	TCP	Outbound
IMAP4	Interactive Mail Access Protocol	ISA Server	143	TCP	Outbound
IMAP4 Server	Interactive Mail Access Protocol (IMAP) - Server	ISA Server	143	TCP	Outbound
IMAPS	Secure Interactive Mail Access Protocol	ISA Server	993	TCP	Outbound
IMAPS Server	Secure Interactive Mail Access Protocol - Server	ISA Server	993	TCP	Inbound
IRC	Internet Relay Chat	ISA Server	6667	TCP	Outbound
Kerberos-Adm (TCP)	Kerberos administration (TCP)	ISA Server	749	TCP	Outbound
Kerberos-Adm (UDP)	Kerberos administration (UDP)	ISA Server	749	UDP	Send/Receive
Kerberos-IV	Kerberos IV authentication	ISA Server	750	UDP	Send/Receive
Kerberos-Sec (TCP)	Kerberos V authentication (TCP)	ISA Server	88	TCP	Outbound

TABLE 6.2   Continued

Built-in Protocol	Description	Defined by	Port No.	Protocol Type	Direction
Kerberos-Sec (UDP)	Kerberos V authentication (UDP)	ISA Server	88	UDP	Send/Receive
LDAP	Lightweight Directory Access Protocol	ISA Server	389	TCP	Outbound
LDAP GC (Global Catalog)	Lightweight Directory Access Protocol global catalog	ISA Server	3268	TCP	Outbound
LDAPS	Secure Lightweight Directory Access Protocol	ISA Server	636	TCP	Outbound
LDAPS GC (Global Catalog)	Secure Lightweight Directory Access Protocol global catalog	ISA Server	3269	TCP	Outbound
Microsoft SQL Server	Microsoft SQL Server protocol	ISA Server	1433	TCP	Inbound
MMS – Windows Media	Microsoft Media Streaming protocol – Client	App. filter	1755	Mixed	Mixed
MMS – Windows Media Server	Microsoft Media Streaming protocol – Server	App. filter	1755	Mixed	Mixed
MSN	MSN Internet Access protocol	ISA Server	569	TCP	Outbound
MSN Messenger	MSN Messenger protocol	ISA Server	1863	TCP	Outbound

TABLE 6.2 Continued

Built-in Protocol	Description	Defined by	Port No.	Protocol Type	Direction
Net2Phone	Net2Phone protocol	ISA Server	6801	UDP	Send
Net2Phone Registration	Net2Phone Registration protocol	ISA Server	6500	TCP	Outbound
NetBIOS Datagram	NetBIOS Datagram protocol	ISA Server	138	UDP	Send
NetBIOS Name Service	NetBIOS Name Service protocol	ISA Server	137	UDP	Send/Receive
NetBIOS Session	NetBIOS Session protocol	ISA Server	137	TCP	Outbound
NNTP	Network News Transfer Protocol (NNTP)	ISA Server	119	TCP	Outbound
NNTP Server	Network News Transfer Protocol - Server	ISA Server	119	TCP	Inbound
NNTPS	Secure Network News Transfer Protocol	ISA Server	563	TCP	Outbound
NNTPS Server	Secure Network News Transfer Protocol - Server	ISA Server	563	TCP	Inbound
NTP (UDP)	Network Time Protocol (UDP)	ISA Server	123	UDP	Send/Receive
PNM RealNetworks protocol (Client)	RealNetworks Streaming Media Protocol (PNM) – Client	App. filter	7070	TCP	Outbound

TABLE 6.2 Continued

Built-in Protocol	Description	Defined by	Port No.	Protocol Type	Direction
PNM RealNetworks protocol (Server)	RealNetworks Streaming Media Protocol (PNM) – Server	App. filter	7070	TCP	Inbound
POP2	Post Office Protocol v.2	ISA Server	109	TCP	Outbound
POP3	Post Office Protocol v.3	ISA Server	110	TCP	Outbound
POP3 Server	Post Office Protocol v.3 – Server	ISA Server	110	TCP	Inbound
POP3S	Secure Post Office Protocol v.3	ISA Server	995	TCP	Outbound
POP3S Server	Secure Post Office Protocol v.3 - Server	ISA Server	995	TCP	Inbound
Quote (TCP)	Quote of the day (TCP)	ISA Server	17	TCP	Outbound
Quote (UDP)	Quote of the day (UDP)	ISA Server	17	UDP	Send/Receive
RADIUS	Remote Authentication Dial-In User Service	ISA Server	1812	UDP	Send/Receive
RADIUS Accounting	Remote Authentication Dial-In User Service accounting	ISA Server	1813	UDP	Send/Receive
RDP (Terminal Services)	Remote Desktop Protocol (Terminal Services)		3389	TCP	Outbound
RIP	Routing Information Protocol		520	UDP	Send/Receive

TABLE 6.2 Continued

Built-in Protocol	Description	Defined by	Port No.	Protocol Type	Direction
Rlogin	Remote login protocol		513	TCP	Outbound
RTSP	Real Time Streaming Protocol – Client	App. filter	554	TCP	Outbound
RTSP Server	Real Time Streaming Protocol – Server	App. filter	554	TCP	Inbound
SMTP	Simple Mail Transfer Protocol (SMTP)	ISA Server	25	TCP	Outbound
SMTP Server	Simple Mail Transfer Protocol – Server	ISA Server	25	TCP	Inbound
SMTPS	Secure Simple Mail Transfer Protocol	ISA Server	465	TCP	Outbound
SMTPS Server	Secure Simple Mail Transfer Protocol (SMTP) – Server	ISA Server	465	TCP	Inbound
SNMP	Simple Network Management Protocol (SNMP)	ISA Server	161	UDP	Send/Receive
SNMP Trap	Simple Network Management Protocol - Trap	ISA Server	162	UDP	Send/Receive
SSH	Secure Shell protocol	ISA Server	22	TCP	Outbound

TABLE 6.2   Continued

Built-in Protocol	Description	Defined by	Port No.	Protocol Type	Direction
Telnet	Telnet protocol	ISA Server	23	TCP	Outbound
Telnet Server	Telnet protocol - Server	ISA Server	23	TCP	Inbound
TFTP	Trivial File Transfer Protocol	ISA Server	69	UDP	Send
Time (TCP)	Time protocol (TCP)	ISA Server	37	TCP	Outbound
Time (UDP)	Time protocol (UDP)	ISA Server	37	UDP	Send/Receive
Whois	Nickname/ Whois protocol	ISA Server	43	TCP	Outbound

Adding a Protocol Definition

Let's say you want to add Cisco's Gateway Discovery Protocol that uses TCP port 1997. To add this protocol definition for arrays or for a standalone ISA Server, begin in the ISA Management console, go to Servers and Arrays, <*your server name*>, Policy Elements, Protocol Definitions. To begin with an enterprise policy, go to the ISA Management console, Enterprise, Policy Elements, Protocol Definitions. After you have reached your starting point, use the following procedure to add a protocol definition:

1. Right-click Protocol Definitions and click on New, then click Definition to start the New Protocol Definition Wizard.

2. Enter a name for the New Protocol Definition, for example `Cisco GDP`.

3. In the Primary Connection Information screen, enter the following information:

   Port number: 1997

   Protocol type: TCP

   Direction: Inbound

4. On the Secondary Connections screen, select the No option.

5. Click Finish to complete the wizard.

TIP

If the protocol you are using requires additional connections after the initial connection has been made, configure secondary connections on the Parameters tab. You may configure more than one secondary connection for a given definition.

Modifying and Deleting a Protocol Definition

To modify a protocol definition for arrays, begin in the ISA Management console, go to Servers and Arrays, *<your server name>*, Policy Elements, Protocol Definitions. To begin with an enterprise policy, go to the ISA Management console, Enterprise, Policy Elements, Protocol Definitions. After you have reached your starting point, use the following procedure to modify a user-defined protocol:

1. Right-click Protocol Definitions and select Properties.
2. On the General tab, you can edit the name or add/edit the description of the protocol.
3. On the Parameters tab, you can add a secondary connection that will be used after the connection has been made on the initial connection.

TIP

Unlike most of the other wizards that you have seen so far, the New Protocol Definition Wizard doesn't allow you to enter a description. It only allows entering a name. After the wizard is complete, go back into the Properties of the definition and enter a definition on the General tab.

As mentioned earlier, you can only delete the protocol definitions that you create as an administrator; built-in definitions cannot be modified or deleted.

To delete a protocol definition, right-click on the protocol definition and select Delete. Click Yes to confirm the deletion.

CAUTION

When you delete a protocol definition, pay close attention to the dialog box that is displayed. If you delete a protocol definition and a rule is configured to use the definition, ISA Server will not start.

Schedules

If you use any type of personal organizer, you know that most of them come with the capability to schedule appointments. Some of the better ones, however, give you the capability to schedule on a recurring basis. For example, if you enter someone's birthday, many of the better organizers allow you to schedule it yearly, and the birthday is entered into your calendar every year automatically. Better yet, if you have a meeting every other Thursday at 9 a.m., some organizers enable you to set a schedule that sets your biweekly meetings automatically. This eliminates your having to figure each meeting out individually and entering it multiple times into your calendar.

Schedules work with the rules. After you have created rules, you apply schedules to them to determine the times that the rules are going to be in effect. Schedules can be applied to site and content rules, bandwidth rules, and protocol rules.

> **NOTE**
>
> ISA Server enables you to create schedules, but it comes with two built-in schedules:
> - Weekends: All day Saturday and Sunday
> - Work Hours: Monday through Friday, from 9 a.m. to 5 p.m.

Adding a Schedule

To add a schedule for an array, start out in the ISA Management console, go to Servers and Arrays, <*your array name*>, Policy Elements, Schedules. To begin the procedure for adding a schedule in an enterprise policy, in the ISA Management console, go to Enterprise, Policy Elements, Schedules. After you have arrived at your starting point, add a schedule using the following procedure:

1. Right-click Schedules and select New, Schedule.
2. On the New Schedule screen, enter a name for the schedule and type an optional description, as shown in Figure 6.13. Also select the active hours, such as Monday through Friday 1 p.m. to 5 p.m.

Modifying and Deleting a Schedule

If you need to modify an existing schedule, use the following procedure. As in most procedures you have encountered throughout the chapter, you can begin your process in an array or in an enterprise policy. To modify a schedule for arrays, begin in the ISA Management console, go to Servers and Arrays, <*your array name*>, Policy Elements, Schedules. For an enterprise policy, in the ISA Management console, go to Enterprise, Policy Elements, Schedules. After you have reached your starting point, use the following procedure to modify a schedule:

1. Right-click Schedules and select Properties.
2. On the General tab, you can edit the name and the description of the schedule.
3. On the Schedule tab, modify the schedule as needed, as shown in Figure 6.14.

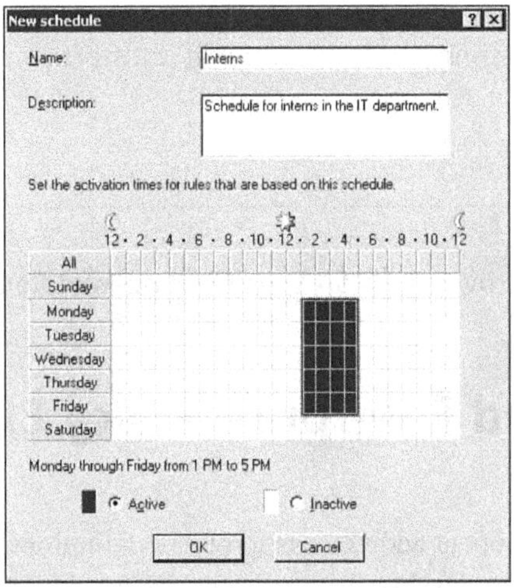

FIGURE 6.13
Creating a new schedule.

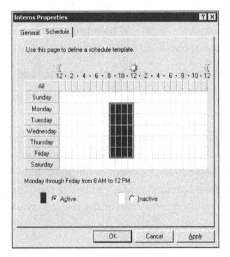

FIGURE 6.14
Modifying the properties of an existing schedule.

To delete a schedule, right-click on the schedule and select Delete. Click Yes to confirm the deletion.

CAUTION

Throughout the chapter you have been cautioned that deleting items will give you a warning stating that if any element you delete is used in a rule, ISA will not start. When you delete a schedule, the same applies. If you delete a schedule and a rule is configured to use the definition, ISA Server will not start.

NOTE

The built-in schedules provided by ISA Server can be modified and deleted.

Using Array and Enterprise Policy Elements Together

Schedules, destination sets, client address sets, protocol definitions, and content groups can be created at either the enterprise level or the array level. Bandwidth priorities and dial-up entries can only be created at the array level.

You create enterprise-level policy elements within your enterprise. If you are creating enterprise-level rules, you may use these policy elements with those rules.

However, if you are using both array-level and enterprise-level policy elements, you can use your array-level rules with enterprise-level policy elements, but not vice versa.

With standalone servers, only array-level policy elements are used.

Summary

This chapter introduced you to policy elements and their role in ISA Server. The seven types of policy elements available to ISA Server—bandwidth priorities, client address sets, content groups, destination sets, dial-up entries, protocol definitions, and schedules—were introduced. In addition, instructions on how to add, modify, and delete these policy elements were also discussed. Finally, information on using array and enterprise policy elements together was given.

Careful planning and implementation of these policy elements can ease the administration burden and provide effective security on your corporate network.

In the next chapter, you will learn how to configure server publishing and Web publishing for internal and external clients, publish rules, and establish listeners. We will also look at various publishing scenarios.

Implementing Publishing

IN THIS CHAPTER

- Hardware Requirements for Publishing   176
- Web Publishing Concepts   177
- Server Publishing Concepts   186
- Running Additional Services on an ISA Server Computer   195
- Publishing a Mail Server   198
- Summary   203

Chapter 7 will focus on Web Publishing and Server Publishing concepts and configuration. You will learn how to properly deploy publishing servers in a secure fashion in your environment. When an ISA Server is acting as a firewall, the configuration on the server itself requires special attention. You will learn how to configure the browser and run certain other services on the ISA Server computer. Additional topics that will be covered include Server Publishing rules, listeners, configuring clients for Server Publishing, and publishing a mail server.

Publishing Terminologies

Microsoft uses the term *Web Publishing* in ISA Server when Web contents on internal Web servers are published for the Internet users. Web Publishing is also known as *reverse proxy*. The term *Server Publishing* is used when all other services are published for the Internet users, such as Exchange or SMTP. In this book, the terms *publishing servers* or *published servers* will be used when there is a need to refer to both Web Publishing and Server Publishing together.

Let's look first at the hardware requirements for publishing servers in general. Then you will be introduced to the Web Publishing concepts, followed by the Server Publishing concepts.

Hardware Requirements for Publishing

This section will limit the publishing requirements to the ISA Server computer. The hardware requirements for the published server will depend on the type of services that are running on the published server. Obviously, the hardware requirements for an Exchange or a SQL Server will be different than, for instance, an FTP server or a Web server. To determine the requirements for a published server, you need to observe how frequently the Internet clients are requesting objects from a published server. In other words, you need to initially estimate the number of requests (hits) per second that you anticipate on the published server. The tables in Chapter 2, "ISA Server Installation and Configuration," cover more details on hardware requirements.

As you learned in Chapter 5, "ISA Acceleration Concepts," you can configure reverse caching for external clients. This helps Internet clients to access objects on the internal servers quickly from ISA Server's cache. Depending on the size of the contents that are published, you will need, at minimum, the amount of memory in the ISA Server computer to match the size of the published contents. For example, if you are publishing 500MB of objects, you will need a minimum of 512MB of RAM in the ISA Server to handle all the cached contents. Needless to say, you should be pretty generous with the amount of memory in the ISA Server, because other services on the server will also consume memory.

The best thing to do is monitor your server for publishing activities on a regular basis, then adjust the hardware accordingly.

For more information on hardware requirements, see Chapter 2.

Web Publishing Concepts

Web Publishing enables you to place your Web server inside the ISA Server and make the contents available to the external clients on the Internet. The contents are published securely, because the ISA Server computer acts as an intermediary and forwards all requests on behalf of the Web server.

Here's how the process works. The Internet clients send a request to communicate with the published Web server. The request is sent to the Web server, but because the published IP address belongs to the ISA Server computer, it intercepts the request and then forwards it to the Web server based on the Web Publishing rules on the ISA Server. When the Web server sends the response back to the Internet client, the ISA Server grabs the request, translates some information in the request so the Internet client sees that the response is coming back from ISA Server's IP address—the only address visible to external clients.

Web Publishing Rules

The Web Publishing rules on the ISA Server determine how the inbound HTTP requests from the clients should be processed, and how the server should respond on behalf of the Web server without compromising security. Typically, the client requests are forwarded to an internal Web server; but if the page is available in the ISA Server computer's cache, the page is provided from the server's cache.

Rules determine what to do with the inbound requests. You can create destination sets that generally include your ISA Server computer's external name. You can also create client sets which normally include the IP addresses of the Internet clients. With destination and client sets, you can control the flow of traffic and essentially filter out requests to meet your security needs.

ISA Server includes a default Web Publishing rule that discards all requests. The server processes each inbound request and forwards the requests based on the Web Publishing rules. If none of the rules apply to the request, or if there is no other rule besides the default rule, the default rule is applied. The default rule discards the requests and is always applied at the end. Therefore, as long as there is a rule that matches the request, the rule is forwarded accordingly; otherwise, the last rule in order (the default rule) is applied, and the request is discarded.

7

IMPLEMENTING
PUBLISHING

> **TIP**
>
> If you right-click Web Publishing Rule and the option to create a new rule is not available, it's probably because the enterprise policy settings are not configured to allow publishing. To allow publishing, log on as enterprise administrator. Right-click the name of your array and then click Properties. On the Policies tab, ensure that the Use Custom Enterprise Policy Settings option is selected, and then check the box Allow Publishing Rules.

Creating a Web Publishing Rule

Let's say you want to create a Web Publishing rule that will allow only Boeing employees to access a Web server that is located on the internal network of your company. To create a new Web Publishing rule, use the following procedure:

1. In the ISA Management console, go to Servers and Arrays, *<your server name>*, Publishing, Web Publishing Rules.

2. Right-click Web Publishing Rules, and click on New, Rule.

3. In the New Web Publishing Rule Wizard, type the name for the rule, for example Boeing Clients.

4. On the Destination Sets screen, you can choose to apply this rule to one of the following:

   • All Destinations

   • All Internal Destinations

   • All External Destinations

   • Specified Destination Set

   • All Destinations Except Selected Set

   You want the rule to be applied to a specific destination set that includes only Boeing employees. Select Specified Destination Set from the drop-down box, as shown in Figure 7.1.

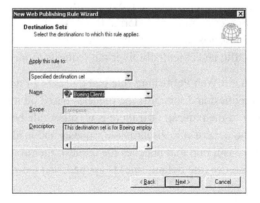

FIGURE 7.1
Applying a Web Publishing rule to a specific destination set.

5. On the Client Type screen, select Specific Users and Groups.

6. On the Users and Groups screen, click Add and then add the Boeing Employees group. You want this rule to be applied only to the Boeing users, as shown in Figure 7.2.

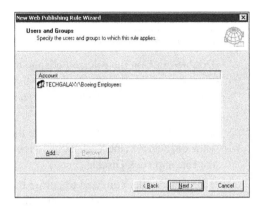

FIGURE 7.2

Applying a Web Publishing rule to a specific group.

7. On the Rule Action screen, click Redirect the Request To This Internal Web Server (Name Or IP Address) and type the fully qualified domain name (for example mars.techgalaxy.net), or the IP address of the Web server that is hosting the contents for the Boeing employees, as shown in Figure 7.3.

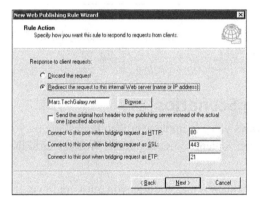

FIGURE 7.3

Redirecting a request to a specific Web server.

8. Click Finish on the last screen to complete the wizard.

You can modify, disable, enable, or delete a Web Publishing rule. Table 7.1 summarizes the procedures.

TABLE 7.1   Modifying, Disabling, Enabling, and Deleting a Web Publishing Rule

Action	Description
To modify a rule	Double-click on the rule and change the name or the description on the General tab. On the Destination tab, you can add additional domains, IP address ranges, or a path to specific folders.
To disable a rule	To disable a rule, you need to ensure that you have the Advanced view enabled. On the View menu, click on Advanced. Right-click the rule and click Disable.
To enable a rule	To enable a rule, you need to ensure that you have the Advanced view enabled. On the View menu, click on Advanced. Right-click the rule and click Enable.
To delete a rule	Right-click the rule and click Delete. Make sure that no other rule is using this element, or else the ISA Server will not start. You can only delete the rules that you create; the default rule cannot be deleted or modified.

NOTE

Web Publishing rules can only be created at the array level. They are not available at the enterprise level.

Web Publishing Scenarios

There are a couple of ways you can implement Web Publishing on your network. In either case, you can publish Web contents on your internal Web server to the Internet clients in a secure manner.

Regardless of the implementation that you use, you must configure the ISA Server computer to listen to incoming Web requests. You might be wondering whether a Web server can use routing and packet filtering to achieve more or less the same results. You could use routing, but that routes the Web requests directly to a server. When you use Web Publishing, ISA Server acts as an intermediary and intercepts all the requests before processing them. In general, routing is used for communication between two TCP/IP addresses; they could either be two internal or two external addresses. Publishing, on the other hand, is used for communication between an internal and external network.

Dealing With DNS Issues

When dealing with published servers, you need to consider the DNS issues. How will the external clients resolve their names? If the DNS server is an internal server, then, like a Web server, it also needs to publish the information for external clients. You should configure Server Publishing on the ISA Server computer so it can publish the internal DNS Server. On the DNS server, simply ensuring that it is a SecureNAT client will eliminate the need for any additional configuration.

Let's consider the following two scenarios. In the first Web Publishing scenario, a Web server is located inside the ISA Server computer on the private network. In the second scenario, the Web services will be published on the ISA Server computer itself.

Publishing a Web Server Inside the Private Network

Let's say you want to publish two Web servers on the techgalaxy.net domain's internal network, one for trainers and the other for consultants. You want trainers to access the Web contents from the Internet using `http://www.techgalaxy.net/trainers`, and the consultants to use `http://www.techgalaxy.net/consultants`. Figure 7.4 shows a graphical layout of the scenario. Here's how you can publish these Web servers:

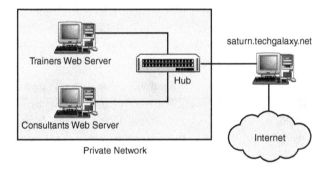

FIGURE 7.4

Publishing a Web server located inside a private network.

1. Create a global group called Trainers Group and add the appropriate users.
2. Create a global group called Consultants Group and add the appropriate users.
3. Create a destination set called Trainers Destination. Include the server name, for example `saturn.techgalaxy.net`, and the path `/trainers/*`.
4. Create a destination set called Consultants Destination. Include the server name, for example `saturn.techgalaxy.net`, and the path `/consultants/*`.

7

IMPLEMENTING
PUBLISHING

> **CAUTION**
>
> On certain pages, the ISA Server Help file instructs you to use backslashes "\" instead of the forward slashes "/." Do not use backslashes. The screen instructions (see Chapter 6, Figure 6.10) are correct, and you must use the forward slashes when you specify the path.

5. On the ISA Server computer, configure the Incoming Web Requests by specifying the *external* IP address of the ISA Server computer.

6. Configure a Web Publishing rule for Trainers. Set the Destination Set to Trainers Destination. You created the set in Step 3. Apply the set to the Trainers Group. On the Action tab, use Redirect the Request To This Internal Web Server and direct the rule to Trainers Server.

7. Configure a Web Publishing rule for Consultants. Set the Destination Set to Consultants Destination. You created the set in Step 4. Apply the set to the Consultants Group. On the Action tab, use Redirect the Request To This Internal Web Server and direct the rule to Consultants Server.

You have now configured your Web servers to publish contents for Trainers and Consultants. You might want to consider one final tweak. The trainers and consultants will use the domain name when they try to access the objects on the internal Web servers. Make sure that on your DNS server you are using a fully qualified domain name to map the IP address of the ISA Server computer.

Publishing a Web Server on the ISA Server Computer

Figure 7.5 shows the second scenario, wherein the ISA Server is also the Web server that needs to be published to the external clients.

In this scenario, let's first examine how the ports are configured on the ISA Server computer by default. On its external interface, ISA Server does not listen to inbound requests. You should configure ISA Server to listen on port 80, as shown in Figure 7.6. For outbound requests, ISA Server listens on port 8080 by default, as shown in Figure 7.7.

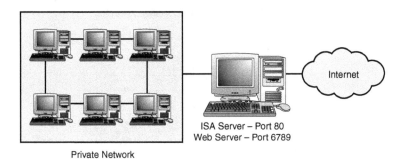

Private Network

FIGURE 7.5

Publishing a Web server on an ISA Server computer.

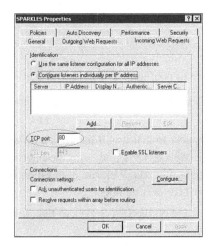

FIGURE 7.6

The default port for inbound requests.

In this scenario, the ISA Server computer is also running Web services. By default, a Web server also uses TCP port 80, which will cause a conflict with the port that ISA Server is listening to on the external interface. Luckily, the solution is rather simple. Configure the Web server to listen on a port other than the default TCP port 80. For example, configure the Web server to listen on port 6789, then create a Web Publishing rule that forwards the request to the Web server on this port.

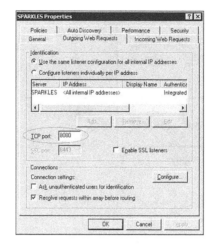

FIGURE 7.7
The default port for outbound requests.

Here's a step-by-step procedure to configure an ISA Server that is also running Web services:

1. Verify that ISA Server is listening on TCP port 80 for inbound requests, as shown in Figure 7.6.

2. Modify the Web server's port so that it will listen on a different unused port, such as TCP port 6789. To modify the Web server's port, start the Internet Services Manager MMC in Administrative Tools. Right-click the Web site in question and select Properties. On the Web Site tab, modify the TCP port number.

3. Create a Web Publishing rule on the ISA Server so that it will forward the requests to the Web server on port 6789.

Now the Internet clients will request Web contents on the standard TCP port 80. The ISA Server listens on port 80, and then realizing it's a Web request, forwards it to the Web server on port 6789. The Web server services the request and ISA Server sends the response back to the client.

Redirecting HTTP and SSL Requests

Both HTTP and SSL requests can be redirected as HTTP, SSL, or FTP requests. This enables you to have more control over your resources and security. Let's first examine how the HTTP requests can be redirected, followed by the process to redirect SSL requests.

To redirect HTTP requests, use the following procedure:

1. In the ISA Management console, go to Servers and Arrays, *<your server name>*, Publishing, Web Publishing Rules.

2. On the View menu, verify that Advanced is checked.

3. In the right-hand pane, right-click the rule you wish to modify and click Properties.

4. On the General tab, ensure that the Enable box is checked.

5. On the Bridging tab, decide how you wish to redirect the requests under the section Redirect HTTP Requests As. The choices are HTTP, SSL, or FTP requests, as shown in Figure 7.8. If you choose SSL, the ISA Server will open a secure channel to the server.

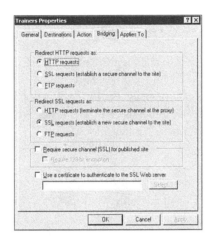

FIGURE 7.8
Redirecting HTTP and SSL requests.

To redirect SSL requests, use the following procedure:

1. In the ISA Management console, go to Servers and Arrays, <*your server name*>, Publishing, Web Publishing Rules.

2. On the View menu, verify that Advanced is checked.

3. In the right-hand pane, right-click the rule you wish to modify and click Properties.

4. On the General tab, ensure that the Enable box is checked.

5. On the Bridging tab, decide how you wish to redirect the requests under the section Redirect SSL Requests As. The choices are HTTP, SSL, or FTP requests, as shown in Figure 7.8.

6. If you select SSL, then check the box Use a Certificate To Authenticate To the SSL Web Server and click on Select to add the certificate that will be used.

7. Notice that if you select Require Secure Channel (SSL) For Published Site, then you can also select a higher-level encryption by checking the box Require 128-bit Encryption. For more information, see the following tip.

TIP

Windows 2000 installs 128-bit encryption automatically when you install Service Pack 2. If you don't have Service Pack 2, you can still upgrade your Windows 2000 computer to 128-bit encryption by downloading a high-encryption pack from Microsoft at no charge at http://www.microsoft.com/windows2000/downloads/recommended/encryption/.

Server Publishing Concepts

The term *Server Publishing* refers to making resources on your private network and internal servers available to external Internet clients. There are several services that you might want to publish to the clients outside your company. For example, an organization such as the Internal Revenue Service (IRS) might want to publish a File Transfer Protocol (FTP) server to the public so they can download IRS forms and publications.

NOTE

Server Publishing Rules are available only when ISA Server is installed in Firewall or Integrated mode.

When you publish servers to external clients, you are not compromising network security. The IP address of the ISA Server computer is the only address external clients can see. The Internet clients send a request to communicate with the published server (for example, an FTP server). The request is sent to the FTP server, but because the published IP address belongs to the ISA Server computer, it intercepts the request and then forwards it to the FTP server. When the FTP server sends the response back to the Internet client, the ISA Server grabs the request and translates some information in the request so the Internet client sees that the response is coming back from ISA Server's IP address—the only address visible to external clients.

To publish servers inside the internal network, you configure Server Publishing rules. Rules determine how the requests (inbound or outbound) should be handled by the server.

NOTE

Web Publishing rules are used to publish HTTP, HTTPS, and FTP contents. Server Publishing rules are used to publish contents other than the aforementioned, such as a database server or an SMTP server.

Configuring Server Publishing

Configuring a server that needs to be published is pretty simple. Published servers are configured as SecureNAT clients, so the configuration required on the server is minimal. All you need to do is ensure that the ISA Server computer is configured as the default gateway on the published server. For example, if your ISA Server computer has an internal IP address of 10.10.10.1, and your SQL Server has an IP address of 10.10.10.125, you will configure 10.10.10.1 as the default gateway on the SQL Server. The SQL Server will act as a SecureNAT client to service the requests of Internet clients. The SQL Server should have a static IP address and, just like any other SecureNAT client on the network, will use DNS to resolve host names.

Server Publishing Rules

For the most part, the concepts of Server Publishing are similar to Web Publishing concepts. The main difference is that with Server Publishing rules, you can filter the contents and then forward it to the internal server. With Web Publishing rules, you simply forward the clients' requests to the Web server without filtering it.

As mentioned earlier, Server Publishing rules are used to publish contents other than those published by Web Publishing rules; namely HTTP, HTTPS, and FTP. This simply means that you can publish contents on just about any computer inside the private network. For example, you can publish a messaging server, such as Exchange, on the private network to the external clients. The security is not compromised, because the external clients communicate with the ISA Server computer and therefore do not have direct access to a published server inside your network.

Creating a Server Publishing Rule

Let's say that your organization needs to provide FTP access to a business partner named Starbucks. The Starbucks employees will be accessing your FTP server to download files. You want to create a Server Publishing rule that will allow only Starbucks employees to access this FTP server that is located on your internal network. To create a new Server Publishing rule, use the following procedure:

1. In the ISA Management console, go to Servers and Arrays, *<your server name>*, Publishing, Server Publishing Rules.

2. Right-click Server Publishing Rules, and click on New, Rule.

3. In the New Server Publishing Rule Wizard, type the name for the rule, for example Starbucks FTP.

4. On the Address Mapping screen, type the IP address of the FTP server that needs to be published. Also, enter the IP address of the external interface of the ISA Server computer, as shown in Figure 7.9.

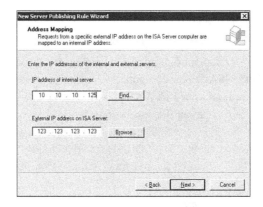

FIGURE 7.9

Configuring address mapping for a Server Publishing rule.

5. In the Protocol Settings screen, select a protocol that you wish to use for the Server Publishing rule, for example FTP Server.

6. On the Client Type screen, you can apply the rule to Any Request or Specific Computers (Client Address Sets). Because you intend to publish the FTP server only for Starbucks employees, you will select the Specific Computers option.

7. On the Clients Sets screen, click Add and select the Starbucks client address set, as shown in Figure 7.10. You should create client address set(s) beforehand; if you haven't, go ahead and create the set(s) now and then restart the wizard.

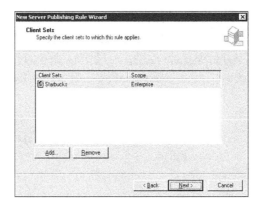

FIGURE 7.10

Specifying a client address set for a Server Publishing rule.

8. Click Finish on the last screen to complete the wizard.

You can modify, disable, enable, or delete a Server Publishing rule. Table 7.2 summarizes the procedures.

TABLE 7.2 Modifying, Disabling, Enabling, and Deleting a Server Publishing Rule

Action	*Description*
To modify a rule	Double-click on the rule and change the name or the description on the General tab. On the Action tab, you can change the mapped IP addresses of the servers, or the mapped server protocol. On the Applies To tab, you can modify the client address sets.
To disable a rule	To disable a rule, you need to ensure that you have the Advanced view enabled. On the View menu, click on Advanced. Right-click the rule and click Disable. Another method to disable a rule is to uncheck the Enable box on the General tab.
To enable a rule	To enable a rule, you need to ensure that you have the Advanced view enabled. On the View menu, click on Advanced. Right-click the rule and click Enable. Another method to enable the rule is to check the Enable box on the General tab.
To delete a rule	Right-click the rule and click Delete. Make sure that no other rule is using this element or else the ISA Server will not start.

7

NOTE

Server Publishing rules can only be created at the array level. They are not available at the enterprise level.

Server Publishing Scenarios

Let's consider three Server Publishing scenarios. In the first scenario, the server will be published in a three-homed DMZ. In the second scenario, the server will be published on a back-to-back DMZ, and in the third scenario, the server will be published on the ISA Server computer itself.

Server Publishing on a Three-Homed DMZ Network

1. Create an IP packet filter in the ISA Management console, Servers and Arrays, *<your server name>*, Access Policy, IP Packet Filters.
2. Right-click IP Packet Filters, and click on New, Filter.

3. In the New IP Packet Filter Wizard, type the name for the filter, for example Starbucks SMTP.

4. On the Servers screen, check the option All ISA Server Computers In the Array, as shown in Figure 7.11.

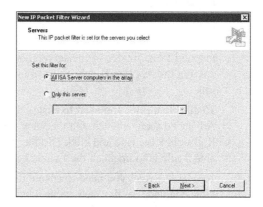

FIGURE 7.11

Configuring an IP packet filter for servers.

5. On the Filter Mode screen, select Allow Packet Transmission, as shown in Figure 7.12.

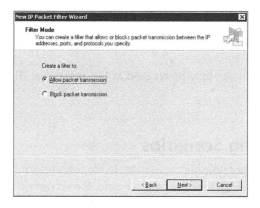

FIGURE 7.12

Configuring the filter mode for an IP packet filter.

6. On the Filter Type screen, select Custom.

7. On the Filter Settings screen, configure the following settings as shown in Figure 7.13.

   • IP Protocol: TCP

   • Direction: Both

- Local Port: Fixed port
- Port Number: 25
- Remote Port: All ports

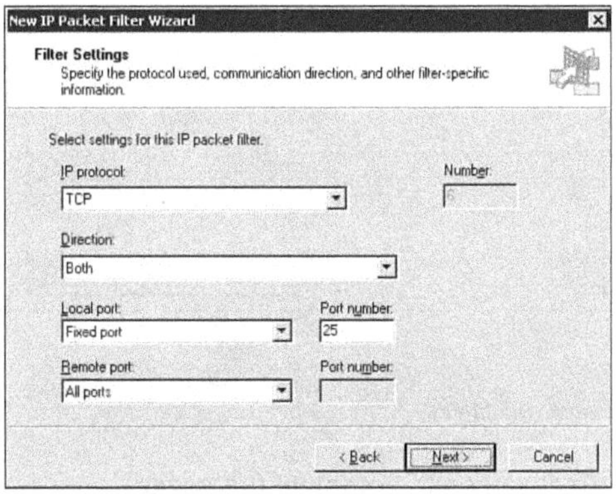

FIGURE 7.13

Configuring filter settings for an SMTP server.

8. On the Local Computer screen, select This Computer (On the Perimeter Network) because you want to publish the SMTP server in the perimeter (DMZ) network. Also, type the IP address of the SMTP server, as shown in Figure 7.14.

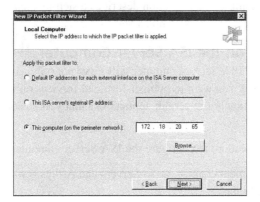

FIGURE 7.14

Publishing a server in the DMZ.

9. On the Remote Computers screen, apply the packet filter to All Remote Computers, as shown in Figure 7.15.

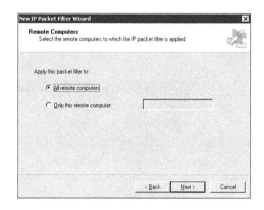

FIGURE 7.15
Applying a packet filter to all remote computers.

   10. Click Finish on the final screen to complete the wizard.

The Starbucks employees will now be able to access the published SMTP server in the three-homed DMZ network.

Server Publishing on a Back-to-Back DMZ Network

In a back-to-back DMZ scenario, you don't need to create IP packet filters. Simply use an existing Server Publishing rule, or create a rule as described in the section Creating a Server Publishing Rule. The example in that section describes a step-by-step procedure on configuring a Server Publishing rule for Starbucks employees.

Server Publishing on the ISA Server Computer

In this third scenario, the ISA Server computer will serve not only as a firewall, but also as a published server. Let's say you want to publish Terminal services on the ISA Server computer, so that the clients can remotely run certain applications that you've configured for them on the ISA Server computer.

Here's a step-by-step procedure to configure the ISA Server computer:

   1. In the ISA Management console, go to Servers and Arrays, *<your server name>*, Access Policy, IP Packet Filters.

   2. Create a packet filter using the following configuration settings for each screen described here:

      • Server: Only this server, select ISA Server computer

      • Filter Mode: Allow packet transmission

- Filter Type: Custom
- IP Protocol: TCP
- Direction: Inbound
- Local Port: Fixed
- Port Number: 3389
- Remote Port: All ports
- Local Computer: This ISA server's external IP address
- Remote Computers: All remote computers

3. Click Finish on the final screen to complete the wizard.

Your employees will now be able to access the published Terminal services on the ISA Server computer remotely, and will be able to run the desired applications based on their access permissions.

Establishing Listeners for Inbound Web Requests

ISA Server *listeners* define how it listens for inbound HTTP and SSL requests from the clients. Without listeners, all inbound requests are discarded. Listeners are also used with authentication. You configure listeners to authenticate users so they can gain access to resources on the network. This authentication has to do with the ISA Server, which gives access to the clients so it can pass the requests to the Web server. If the published Web server requires authentication, that authentication is applied in addition to the ISA Server authentication.

To configure listeners for inbound Web requests, follow the procedure described here:

1. In the ISA Management console, go to Servers and Arrays, *<your server name>*.

2. Right-click the server name, or the name of the array and select Properties.

3. On the Incoming Web Requests tab, you can either select Use The Same Listener Configuration For All IP Addresses or Configure Listeners Individually Per IP Address, as shown in Figure 7.16.

4. If you select Use The Same Listener Configuration For All IP Addresses, the ISA Server will listen for inbound requests on all IP addresses on the internal and external interface of the ISA Server computer.

5. Click Edit to configure additional parameters, as shown in Figure 7.17. You can enter a display name and configure several authentication parameters.

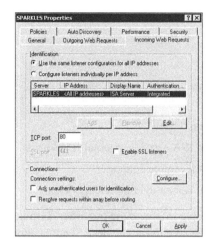

FIGURE 7.16

Configuring a listener for incoming Web traffic.

TIP

To learn more about the authentication methods used by IIS, check out the article "Internet Information Services 5.0 Authentication Methods" at
`http://www.win2000mag.com/Articles/Print.cfm?ArticleID=8443.`

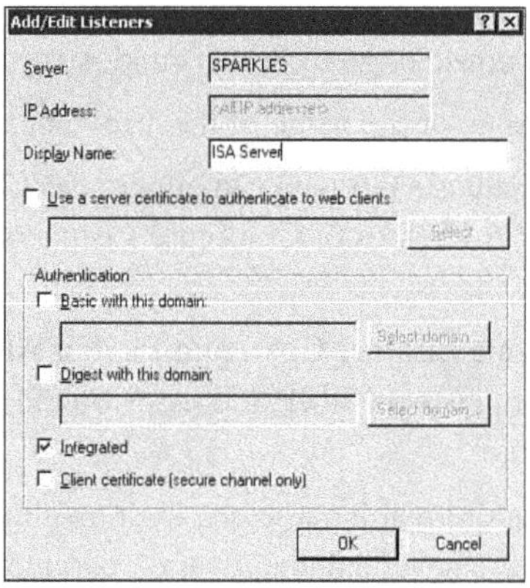

FIGURE 7.17

Configuring additional listener parameters.

6. If you select Configure Listeners Individually Per IP Address, the ISA Server will listen for inbound requests on specific IP addresses on the internal and external interface of the ISA Server computer.

7. If you have configured a certificate for listeners, you can check the box Enable SSL Listeners. This will enable ISA Server to listen to SSL requests on the default port 443. You may modify the default HTTP and SSL ports based on your network configuration.

8. Under Connections Settings, you can require authentication for gaining access to the ISA Server computer by checking the box Ask Unauthenticated Users For Identification.

TIP
Do not enable the option Ask Unauthenticated Users For Identification on the Incoming Web Requests tab for servers that are published to the general public, such as Web servers. For Web servers, you should control authentication by configuring it on the Web server itself, instead of checking this option. This option is typically used for limited publishing scenarios, such as publishing a Web server only for business partners or vendors.

9. Under Connection Settings, you can also specify that the ISA Server should resolve a request from Web Proxy clients within an array first, before it routes it based on the routing policy. To enable this option, check the box Resolve Requests Within Array Before Routing.

Normally, you would want to configure listeners individually per IP address and specify the IP address of the external network card on the ISA Server computer.

Running Additional Services on an ISA Server Computer

Depending on your network configuration, some organizations may run additional services on the ISA Server computer, instead of running them on the internal or DMZ network. This is especially true for smaller organizations and small office/home office (SOHO) networks that can't afford additional servers for various services.

When you configure rules on the ISA Server to allow clients to access resources, ISA Server opens and closes the ports dynamically to let the packets through. However, when you configure services that are installed on the ISA Server computer, instead of creating rules, you create IP packet filters. IP packet filtering opens the port statically, and directs the packets to the appropriate ports. This allows communications on those ports while still permitting you to take advantage of all the ISA Server features, such as Firewall, Web, and Cache services. You have

7

**IMPLEMENTING
PUBLISHING**

already learned how to configure Terminal services in a previous example. Let's look at a couple of examples of configuring additional services on an ISA Server computer.

Configuring IIS to Run On an ISA Server Computer

To configure Internet Information Services to run on an ISA Server computer, create a packet filter using the procedure described here:

1. In the ISA Management console, go to Servers and Arrays, *<your server name>*, Access Policy, IP Packet Filters.

2. Create a packet filter using the following configuration settings for each screen described here. See Figure 7.18 for filter settings.

    - Server: Only this server, select ISA Server computer
    - Filter Mode: Allow packet transmission
    - Filter Type: Custom
    - IP Protocol: TCP
    - Direction: Inbound
    - Local Port: Fixed
    - Port Number: 80
    - Remote Port: All ports
    - Local Computer: This ISA server's external IP address
    - Remote Computers: All remote computers

3. Click Finish on the final screen to complete the wizard.

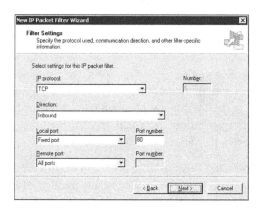

FIGURE 7.18
Configuring IIS to run on an ISA Server computer.

Configuring Outlook Express to Run On an ISA Server Computer

To configure Outlook Express on an ISA Server computer so you can access Post Office Protocol version 3 (POP3), Simple Mail Transport Protocol (SMTP), and Network News Transfer Protocol (NNTP) servers on the Internet, create packet filters using the procedure described here:

1. In the ISA Management console, go to Servers and Arrays, *<your server name>*, Access Policy, IP Packet Filters.

2. You will need to create three packet filters, one for each protocol that will be used. For the POP3 protocol, create a packet filter using the following configuration settings for each screen described here:

   - Server: Only this server, select ISA Server computer
   - Filter Mode: Allow packet transmission
   - Filter Type: Custom
   - IP Protocol: TCP
   - Direction: Both
   - Local Port: Dynamic
   - Remote Port: Fixed
   - Port Number: 110
   - Local Computer: Default IP addresses for each external interface on the ISA Server computer
   - Remote Computers: All remote computers

3. For the SMTP protocol, use the following settings:

   - Server: Only this server, select ISA Server computer
   - Filter Mode: Allow packet transmission
   - Filter Type: Custom
   - IP Protocol: TCP
   - Direction: Both
   - Local Port: Dynamic
   - Remote Port: Fixed
   - Port Number: 25
   - Local Computer: Default IP addresses for each external interface on the ISA Server computer
   - Remote Computers: All remote computers

4. For the NNTP protocol, use the following settings:
   - Server: Only this server, select ISA Server computer
   - Filter Mode: Allow packet transmission
   - Filter Type: Custom
   - IP Protocol: TCP
   - Direction: Both
   - Local Port: Dynamic
   - Remote Port: Fixed
   - Port Number: 119
   - Local Computer: Default IP addresses for each external interface on the ISA Server computer
   - Remote Computers: All remote computers

5. Click Finish on the final screen for each packet filter to complete the wizard.

Publishing a Mail Server

ISA Server comes with a Mail Server Security Wizard that allows you to publish a mail server on your network. The wizard automatically configures the appropriate Server Publishing rules and protocol rules for you. Publishing a mail server allows you to publish services that utilize protocols such as POP3, IMAP4, NNTP, and SMTP. The wizard creates different protocol rules, depending on the settings you select, to allow outbound mail traffic.

If you are running the wizard on the ISA Server computer, the wizard will create packet filters instead of publishing rules. It will also allow you to apply content filtering on incoming mail traffic. If the SMTP application filter is not enabled, the wizard will enable it so you can filter out incoming SMTP messages using advanced content filtering.

TIP

Enabling advanced content filtering, such as filtering by mail attachments, requires an ISA Server component known as *Message Screener*. Message Screener must be installed on the computer running IIS with an optional SMTP Server component. Although you can run Message Screener either on the ISA Server or on another computer, for performance reasons you should run Message Screener on a separate computer.

To run the Mail Server Security Wizard, use the following procedure:

1. In the ISA Management console, go to Servers and Arrays, *<your server name>*, Publishing, Server Publishing Rules.

2. Right-click on Server Publishing Rules and click Secure Mail Server to start the Mail Server Security Wizard.

NOTE

If you don't see the Secure Mail Server option when you right-click the Server Publishing Rules under your array, it's probably because publishing is not enabled in the enterprise policy settings. Enable publishing on the Policies tab of your server or array's Properties.

---

3. On the Mail Services Selection screen, choose the services that you would like to publish, as shown in Figure 7.19.

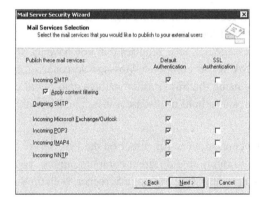

FIGURE 7.19

Running the Mail Server Security Wizard.

4. On the ISA Server's External IP Address screen, enter the external IP address of the ISA Server computer. This IP address must not be in the LAT.

5. On the Internal Mail Server screen, you will specify where the mail services are running. If the mail server is located on a computer other than the ISA Server computer, enter its IP address. Otherwise, if the mail service is running on the ISA Server computer, select On the Local Host, as shown in Figure 7.20.

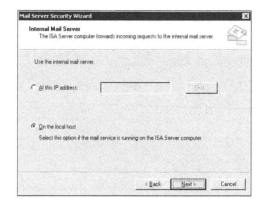

FIGURE 7.20

Forwarding requests to the internal mail server.

6. Click Finish to complete the wizard.

Configuring Message Screener

You can install Message Screener either during the initial installation of ISA Server, or add it later on. This service is part of the Add-in services that could be installed by running the ISA Server setup program. Message Screener requires that you have an SMTP or related service already installed on the ISA Server computer. Message Screener's job is, like its name says, to screen the messages by using the SMTP filter settings configured on the ISA Server computer. Unless a rule requires it to hold or discard a message, Message Screener will forward the message.

Message Screener can be configured to run either on the ISA Server computer or on a different computer. It is preferable to run it on a different computer, unless you don't expect much SMTP traffic. Let's look at configuring Message Screener, both on the ISA Server and another computer.

Here's a step-by-step process to configure Message Screener on the ISA Server computer:

1. Ensure that the IIS and SMTP services are running on the ISA Server computer. If not, install and configure the services. Message Screener requires that these services be available on the same computer where it is running.

2. In the Internet Services Manager, configure the Default SMTP Virtual Server to listen only on the internal IP address of the ISA Server computer. By default, the SMTP Virtual Server can respond to all the IP addresses. Also, configure the SMTP server to accept

inbound messages from all domains and to forward the messages to your internal mail server. For example, if you are running an Exchange server on your private network, configure the SMTP server so it will accept all messages from the Internet and then forward it to your Exchange server.

3. Run the ISA Server Setup program from Control Panel, Add/Remove Programs and install Message Screener from the Add-in services option.

4. Run the Secure Mail Server Security Wizard and use the internal IP address of the ISA Server computer to publish the SMTP server.

5. In the ISA Management console, go to Server and Arrays, *<your computer name>*, Extensions, Application Filters.

6. In the right-hand pane, right-click SMTP Filter and click Properties.

7. On the General tab, ensure that the box Enable This Filter is checked. If not, check the box.

NOTE

The ISA Server CD contains a very useful document that covers advanced SMTP filter configuration options. The document is located in the \support\docs folder and is called smtpfilter.htm.

Configuring the Message Screener on a Different Computer

In the previous section, we looked at configuring Message Screener on the ISA Server computer. Let's now look at how Message Screener is configured on a different computer. As previously mentioned, this second method is the recommended method.

Here's a step-by-step process to configure Message Screener on a computer other than the ISA Server computer:

1. Ensure that IIS and SMTP service is running on the designated computer. If not, install and configure the services.

2. Configure the SMTP server to accept inbound messages from all domains and to forward the messages to your internal Exchange server.

3. Run the ISA Server Setup program on the SMTP server from Control Panel, Add/Remove Programs, and install only Message Screener from the Add-in services option. You do not need to install any other components other than Message Screener.

4. If Message Screener and the ISA Server computer are not part of the same Active Directory forest, or if ISA Server is running as a standalone server, then on the SMTP Server, run the SMTPCred.exe tool available on the ISA Server CD in the \ISA\I386 folder. Specify the ISA Server's name, how often Message Screener should retrieve the information from the ISA Server computer, and a regular user account.

5. Run the Secure Mail Server Security Wizard and publish the SMTP server.

6. On the ISA Server computer, enable Message Screener to gain access to the ISA Server computer by configuring the Distributed COM on the ISA Server computer. This is necessary because the SMTP filter uses Distributed COM to transmit data.

7. To configure DCOM, at the command prompt type dcomcnfg.exe.

8. On the Applications tab, select VendorData Class and then click Properties, as shown in Figure 7.21.

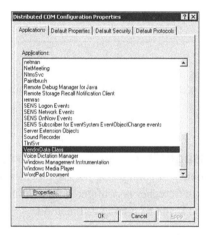

FIGURE 7.21
Configuring DCOM on the ISA Server computer.

9. On the Security tab, select the options Use Custom Access Permissions, Use Custom Launch Permissions, and Use Custom Configuration Permissions, as shown in Figure 7.22. For each of these settings, click Edit and then configure the settings as follows:

- For access permissions: Add Everyone, Allow Access
- For launch permissions: Add Everyone, Allow Launch
- For configuration permissions: Add Everyone, Full Control

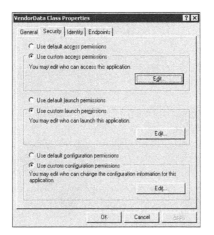

FIGURE 7.22

Configuring DCOM security on an ISA Server computer.

Summary

This chapter introduced Web Publishing and Server Publishing concepts. You learned how to create Web Publishing and Server Publishing rules, and establish listeners. To understand the concepts better, Web Publishing and Server Publishing scenarios were used with step-by-step instructions on configuring the ISA Server computer in each scenario.

You were also introduced to publishing a mail server. In the last section you learned how to install and configure Message Screener, both on the ISA Server computer and on a separate computer.

The next chapter will discuss monitoring, alerts, and reporting.

Monitoring, Alerts, and Reporting

IN THIS CHAPTER

- Monitoring Performance   206
- Tips for Monitoring Performance   211
- Using Alerts   214
- Logging and Reporting   222
- Summary   236

Monitoring the performance of your ISA Server offers several advantages. Besides being able to keep track of trends and troubleshoot any potential problems, you are also able to optimize your server configuration, analyze the effect of services and their impact on network resources, and plan for any future modifications.

In this chapter, you will learn how to monitor your ISA Server computer and configure alerts so you can be notified of important changes to the server, especially any security breaches that could have an adverse affect on your network. In addition, you will also learn how to generate reports. After all, collecting data doesn't do any good if you don't have a nice way to interpret it. Reports allow you to do just that.

Let's begin with an introduction to performance monitoring concepts, including the establishment of a baseline. Then you will learn about the performance counters in more detail, followed by some tips. The section on monitoring will be closed with a discussion on bottlenecks in four major areas: memory, hard disk, processor, and network.

Monitoring Performance

Understanding how your ISA Server is performing is more important than a lot of administrators realize. Analyzing the effect of server workload, fine tuning configurations, and keeping track of trends are all crucial elements of managing an ISA Server computer.

ISA Server includes a number of performance counters that are available to you when the server is installed. These counters can be used to analyze various components of ISA Server. For example, a higher percentage of the Cache Hit Ratio counter would indicate that the caching component of ISA Server is performing well, because the users are retrieving most of the information from the cache. For end users, this would result in a faster response time. However, before you start monitoring your ISA Server, you must establish a baseline.

Establishing a Baseline

A *baseline* is defined as the performance of your ISA Server that is acceptable to you when the system is running standard services under normal conditions with an average workload. Baselines are completely dependent on your own environment. What's acceptable to one organization may not, and most likely will not, be acceptable to another organization.

To better understand the concept of baseline, let's consider the following example. Let's say you monitor your network traffic and the Network Utilization counter consistently shows a value of 18%. What does this mean? Is 18% a good number? Is it too high? Is it too low? Well, the answer is "it all depends." If your network normally operates at 28% utilization, then you can say that the 18% value seems to be pretty good. On the contrary, if the network normally operates at 6% utilization, the 18% utilization could mean that you have some serious problems. But how do you know what's good and what's bad? The answer is baseline. As you can probably tell, an 18% network utilization can be a matter of concern for one organization, while the network administrator of another organization might consider it a blessing. The numbers for network utilization are simply used here to illustrate the baseline concept.

Performance Counters

You will monitor performance counters with the ISA Server Performance Monitor. By default, several counters are pre-installed, but additional counters can be added in each of the six available categories. Just to avoid any confusion, we are talking about ISA Server Performance Monitor, which is a customized version of the System Monitor in Windows 2000. See the sidebar for more details. With System Monitor, you can't add additional counters to the pre-configured list. However, applications or services, such as Exchange, Active Directory, or SQL Server, can add their own performance objects. The six available categories are:

- Bandwidth Control counters
- Cache counters
- Firewall Service counters
- H.323 Filter counters
- Packet Filter counters
- Web Proxy Service counters

To access ISA Server Performance Monitor, click on Start, Programs, select the Microsoft ISA Server group, and then click on ISA Server Performance Monitor. Figure 8.1 shows a sample ISA Server Performance Monitor. Notice that the Object heading lists the service to which the counter belongs. For example, the highlighted Memory Usage Ratio Percentage counter belongs to the ISA Server Cache.

You can either use the ISA Server Performance Monitor, as indicated earlier, or use the Performance console under Start, Programs, Administrative Tools. The advantage of running the ISA Server Performance Monitor is that you don't have to manually add individual counters because it is already pre-configured for ISA Server. As mentioned previously, you are not limited to the counters that are pre-installed in ISA Server Performance Monitor; you can add additional counters to customize this tool. This pre-configured MMC is simply a subset of the complete Performance console.

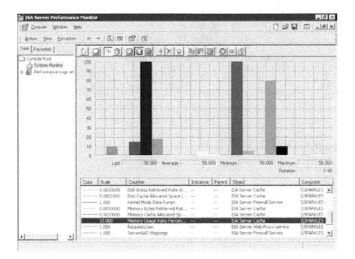

FIGURE 8.1
The ISA Server Performance Monitor.

Would the Real Monitor Please Stand Up?

What you might find interesting (or confusing, depending on your perspective) is the way Microsoft has mixed Performance Monitor and System Monitor in Windows 2000. For example, when you run the ISA Server Performance Monitor tool, as shown in Figure 8.1, you are running the System Monitor, and not the Performance Monitor. Notice the title of the MMC at the very top, and notice what the highlighted tool under Console Root shows. In other words, Microsoft has changed the name of the tool to System Monitor, but decided to keep the old name (Performance Monitor) that starts it. Hmmm? It's similar to buying an Acura; it's sold under the name Acura, but in reality what you are really buying is a Honda, because the engine and parts are all produced by Honda. Go figure! Then there's a Performance console that you start from the Administrative Tools. This is a generic tool, so the title only says Performance—not Performance Monitor, but you still run System Monitor. In Windows NT the tool was known as Performance Monitor, so when you typed `perf-mon` at the command prompt, you started Performance Monitor. Now in Windows 2000 when you type `perfmon`, you get System Monitor. Got it? Good! But wait, there's more. Things weren't complicated enough so Microsoft decided to add another Performance Monitor in Windows 2000 Resource kit, known as Performance Monitor 4 (`perfmon4.exe`). This is the old NT Performance Monitor and is supposed to do things that the standard Windows 2000 System Monitor, which is called Performance, can't do. Clear as mud? I thought so.

The following is an alphabetical catalogue of the common default ISA Server 2000 counters:

- Active sessions
- TCP connections
- Active UDP connections

We'll take a deeper look at each of these counters in the next few sections.

Active Sessions

When the clients are using the Firewall service, the client sessions can be monitored. This counter is used to count the number of active sessions for the Firewall service. For example, a drastic decrease in a number of active sessions could potentially be a matter of concern.

Active TCP Connections

This counter is used to count the number of active TCP connections for the Firewall service. These are the connections that are currently passing data on the wire.

Active UDP Connections

This counter is used to count the number of active UDP connections for the Firewall service. These are the connections that are currently passing data on the wire.

Cache Hit Ratio (%)

This Web Proxy service counter is used to measure the effectiveness of cache. It indicates the percentage of ISA Server Web Proxy clients that have been served from the cache out of the total number of clients served by the server. A higher percentage of cache hit ratio means that the users are retrieving a large number of objects from the cache. Lower numbers indicate slower response time for users. A value of zero indicates that caching is disabled. This counter is related to the next counter, the Cache Running Hit Ratio (%).

Cache Running Hit Ratio (%)

This Web Proxy service counter is rather similar to the one listed previously. The difference between the two counters is that this counter measures the ratio for the last 10,000 requests, while the Cache Hit Ratio(%) counter is used to measure this ratio from the last time the Web Proxy service was started. In other words, the previous counter was an overall total, whereas this counter measures only the last 10,000 requests.

Client Bytes Total/Sec

This is a Web Proxy service counter that is used to measure the total rate for all the bytes transferred per second between the Web Proxy clients and the Web Proxy service. It will help you determine the load on the Web Proxy service. Higher numbers indicate that your server may be too busy and you may have to consider additional resources to service the clients.

Current Average Milliseconds/Request

This is a Web Proxy service counter that is used to measure the average time in milliseconds taken by the server to service a request. Higher values indicate slower responses. Lower values mean the clients don't have to wait too long for the requests to be processed.

Current Users

This is a Web Proxy service counter that is used to measure how many users are using the Web Proxy service at a given time. Obviously, you'll need to monitor this counter at different times of the day to get a better overall picture of server usage. This counter can also be useful if you want to find out how many users are currently connected to the Web Proxy service before rebooting the server or stopping the service.

Disk Cache Allocated Space (KB)

This is a cache counter that indicates how much disk space is being used by the ISA Server disk cache out of the total amount that was allocated for disk caching. Higher values indicate that you may want to consider increasing the size of the disk cache if you are getting too close to the total allocated space.

Max URLs Cached

This is a cache counter that shows the maximum number of URLs that are stored in the ISA Server cache. Do not confuse this with the "URLs in cache" counter that shows the number of URLs currently in cache.

Memory Cache Allocated Space (KB)

This is a cache counter that is similar to the disk cache allocated space counter listed previously, except that it's for memory. It indicates the amount of space that is being used by the memory cache out of the total memory allocated for memory caching on the ISA Server computer.

Memory Usage Ratio Percent (%)

This is a cache counter that indicates the ratio between the amount of cache that was retrieved by the clients from the memory and the amount of total cache retrieved by the clients. If the percentages are higher, you might want to allocate more memory to cache. Lower numbers indicate that you will be better off allocating some memory resources to other services. For caching, this is an excellent counter to keep an eye on.

Requests/Sec

This is a Web Proxy service counter that indicates the number of inbound requests per second from Web Proxy clients. Higher numbers mean that ISA Server is too busy and might not be able to handle all the requests, in which case you might have to add additional resources to service the clients.

SecureNAT Mappings

This is a Firewall service counter that is used to keep track of the number of mappings created by SecureNAT clients.

Total Dropped Packets

This is a packet filter counter that measures the total number of dropped or filtered packets on the ISA Server computer. This counter lists all dropped packets, regardless of whether the packets were dropped by the client, the network interface card, or for any other reason.

URL Commit Rate (URL/sec)

This is a cache counter that measures the rate at which the URLs are written to the cache. This counter has to be compared to some additional counters before you take some decisive actions. For example, you might want to keep an eye on some hard disk and memory counters before reaching any conclusions.

URLs in Cache

This cache counter is used to measure the number of URLs that are in ISA Server cache at any given time. If you are looking for the cumulative number of URLs in cache, then use another counter called Total URLs Cached.

Tips for Monitoring Performance

When monitoring the performance of your ISA Server computer, try not to jump to conclusions by looking at only a single counter. There are at least four areas that you should concentrate on:

- Memory
- Hard disk
- Processor
- Network

Simply examining one area can sometimes be deceiving. Therefore, it is best that you look at all four of these areas before you reach a conclusion. For example, if you notice that your hard disk is thrashing and you look at only the disk counters to conclude that you need to upgrade your hard disk, you might be jumping the gun. The real problem might be that you don't have enough memory, which is causing the information to be swapped to the pagefile frequently. This might give you the false impression that the disk subsystem is the bottleneck, although in reality it's the memory that is the culprit. Whether you are capacity planning, troubleshooting, or analyzing your ISA Server computer, you should keep in mind that performance monitoring is an art, not a science.

Let's look at the four major areas and see how you can identify the bottlenecks in each of them.

Memory Bottlenecks

Memory issues are generally easy to spot in Windows 2000. Does the server in question frequently page application requests to the hard disk? If so, you might have a memory issue. Does the server in question fail the memory check at the Power On Self Test (POST)? If so, you might have a memory problem. Does the server in question have Operating System instabilities that don't seem to be tied to a specific application-level problem? Again, it could lead to a memory problem. Some of the memory issues can be corrected by installing the latest service packs.

Although many memory-related problems can be traced back to the preceding issues, sometimes the problem is configuration-oriented. A memory bottleneck can occur when certain memory-related options (such as memory cache) are not configured properly.

The value of following performance counters is directly associated with the memory configuration of the ISA Server, and will help you identify memory bottlenecks.

- *Total Memory Bytes Retrieved (KB)*—This ISA Server Cache performance counter is a measurement of the total number of bytes that have been retrieved from the memory cache in response to client requests.

  Low numbers for this counter may indicate an inefficient use of memory. High numbers for this counter may indicate that more memory should be allocated to the cache.

- *Total Memory URLs Retrieved*—This Cache performance counter is a measurement of the total number of URLs that have been retrieved from the memory cache in response to client requests.

  Low numbers for this counter may indicate an inefficient use of memory. High numbers for this counter may indicate that more memory should be allocated to the cache.

- *Requests/Sec*—This Web Proxy Service performance counter measures the rate per second at which the inbound requests are being made to the Web Proxy service. A higher value means that you might need to reserve additional resources to service the Web Proxy clients' requests.

Hard Disk Bottlenecks

A poor-performing cache points right to the disk subsystem in all but the rarest cases. Disk bottlenecks are perhaps the biggest factor in overall lackluster performance. To watch for potential disk issues, keep your eye on the following counters:

- *Disk Failure Rate (Fail/Sec)*—This Cache performance counter measures the total number of disk *I/O failures* per second.

  An I/O failure is the inability of the ISA Server computer to read or write to the disk cache. This counter, along with the Total Disk Failures counter is useful in determining serious disk cache problems.

- *Total Disk Failures*—This Cache performance counter measures the total number of times the Web Proxy service failed to read or write to the disk cache because of an I/O failure.

  A low number here means that a disk is performing up to par. A high number means that there are issues with the cache disk (it is too slow, too small, or the cache is improperly configured).

Processor Bottlenecks

When all other resource allocation options have been exhausted and the ISA Server is still not performing well, consider replacing the processor or perhaps going with different processor architecture. A Pentium III processor will outperform a Pentium II processor at the same clock speed because of architecture enhancements in the Pentium III. Something to keep in mind here is that when using a multiprocessor computer with more than two processors, make sure to use the HAL from the manufacturer, and not the default Microsoft multiprocessor HAL. The default HAL has some known performance issues when using more than two processors. Also, when dealing with processor bottlenecks, ensure that you are using the latest service pack. Most of the known bugs are fixed in the latest service packs.

To troubleshoot processor bottlenecks, keep an eye on the following processor counters:

- *% Processor Time*—This processor counter indicates the time in percentage that the processor is executing a non-idle thread. *Idle threads* are threads that are consuming processor cycles when it has nothing else to do. The calculation is based on the time the processor takes executing the idle thread and subtracted from 100%.

  A consistent value of 80% or higher indicates that the processor is the bottleneck. Determine the process that is the culprit. You may consider upgrading to a faster processor, or adding an additional processor to resolve the processor bottleneck.

- *Interrupts Per Second*—During normal operation, several devices generate interrupts. For example, the system clock sends an interrupt to the processor every 10 milliseconds to communicate with the processor. Similarly, the hard drives, network cards, mice, and other devices interrupt the processor to get its attention. The Interrupts/sec counter is the average number of hardware interrupts per second received by the processor.

  If you see a big increase in the values of this counter without an increase in the system activity, the problem is most likely with your hardware. Try to isolate the culprit device.

Network Bottlenecks

Certain performance issues are network-related. If the internal network is not robust enough to handle the capacity of incoming client requests, response times will suffer. Additionally, if outbound bandwidth is insufficient, performance will be less than optimal. Watch the following counters to get an indication of network performance and to identify network bottlenecks.

8

MONITORING,
ALERTS, AND
REPORTING

- *Upstream Bytes Received/Sec*—This Web Proxy Service performance counter measures the rate per second at which the Web Proxy Service receives data from the remote servers on the Internet.

  The counter is dependent on the connection bandwidth. For example, if the values of this counter are consistently low, then you might have a bottleneck caused by a slow Internet connection. You might need to do a little more leg work and monitor some additional counters before you are convinced that you should upgrade to a faster connection.

- *Upstream Bytes Sent/Sec*—This Web Proxy Service performance counter measures the rate per second at which the Web Proxy Service sends data to remote servers on the Internet.

  This counter is similar to the preceding counter, except that it measures sent bytes rather than received bytes. Therefore, it is also dependent on the connection bandwidth. Consistently low values for this counter indicate a bottleneck related to the slow Internet connection.

- *Failing Requests/Sec*—This Web Proxy Service performance counter measures the rate per second at which the Web Proxy client requests have failed.

  You should compare this counter with the Requests/Sec counter. If the value of this counter is rather high compared to the total Requests/Sec, you definitely have a problem. There are several configuration areas that you can explore to resolve this bottleneck. Try modifying the configuration settings for Incoming Web Requests in the properties dialog box of your ISA Server computer or array in the ISA Management console. Pay special attention to the connections settings. Another area to focus on is your connection bandwidth. If this doesn't resolve the problem, then look at your bandwidth rules. Pay close attention to bandwidth priorities. They might need some tweaking.

Using Alerts

The ISA Server alert service is used to notify you when certain predetermined events occur. Alerts can be configured to set off a series of actions when certain events take place. The alert service acts as a filter and watches for certain events that you have configured. As soon as the event takes place, the alert service takes the appropriate actions.

The alert service gives you a lot of control over what actions to take. For example, you can decide how many events should occur before you receive an alert from the ISA Server, how long it should wait before issuing an alert, and how frequently the events occur before an alert is issued. Once the alert condition is met, you can configure the ISA Server to take one of several possible actions. For example, you can configure the service to send you an e-mail message, log the event in the event log, take a specific action, and stop or start one of the ISA Server services.

ISA Management can be used to view all the alerts that ISA Server supports out of the box (see Figure 8.2), and to configure which actions should occur when an event takes place. For example, you can configure ISA Server to send you an e-mail if someone is running a port scanner on your ISA Server computer.

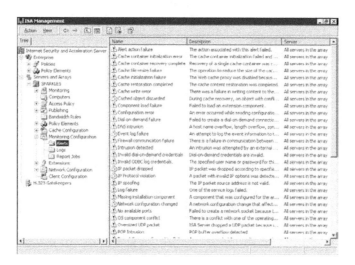

FIGURE 8.2
Viewing alerts in ISA Management console.

Creating Alerts

To create an alert, follow the procedure described here:

1. In the ISA Management console, go to Servers and Arrays, *<your server name>*, Monitoring Configuration, Alerts.

2. Right-click Alerts, click on New, and then click Alert to start the New Alert Wizard.

3. On the welcome screen, enter a name for the Alert, for example Intrusion.

4. On the Server screen, either select the Any Server or the This Server option. If you select the This Server option, select a particular server from the drop-down box.

5. On the Events and Conditions screen, choose an Event from the drop-down box, for example Intrusion Detected, as shown in Figure 8.3. Under Additional Condition, select an appropriate option from the drop-down box, for example Any Intrusion.

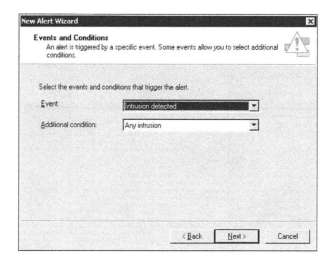

FIGURE 8.3

Configuring an event and a condition for an alert.

NOTE

When configuring the events that trigger an alert, some of the options allow you to enter an Additional Condition. For example, if you select Intrusion Detected as an event, as shown in Figure 8.3, you can select one of the following additional conditions: Any Intrusion, All Port Scan Attack, Well-Known Port Scan Attack, IP Half Scan Attack, Land Attack, Ping of Death Attack, UDP Bomb Attack, and Windows Out-of-Band Attack.

---

6. On the Actions screen, select an action that you want the alert service to perform when an intrusion is detected, as shown in Figure 8.4. Depending on the options you select on this screen, you will be presented with additional screens. For demonstration purposes, select all the options on this screen.

7. On the Sending E-mail Messages screen, enter the appropriate options for the SMTP server and the person you want to be notified, as shown in Figure 8.5.

8. On the Running a Program screen, enter the path to the program. You can run the program either with the local system account or a specific user account, as shown in Figure 8.6.

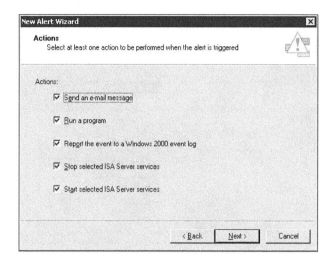

FIGURE 8.4

Configuring an action for an alert.

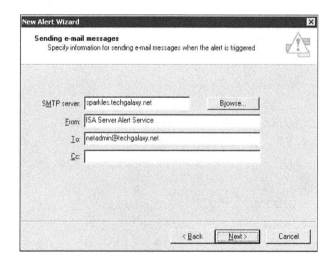

FIGURE 8.5

Configuring e-mail options for an alert.

9. On the Stopping Services screen, you can decide which service(s) to stop when an alert occurs, as shown in Figure 8.7.

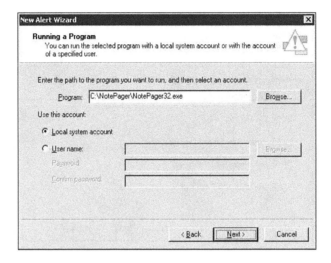

FIGURE 8.6

Configuring to run a program when an alert occurs.

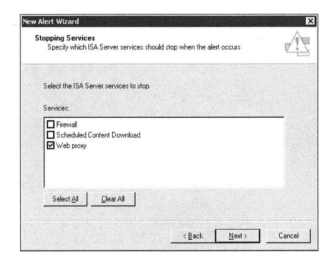

FIGURE 8.7

Stopping ISA Server services when an alert occurs.

10. Depending on the service(s) that you stopped in the previous screen, you will start the service(s) on the following Starting Services screen.

11. On the final screen, click Finish to complete the wizard.

> **NOTE**
>
> If an alert with the same event GUID is already defined, ISA Server will inform you that you can't create a new alert. For example, because of the default alerts that already exist, you may not be able to create a new alert as described previously if you select Any Server in Step 4. However, you will be able to create a new alert if you use the This Server option to specify a specific server.

Modifying Alerts

Once an alert has been configured, you can go back and modify the alert. To modify an alert, right-click the alert and select Properties. On the General tab, you can modify the name of the alert and enable (or disable) it, as shown in Figure 8.8. You can also enter a description for the alert, an option that is not available during the creation of the alert. On the Events and Actions tabs, you can make additional changes. These options are discussed in the next two sections.

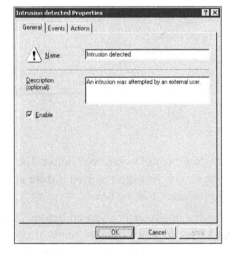

FIGURE 8.8
Modifying an alert.

Configuring Alert Thresholds

When you are monitoring performance counters, you need to determine what the acceptable values are for each counter. Based on your baseline, when the values reach a certain threshold, you might have a problem. Luckily, you can configure your system to alert you when these thresholds are reached.

To configure alert thresholds, follow the procedure described here:

1. In the ISA Management console, go to Servers and Arrays, *<your server name>*, Monitoring Configuration, Alerts.

2. Right-click the alert that you want to configure and select Properties.

3. On the Events tab, configure the threshold options under Actions Will Be Executed When The Selected Conditions Occur, as shown in Figure 8.9.

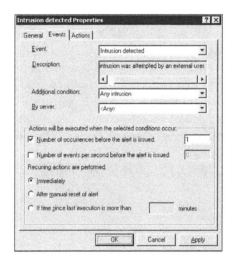

FIGURE 8.9

Configuring alert conditions and thresholds.

4. Specify a number in the Number of Occurrences Before The Alert Is Issued box. For example, if you want the alert to be triggered even if there is a single intrusion that is detected by the ISA Server, enter 1 in the box.

5. Enter a value in the Number of Events Per Second Before The Alert Is Issued box. The options in Steps 4 and 5 work together. In other words, if you type a value in both the boxes, the alert will only be issued if both the limits are reached.

6. After the conditions are met, the recurring actions can be performed by selecting one of the following three options:

    *   Immediately

    *   After Manual Rest of Alert

    *   If Time Since Last Execution Is More Than *X* Minutes (where *X* is the time that has passed before the alert should be reissued)

Configuring Alert Conditions

As an administrator, you can decide which events can trigger alerts. In addition, you can also select additional conditions that can trigger an alert (see Figure 8.9). You also have the option to limit the event to a specific server in the array.

To configure alert conditions, follow the procedure described here:

1. In the ISA Management console, go to Servers and Arrays, *<your server name>*, Monitoring Configuration, Alerts.
2. Right-click the alert that you want to configure and select Properties.
3. On the Events tab, you can configure a different event from the drop-down box under Event, as shown in Figure 8.9.
4. Under Additional Condition, you can select a different option. For example, if you were mainly concerned about port scans, instead of Any Intrusion, you would select All Port Scan Attack.
5. Under By Server, select a specific server; or for an array, choose Any.

Configuring Alert Actions

When an alert condition is met, you can configure the server to take one of several actions. For example, you can send an e-mail, run a specific program, log the event in the Windows 2000 event log, or stop or start one of the several ISA Server services.

To configure alert actions, follow the procedure described here:

1. In the ISA Management console, go to Servers and Arrays, *<your server name>*, Monitoring Configuration, Alerts.
2. Right-click the alert that you want to configure and select Properties.
3. On the Actions tab, you can configure the e-mail options, as shown in Figure 8.10.
4. Under the Program section, specify the program that you want to execute when an alert is triggered. The program can be executed either under the local system account credentials, or a specific user account.
5. Check the box Report to Windows 2000 Event Log, if you want to log the event. You can also stop or start individual services by checking the appropriate boxes and then using the Select button to choose specific services.

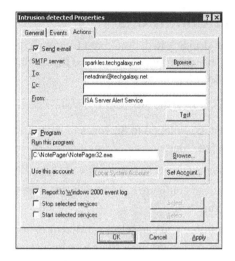

FIGURE 8.10

Configuring alert actions.

Logging and Reporting

The logging feature in ISA Server allows you to monitor the server's activities. You can examine how the server responds to inbound and outbound requests by logging events in the logs. In addition to *file format*, logs are also supported in *database format* and are meant to monitor access and security activities on the ISA Server computer.

Logs are generated for each server in an array. However, the logging information from all the servers is centralized into a single log and then presented as a single report by the ISA Server. This makes it convenient for administrators to analyze the logs for security, troubleshooting, and performance.

You can configure logs for the following three services in ISA Server, as shown in Figure 8.11:

- Packet filters
- ISA Server Firewall service
- ISA Server Web Proxy Service

The reporting feature of ISA Server is an excellent tool with which to analyze ISA Server traffic without wasting too much time writing batch files, custom scripts, or special utilities.

Reports can be scheduled to run at specified intervals, and can be saved in the \ISAReports folder on the ISA Server computer or on a network location.

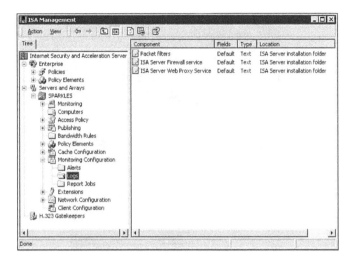

FIGURE 8.11
ISA Server logs.

The report engine combines the logs from all the servers in the array into a database. When a report is requested, relevant information from each database is combined into a single report database, which is viewable only on the ISA Server from which the request was made.

Configuring Logging

To configure logging for a service, use the following procedure:

1. In the ISA Management console, go to Servers and Arrays, *<your server name>*, Monitoring Configuration, Logs.

2. In the right-hand pane, right-click the service that you want to configure and select Properties.

3. On the Log tab, check the box Enable Logging For This Service, as shown in Figure 8.12.

CAUTION

When configuring logging, make sure that the path for the log files is the same on all the servers in an array. The recommended path is the \ISALogs folder in the Microsoft ISA Server installation folder. If you specify a different path, make sure that the path exists on every server in the array, otherwise the ISA Server services will fail.

8

MONITORING,
ALERTS, AND
REPORTING

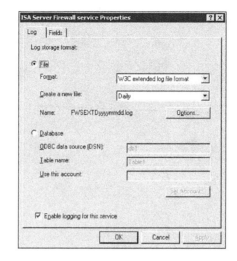

FIGURE 8.12
Enabling logging for a service.

Log Formats Supported by ISA Server

ISA Server supports detailed logs that can be generated in standard file formats like World Wide Web Consortium (W3C) extended, ISA Server, and Open Database Connectivity (ODBC). When logging is enabled, daily, weekly, monthly, or yearly logs are created for every server in an array.

Let's examine the log formats supported by ISA Server.

W3C Extended Log File Format

This file format is useful when working with reporting applications that support the W3C format. This is the default logging format used by ISA Server. This format contains data as well as information about the data format. W3C format provides extended fields that provide additional information. However, it doesn't log any fields that are not selected. It uses the tab character as a delimiter and Greenwich Mean Time (GMT) for date and time fields.

ISA Server File Format

ISA Server file format is useful when you are working with applications that recognize the ISA Server formats. Unlike W3C format, this format contains only the data; information about the data format is not provided. In contrast to the W3C format, it logs all fields, even if they are not selected. However, the empty fields are logged as dashes to indicate that there is no data. ISA Server file format uses the comma character as a delimiter and local system time for date and time fields.

ODBC Format

Notice that the preceding two formats were file formats. ODBC format lets you save logs to a database. Specifically, an ODBC lets you save a log file to an ODBC-compliant database, such as Microsoft SQL Server.

The next two sections present step-by-step instructions on first logging to a file, and then to a database.

Logging to a File

To configure logging to a file, use the following procedure:

1. In the ISA Management console, go to Servers and Arrays, *<your server name>*, Monitoring Configuration, Logs.

2. In the right-hand pane, right-click the service that you want to configure and select Properties.

3. On the Log tab, ensure that the box Enable Logging For This Service is checked.

4. On the Log tab, click File and select a file format, as shown in Figure 8.12. Your options are W3C Extended Log File Format and ISA Server File Format.

5. In Create a New File, decide how often you want the log to be created by selecting daily, weekly, monthly, or yearly.

6. To configure additional options such as the location of the log files and compression, click on the Options button.

7. From the Options screen, modify the location where the logs are stored, as shown in Figure 8.13.

8. By default, the log files are compressed to save disk space and the number of log files that are saved is set to seven. Modify these options if necessary.

9. Click the Fields tab, as shown in Figure 8.14. Select the fields that you want to appear in the logs. You can exclude any field except Time. To quickly select or clear all the fields, use the Select All or Clear All button at the bottom. To switch back to the default fields, use the Restore Defaults button.

8

MONITORING,
ALERTS, AND
REPORTING

NOTE

You can compress log files only on an NTFS partition.

FIGURE 8.13
Modifying the storage location for log files.

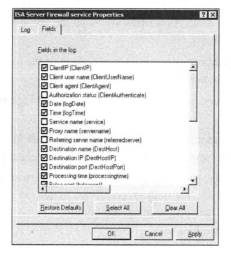

FIGURE 8.14
Selecting fields for a W3C extended log file format.

Logging to a Database

To configure logging to an ODBC database, use the following procedure:

1. In the ISA Management console, go to Servers and Arrays, *<your server name>*,
   Monitoring Configuration, Logs.

2. In the right-hand pane, right-click the service that you want to configure and select Properties.

3. On the Log tab, ensure that the box Enable Logging For This Service is checked.

4. On the Log tab, click Database, as shown in Figure 8.15.

5. In the ODBC Data Source (DSN) field, enter the data source name for the log database.

6. In the Table Name field, enter the name of the database table for the log.

7. In the Use This Account field, click Set Account and then enter a valid account and password.

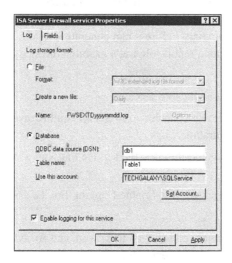

FIGURE 8.15
Logging to an ODBC database.

8

> **CAUTION**
>
> Do not enter spaces in the data source name (DSN) or the table name. Entering spaces may cause the ISA Server services to stop.

Working with Reports

ISA Server can take the data collected in the ISA Server log files and generate reports. Data can be saved in daily or monthly summaries, and these summaries can then be used to generate reports. Reports let you analyze your usage trends, monitor your security, and optimize your servers.

> **NOTE**
>
> Reports generated on one ISA Server in an array are not viewable in the ISA Management console on other members of the array. In other words, the database resides on the ISA Server computer where the report is generated, and can be viewed only on that computer.

Steps Required to Generate and View Reports

As mentioned previously, ISA Server uses the log summaries to create the reports. Therefore, the first step in generating reports is to configure log summaries, because at minimum ISA Server requires one daily summary before it can generate a report. Furthermore, to view a report, you first need to create a report job. Let's examine the steps required to generate and view reports.

1. Enable logging for the applicable service.

   a. In the ISA Management console, go to Servers and Arrays, *<your server name>*, Monitoring Configuration, Logs.

   b. In the right-hand pane, right-click the service that you want to configure and select Properties.

   c. On the Log tab, check the box Enable Logging For This Service.

2. Enable reporting.

   a. In the ISA Management console, go to Servers and Arrays, *<your server name>*, Monitoring Configuration, Report Jobs.

   b. Right-click Report Jobs and select Properties.

   c. On the General tab, check the box Enable Reports, as shown in Figure 8.16.

3. Configure log summaries.

   a. In the ISA Management console, go to Servers and Arrays, *<your server name>*, Monitoring Configuration, Report Jobs.

   b. Right-click Reports Jobs and select Properties.

   c. On the Log Summaries tab, check the box Enable Daily and Monthly Summaries, as shown in Figure 8.17.

4. Create a report job.

   a. In the ISA Management console, go to Servers and Arrays, *<your server name>*, Monitoring Configuration, Report Jobs.

   b. Right-click Report Jobs and select New, then click Report Job.

   c. On the General tab, enter a name and an optional description for the report job, as shown in Figure 8.18.

FIGURE 8.16

Enabling the reporting option.

FIGURE 8.17

Configuring log summaries.

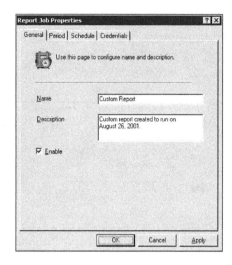

FIGURE 8.18

Creating a report job.

      d. Verify that the Enable box is checked.

      e. On the Period tab, specify how often the report should run, as shown in Figure 8.19.

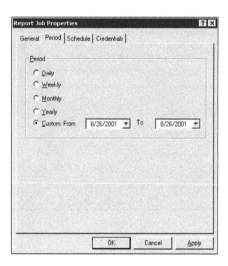

FIGURE 8.19

Specifying the frequency of a report job.

      f. On the Schedule tab, configure the schedule options, as shown in Figure 8.20.

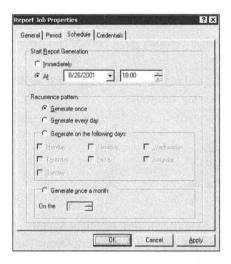

FIGURE 8.20

Scheduling a report job.

g. On the Credentials tab, enter a username and password for a person who has the authorization to access the reports, as shown in Figure 8.21. This will typically be an administrator; however, you may use a different user.

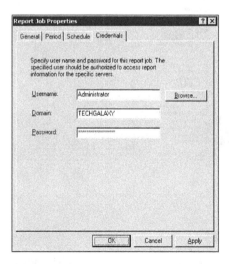

FIGURE 8.21

Configuring credentials for a report job.

h. When you click OK, your report will show up in the right-hand pane.

5. View the report.

   a. In the ISA Management console, go to Servers and Arrays, <*your server name*>, Monitoring, Reports.

   b. There are five predefined reports that you can view, as shown in Figure 8.22. Select from one of the following categories:

- Summary
- Web usage
- Application usage
- Traffic and utilization
- Security

For example, to view a Summary report, highlight Summary and then right-click the applicable report in the right-hand pane and click Open. The report will be opened in a separate window in an HTML format.

FIGURE 8.22
ISA Server's predefined reports.

Managing Reports

In order to manage reports, you need to ensure that you have the proper credentials to access the reports; otherwise, you won't be able to view or modify them. To access the reports on various servers in an array, you must have the appropriate permissions on each server in the array. By default, the Domain Admins group has the proper credentials to access reports on any ISA

Server in an array. This is mainly because the members of this group meet the two prerequisites for accessing the reports. They have local administrative privileges, in addition to the permissions to launch Distributed COM (DCOM) objects on each ISA Server that is a member of an array. If you want another individual to have the rights to manage reports, simply make sure that he or she meets the two aforementioned prerequisites.

> **NOTE**
>
> Reports are normally saved as a set of HTML files, but you can also save them as Excel spreadsheets. For example, to save the custom report that you created in the previous section in Excel format, right-click the report and click Save As. In the Save As field, select Microsoft Excel Workbook (*.xls).

Be patient when generating reports, because it might take a while before the reports are available to you, depending on the contents and your network environment.

Viewing Predefined Reports

There are five predefined reports available to the ISA Server administrators. To view these reports, follow the instructions in Step 5b in the previous section "Steps Required to Generate and View Reports." These reports include the following:

- Summary reports
- Web usage reports
- Application usage reports
- Traffic and utilization reports
- Security reports

The following sections describe each of these predefined reports in more detail. Keep in mind that your report output may vary, depending on the configuration options that you've selected.

Summary Reports

These reports are based on logs from the Firewall and Web Proxy services. They are primarily meant for network administrators or network architects because they contain statistics about network traffic and usage. These reports typically display statistics on topics such as the following:

- Protocols
- Top users
- Top Web sites

- Cache performance
- Traffic
- Daily traffic

Web Usage Reports

These reports are based on Web Proxy service logs. They display the Web usage statistics, such as the top Web sites, HTTP responses, and browsers. These are beneficial to the network administrators or Web administrators. These reports typically display statistics on topics such as the following:

- Top Web users
- Top Web sites
- Protocols
- HTTP responses
- Object types
- Browsers
- Operating systems
- Browsers vs. operating systems

Application Usage Reports

These reports are based on the Firewall service logs. They display information about Internet application usage, such as top application users, top applications, and top destinations. These reports are ideal for network architects or persons responsible for network capacity planning. These reports typically display statistics on topics such as the following:

- Protocols
- Top application users
- Top applications
- Operating systems
- Top destinations

Traffic and Utilization Reports

These reports are based on logs from the Firewall and Web Proxy services. They display Internet usage based on protocol and application. They are great for network administrators and architects who are responsible for planning bandwidth policies. These reports typically display statistics on topics such as the following:

- Protocols

- Traffic
- Cache performance
- Connections
- Processing time
- Daily traffic
- Errors

Figure 8.23 shows a sample of a daily traffic report generated by ISA Server.

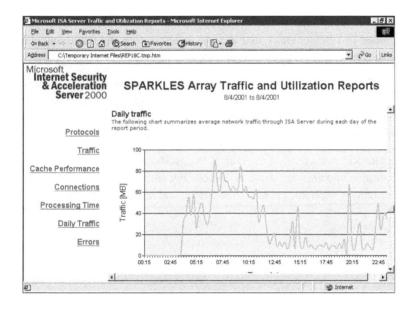

FIGURE 8.23

A sample daily traffic report.

Security Reports

Security reports are perhaps the most important of all the reports. These reports are based on the logs from the Firewall service, Web Proxy service, and packet filters. Security reports are meant for the security or auditing team, network administrators, or anyone responsible for network security. They provide valuable information on security violations, and depending on the security breach, can help track down the culprits or close the security holes. These reports typically display statistics on topics such as the following:

- Authorization failures
- Dropped packets

Summary

This chapter covered the topics of monitoring performance, configuring alerts, and generating reports. ISA Server has an extensive set of monitoring, logging, and reporting tools that are highly configurable and easy to use.

The ISA Server Performance Monitor uses the `Perfmon` interface, which means that administrators who are already familiar with Windows NT's performance monitoring tool will feel right at home. This chapter discussed the concept of baseline and explained several crucial performance counters in detail.

Administrators can set conditions and thresholds so that specific events can trigger alerts. This chapter examined ISA Server alerts, and in addition to creating and modifying alerts, you also learned how to configure alert thresholds and alert conditions.

ISA Server allows you to log server activity and generate reports. The reports are created from the log summaries, which are saved as Web pages. This chapter presented ISA Server's logging and reporting features. ISA Server's five predefined reports were examined, and you were walked through a step-by-step process to generate and view reports.

The next chapter addresses most of the critical troubleshooting areas in ISA Server. It's presented in a question and answer format to address key areas of interest, such as troubleshooting services, connections, sessions, caching, publishing, and authentication, to name a few.

Troubleshooting

IN THIS CHAPTER

- **Troubleshooting Services   238**
- **Using the Event Viewer to Help Troubleshoot ISA Events   243**
- **Troubleshooting Caching   246**
- **Troubleshooting Sessions   249**
- **Troubleshooting Connections   250**
- **Troubleshooting Access   252**
- **Troubleshooting Authentication   255**
- **Troubleshooting Publishing   258**
- **Troubleshooting Dial-Up   259**
- **Summary   260**

This final chapter in the book is devoted to troubleshooting. The key to successful network administration is being good at troubleshooting. No matter how "on top of things" you might be, problems will always arise. The ability to effectively analyze and solve the unexpected problem is what makes you a good network administrator. Let's take a look at several potential problem areas and some steps you can take to solve the problems when they occur.

This chapter will cover the following troubleshooting areas:

- Services
- Event Messages
- Caching
- Sessions
- Connections
- Access
- Authentication
- Publishing
- Dial-up

Let's begin with steps you can take to troubleshoot problems with ISA Services.

Troubleshooting Services

The five "out of the box" services ISA Server comes with include the following:

- ISA Server Control service (`mspadmin.exe`)
- Web Proxy service (`w3proxy.exe`)
- Firewall service (`wspsrv.exe`)
- Scheduled Cache Content Download service (`w3prefch.exe`)
- H.323 Gatekeeper service (`svchost.exe –k iptelsvcs`)

Incorrect configurations are the root cause of most service-level problems with ISA Server. Be very careful when configuring these services, as oversights can be costly. Make sure that you test the configured services, ports, and policies thoroughly before implementing them on your production servers. It is a bad idea to experiment on "live" servers. If you are new to firewalls and security, then consider playing with Firewall as playing with fire. It is easy to get burned unless you take some precautionary measures.

Depending on the configuration changes you make to the ISA Server, you might have to restart one or more services on all the servers in an ISA Server array. Although ISA Server will warn you about the services that need to be restarted, it will be helpful in troubleshooting if you know what configuration changes result in restarting specific services. Table 9.1 lists the changes and the resulting service(s) that must be restarted.

TABLE 9.1 Configuration Changes Requiring a Service Restart

Configuration Modifications	Service(s) Restarted
Modifying IP address of a network card	Firewall, Web Proxy
Modifying port numbers	Web Proxy, Scheduled Content Download
Adding or removing an array server	Web Proxy
Enabling/disabling packet filters	Firewall, Web Proxy
Enabling/disabling application filters	Firewall
Enabling/disabling or changing order of Web filters	Web Proxy
Modifying H.323 Gatekeeper interface	H.323 Gatekeeper
Modifying routing tables	Firewall
Updating SSL Certificates	Web Proxy
Modifying a LAT	Firewall, Web Proxy
Modifying cache size	Web Proxy
Adding/removing disks from ISA cache	Web Proxy
Enabling/disabling CARP	Web Proxy, Scheduled Content Download
Modifying properties a for Web requests	Web Proxy

ISA Server Control Service

The ISA Server Control a service (`mspadmin.exe`) is responsible for the following:

- Spawn alerts and actions
- Stops and restarts the other ISA Server services when necessary
- Makes sure that the configuration of each member server in the array is synchronized
- Deletes old log files
- Updates the client-side configurations files `msplat.txt`, and `mspclnt.ini`

Unlike other ISA Server services, the ISA Server Control service cannot be directly manipulated from the ISA Management console.

To stop or start the ISA Server Control service, type the following at a command prompt:

```
net stop isactrl
net start isactrl
```

You can also use the Services MMC in the Administrative Tools to stop or start this service.

TIP

You will discover that when you stop the ISA Control service, either at the command prompt or using the Services MMC, it stops three additional services: Web Proxy, Firewall and Scheduled Content Download. However, when you start the ISA Server Control service, it doesn't start all the other services automatically. You will have to manually start the services either in Services MMC or in the ISA Management console under Monitoring, Services. If you use the restart option in Services MMC, all four services are automatically stopped and restarted.

Let's take a look at another possible scenario you might encounter with ISA Server services:

- **Why is the ISA Server Control Service failing to initialize on my Server?**

    The solution begins with the fact that you might not have enough system resources on your server. You can use the Task Manager (use the CTL-SHIFT-ESCAPE combination keys) to identify the applications that are consuming most of the resources. Try closing some of the applications. If that doesn't take care of the problem, then reboot the server.

NOTE

ISA Server Control Service will fail to start on a server if the server is part of an array and is then moved out of the array to a different site. In addition, the service will also fail if the server was part of a domain and now is no longer in the same domain as the rest of the array members. In such cases, the server either needs to be moved to an array in the new site, or, in case of a domain, the server should be added to an array in the new domain.

Web Proxy Service

The Web Proxy service (w3proxy) is a service responsible for providing cross-platform Web access. Most popular clients are supported. The list includes the following clients:

- Windows 2000
- Windows 95/98
- Windows NT
- UNIX
- Macintosh

The Web Proxy service can retrieve objects for the clients using FTP, HTTP, Gopher, and HTTPS. The client browsers must be pointing to the ISA Server computer to use this service. The following is a common scenario that you may encounter when working with Web Proxy service:

- **My ISA Server, which meets the minimum hardware requirements, crashed and I had to restart it. I warned my clients that when the box comes back up and the Web Proxy service restarts, Web access might be slow while the 2GB cache is restored. It has been 40 minutes, and most clients are still complaining about slow Internet access,and some even say they can't access the Web at all. Why?**

    You were right in informing your clients that Internet access would be slow while the cache is restored. When you stop the Web Proxy service, the cache contents are not deleted. When you restart the Web Proxy service, the process of restoring cache can take a long time on older hardware with a large cache size. Give it some time. With a 2GB cache size, the restoration could take a couple of hours.

    The fact that some clients are complaining of no Web access at all is also not surprising. Check to see what content they are trying to access. Most likely they are trying to get to information that has been previously cached, but has not been restored yet. Because the cached information is not available, their browsers should be trying to get to the intended site directly. Perhaps with the traffic congestion upon the initial server restart, they were not able to directly access the live content either. If this is the case, have them try again. It should work, although it will be slow until the cache is fully restored. One additional thing I suggest in this case is to upgrade the RAM in the server to at least 512MB. That would give you some performance boost, and would decrease the cache rebuild time.

Firewall Service

The ISA Server Firewall service supports requests made from Firewall clients and SecureNAT clients. Firewall client software is supported on Windows Me, Windows9x, Windows NT, and Windows 2000 computers only. Some 16-bit Winsock applications are supported, but only on

9

Windows NT and Windows 2000. Keep in mind that the Firewall service is available only when ISA Server is installed in Integrated or Firewall mode.

The ISA Management console can be used to stop or start the Firewall service. Let's take a look at a possible trouble point:

- **We are using a chain of ISA Servers on our network. The Firewall clients can successfully access the Internet using their browsers but they can't seem to connect to Internet sites and use Winsock applications. Rebooting doesn't help either. What are we missing?**

    If you are providing Internet access to your Firewall clients through an upstream server and the clients don't have any direct connection to the upstream ISA Server, try configuring Winsock proxy chaining. The routing rules that you have configured only apply to the Web browser requests. You need to make sure that in addition to the routing rules you've also configured Winsock proxy chaining (also referred to as Firewall service chaining). When you configure Firewall service chaining, you make the ISA Server computer act like a Firewall client to an upstream ISA Server.

    To configure firewall service chaining, go to ISA Management console and right-click on Network Configuration. Select Properties and then configure Firewall chaining.

H.323 Gatekeeper Service

The H.323 Gatekeeper and the H.323 protocol filter work together to provide a full-featured and complete communications solution to H.323-registered clients who are using applications such as NetMeeting 3.0. The H.323 protocol filter can be used to configure PBX-like dial plans and call routing scenarios that are based on your client's e-mail address (or other "well-known" aliases). Once configured, clients can participate in audio and video conferences, use remote desktop features, and share files and applications.. H.323 Gatekeeper is mandatory for all inbound calls going through the ISA Server (see Figure 9.1). Outbound calls do not require the H.323 Gatekeeper service, so they can be made without using it.

The ISA Management console can be used to stop or start the H.323 Gatekeeper service.

Here is a scenario involving the H.323 service:

- **I have a client that can do audio conferencing with NetMeeting 3.0, but can't do video. Why not?**

    Check the H.323 packet filter configuration properties and verify that Allow Video is checked. See Figure 9.1 for configuration options.

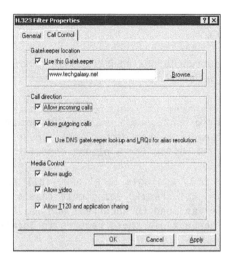

FIGURE 9.1
Configuring H.323 filter properties.

Using the Event Viewer to Help Troubleshoot ISA Events

ISA Server events that are tracked while the product is running can be viewed by using the Event Viewer application. Event Viewer in Windows 2000 is a significant improvement over the Event Viewer in Windows NT. Now you will find a detailed explanation, and in some cases, step-by-step instructions on how to solve the problem. Another cool feature that is now available is the *copy function*. You no longer have to mess with screen shots so you can send the description of the error to the technical support. Figure 9.2 shows a warning from the DNS source with event ID 414. To read the entire description of the message you'll need to scroll down, but luckily you can copy this error to a word processor. The icon in the graphic just below the arrows is the copy icon. Simply click on the icon once and then paste the output in a document.

Here's the full sample output of the messages seen in Figure 9.2. Note the detail that Event Viewer offers you as a measure for troubleshooting:

```
Event Type:      Warning
Event Source:    DNS
Event Category:  None
Event ID:        414
Date:            3/24/2001
Time:            8:49:43 PM
```

```
User:          N/A
Computer:      OPTIPLEX
Description:
The DNS server machine currently has no DNS domain name. Its DNS name is a
➥single label hostname with no domain (example: "host" rather than "host.
➥microsoft.com").

You might have forgotten to configure a primary DNS domain for the server
➥computer. For more information, see either "DNS server log reference" or "To
➥configure the primary DNS suffix for a client computer" in the online Help.

While the DNS server has only a single label name, all zones created will have
➥default records (SOA and NS) created using only this single label name for the
➥server's hostname. This can lead to incorrect and failed referrals when
➥clients and other DNS servers use these records to locate this server by name.


To correct this problem:
 1) open ControlPanel
 2) open System applet
 3) select NetworkIdentification tab
 4) click the "Properties" button and enter a domain name or workgroup name;
➥this name will be used as your DNS domain name
 5) reboot to initialize with new domain name

After reboot, the DNS server will attempt to fix up default records,
➥substituting new DNS name of this server, for old single label name. However,
➥you should review to make sure zone's SOA and NS records now properly use
➥correct domain name of this server.
```

I am sure you will agree that this is far better than the usual "See your systems administrator for help" message that you might be accustomed to.

There are four severity levels for individual event messages. Generally, you'll see only three of them: the informational, error, and warning messages. The four levels are as follows:

- Success
- Informational
- Warning
- Error

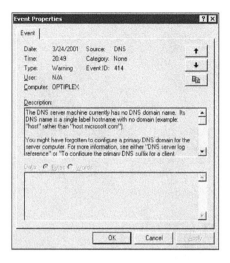

FIGURE 9.2
A sample warning event message.

NOTE

The four severity levels previously listed are different than the five types of events that are logged in the Event Viewer:

- Information
- Warning
- Error
- Success Audit
- Failure Audit

The last two are only available when the security auditing is turned on (by default it is off).

The various categories of event messages are as follows:

- Alert
- Bandwidth
- Caching
- Common service
- Dial-up connection

- Intrusion detection
- ISA Server Control service
- ISA Server Firewall service
- ISA Server Web Proxy service
- Log
- Packet filter
- Server

For a detailed listing of ISA Server 2000 event message IDs for various services visit
`http://www.techgalaxy.net/isaserver.htm`.

Troubleshooting Caching

ISA Server supports caching of frequently requested objects to enhance clients' access to the
Internet. You can implement *forward caching*, where the internal network clients access information on the Internet, or *reverse caching*, where folks on the Internet can access information
residing on your company's internal servers. In addition, you can also configure the Scheduled
Cache Content Download service, which can be used to specify one-time or regularly scheduled downloads of anticipated HTTP contents directly to cache, as seen in Figure 9.3. The
process is handled in the background and when utilized properly, can decrease client bandwidth utilization and increase cache performance.

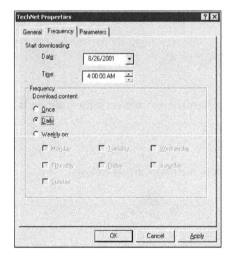

FIGURE 9.3
Scheduled Cache Content Download options.

Here are some potential troublesome scenarios you might encounter with ISA caching:

- **I have configured the ISA Server for caching but it seems like the caching, is not really improving the performance. Am I doing something wrong?**

    ISA Server only caches objects that meet the caching criteria. When the caching is working properly and the clients are retrieving objects from the cache, the clients notice a performance boost. However, if most of the objects that the clients are retrieving are not in the cache, the clients will not notice any performance improvement. What you can do is configure the objects that meet your criteria. For example, you can configure the ISA Server to cache the following objects:

    - Objects that are larger than a specific size
    - Objects that contain a question mark in the URL
    - Objects that do not specify a last modification date

> **NOTE**
>
> By default, objects that are smaller than 12,800 bytes are stored in RAM as well as disk. Objects that are larger are stored only on the disk. You can change the maximum size of objects in RAM. See Chapter 5, "ISA Acceleration Concepts" for more details.

To configure which objects to cache, follow this procedure:

1. In the ISA Server Management console, right-click Cache Configuration and then click on Properties.
2. Click on the Advanced tab and select one of the options for caching, as shown in Figure 9.4. The options shown in the figure are the default options.

> **NOTE**
>
> As a software or Web developer, you should be aware that ISA Server doesn't cache requests that contain the following HTTP request headers:
>
> - `Authorization:` (Unless the server had explicitly permitted the authorization by including the `cache-control: public` header in the response)
> - `Cache-control: no-store`
>
> *continues*

9

TROUBLESHOOTING

In addition, the server also doesn't cache requests that contain the following HTTP response headers:

- `cache-control: no-cache`
- `cache-control: private`
- `pragma: no-cache`
- `www-authenticate`
- `set-cookie`

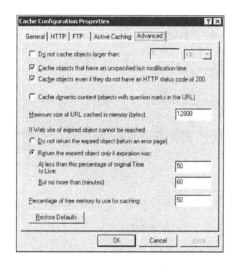

FIGURE 9.4

Configuring advanced caching options.

- **My ISA Server has been running for a while. This morning I noticed that the Web Proxy service failed. I've tried to restart the service but it won't start. Why isn't the Web Proxy service starting, even after rebooting the ISA Server computer?**

Believe it or not, if your cache content file is corrupted, your Web Proxy service will fail to start. Reconfigure the drives that you are using for caching. Here are a couple of recommendations. It is best to configure caching on an NTFS drive that doesn't contain the Windows 2000 and ISA Server system files. In addition, you will have the best results if you format the drive before configuring it for caching. Although Windows 2000 enables you to format drives without assigning a drive letter, ISA Server will not recognize the drive for caching purposes.

> **TIP**
>
> By default, ISA Server sets up a 100MB cache as long as there is at least 150MB of free disk space available. At minimum, you must configure one drive with 5MB for caching. For best results, you should reserve at least 100MB of cache with an additional 0.5MB for each additional Web Proxy client.

- **I installed the ISA Server in Firewall mode. Why isn't the Scheduled Cache Content service starting?**

  The Scheduled Cache Content service will not start because you've installed ISA Server in Firewall mode. Normally, this service is disabled if you install ISA Server in Firewall mode. The Scheduled Cache Content service only runs in Cache or Integrated mode. It is quite possible that you removed the Cache component of ISA Server, and after the reboot, the service got started. To fix this problem, simply reinstall ISA Server, either in Cache or Integrated mode.

Troubleshooting Sessions

Client sessions can be monitored in the ISA Management console under server name, Monitoring, Sessions. Here you can manage client sessions and configure permissions for the sessions object, which defines the type of access for individual users or groups.

Let's look at some troubleshooting areas for scenarios related to sessions.

- **I added a client to a new group that has several restrictions, but the client's level of access did not change. Why not?**

  Just like NT permissions, ISA Server access rules are only applied after the client's security token is renewed. For your restrictions to take effect, have the client log off, then log back on.

- **My dial-up session suddenly dropped. How come?**

  Well, there could be several reasons for a dropped connection, but let's just say for argument's sake that the cause of the disconnection could not be determined. In this case, stop and restart all the ISA Server services. The service will automatically attempt to reconnect the session. You can use the ISA Management console to stop or start the services, as shown in Figure 9.5.

- **Why can I establish an SSL session to some sites, but not to others?**

  The site you are trying to establish a connection to probably has SSL configured on non-standard ports. To enable SSL connectivity to non-standard ports, the ISA Server `FPCProxyTunnelPortRange` COM object needs to be modified with the ISA Server SDK.

9

TROUBLESHOOTING

FIGURE 9.5
Stopping/starting ISA Server services.

NOTE

By default, ISA Server only enables connections on port 443 (HTTPS) and 563 (SecureNews). If a client attempts a connection to a site that is configured for any port other than the preceding default ports, the connection will fail.

Troubleshooting Connections

When it comes to connectivity, there are a wide range of problems that you may have to troubleshoot. Let's look at several scenarios that are related to connections.

- **Users on the internal LAN can connect to external Web sites, but the connection is slow. What could be the problem?**

  Check to see whether IP routing has been enabled on the ISA Server. If not, enable it by going to the properties of the IP Packet Filters under Access Policy, as shown in Figure 9.6. If IP routing is already enabled, check to see whether dynamic packet filtering is turned on. If IP routing is enabled but dynamic packet filtering is not, users may still experience slow connections.

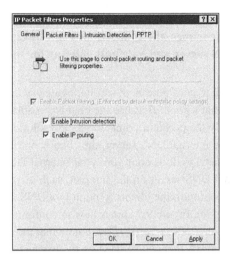

FIGURE 9.6

Enabling IP routing.

- **Although a protocol rule has been created to allow all IP traffic, SecureNAT clients can't connect to a particular site/service/IP port. What could be the problem?**

  The first thing to do here is find out what the user is trying to connect to. Then determine what protocol the user is attempting to use to make the connection, and whether the protocol requires multiple, simultaneous connections.

  The answer to this situation depends on what the user is trying to accomplish. Keep in mind that SecureNAT clients can only make connections with already defined protocols, and any required secondary connections will be refused unless you have created an application filter that uses the protocol in question. If the user is trying to connect to a specific port, create a protocol definition with that port number as the primary port. If the user is trying to connect to a service that utilizes several ports, then create an application filter that identifies all the necessary ports.

  Lack of authentication support could be another reason why the user can't connect. If you want to allow Internet access only for authenticated users, then SecureNAT client won't help. In that case, you should install a Firewall client.

- **Why can't my SecureNAT clients connect to the Internet, even though they have been configured with a proper default gateway?**

  You need to ensure that the SecureNAT clients are configured for DNS in addition to the default gateway.

9

TROUBLESHOOTING

- **Our SecureNAT clients can make connections to the Internet using IP addresses, but when they use the names, the connections can't be established. I have configured an internal DNS server and a default gateway for the clients. What am I missing?**

  Well, you remembered to configure both a default gateway and a DNS server for your SecureNAT clients—that's good. Because the clients are able to resolve addresses using IP addresses, obviously the problem points to name resolution issues—as in DNS. If you are pointing to the internal DNS server, the client won't be able to resolve Internet addresses. What you need to do is configure your internal DNS server to forward requests to an external DNS server on the Internet, such as your ISP's DNS server. Another option is to configure the clients to point to a DNS server that forwards requests to an external DNS server. Figure 9.7 shows how to configure your DNS server to forward requests to another DNS server(s). Please note that the IP address used in Figure 9.7 is not a valid IP address that can be used on the Internet. It is only used for demonstration purposes.

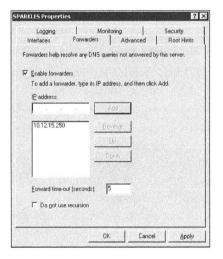

FIGURE 9.7
Forwarding DNS requests to another DNS server.

Troubleshooting Access

If you are an ISA Server administrator, you will definitely encounter access policy issues that you'll have to troubleshoot. The following questions address some of the more common scenarios.

- **Why can't the clients connect to any Web sites on the Internet?**

  Upon initial installation, ISA Server does not permit any traffic in either direction—to or from the Internet. In order to permit your clients to access the Internet, you need to do two things:

  1. Configure at least one site and content rule.
  2. Configure at least one protocol rule.

  After you create a rule and then configure a protocol rule that permits access to the contents, clients will be able to access the Web sites.

  If the clients can't access any Web sites after you have already created a protocol rule, then you might want to check their browser settings and make sure they are using the correct proxy port. By default, ISA Server uses port 8080.

TIP

After you install the ISA Server, it creates a default site and content rule that permits all clients access to all the Web sites on the Internet, 24 hours a day. But this is not enough for clients to connect to the Internet. Assuming you are not using an Enterprise Policy, what you must do is create a protocol rule that will use this default content rule and permit clients to access the Internet using the protocols defined in the rule.

- **When a client attempts to ping a known "live" Web site, he/she gets no response. Why?**

  ICMP requests are disabled by default. To enable ICMP for SecureNAT clients, enable IP routing and create a packet filter that permits ICMP packets to travel in both directions. The inbound ICMP echo requests are disabled by default to protect your server from ping of death attacks. Another reason that a client may not be able to ping a Web site is that the site administrator may have disabled ICMP responses. This will result in a "request timed out" response to the client.

- **Why am I not able to establish a VPN connection to my home computer from my PC at work?**

  The ISA Server administrator needs to enable IP routing and check the PPTP Through ISA Firewall box, as shown in Figure 9.8. PPTP connections cannot be made from a Firewall client or a proxy client without proper configuration. In order for the user to establish the connection, a static route through the ISA server to the destination has to be created.

To configure the enabling of PPTP through the ISA Server computer, in the ISA Server Management console go to the properties of IP Packet Filters under Access Policy and click on the PPTP tab. Check the box PPTP Through ISA Firewall.

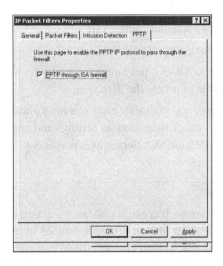

FIGURE 9.8
Enabling PPTP to pass through ISA Server.

- **I disabled the protocol rule that permitted access to RealAudio, but the clients are still using RealAudio. How come?**

  Simply disabling a protocol rule doesn't prevent existing clients from continuing to use the protocol. What you need to do is disconnect existing clients if you want to prevent them from using RealAudio. In other words, although clients will not be able to establish new sessions and new clients will not be able make any connections, the clients with existing RealAudio sessions will continue to use the protocol until either they disconnect the session by logging off, or you disconnect them.

- **Why can't clients use a specific protocol definition even though a protocol rule permits access?**

  You might have disabled an application filter. Enable the application filter; otherwise, all clients that use the protocol definition are blocked, even if the protocol rules permit access.

- **Why can't the clients access Napster through the ISA Server?**

  You need to install a Firewall client on the computers that need access to Napster. Create a protocol definition with the following information:

- Protocol name: Napster
- Initial port: 8875, TCP, Outbound
- Subsequent Connections: 8888-8888, TCP, Outbound
- Subsequent Connections: 6600-6699, TCP, Outbound

Create a protocol rule with this information that permits access to the clients. You should be able to go through your ISA Server and access a computer running Napster without configuring anything in Napster.

> **TIP**
>
> When working with Napster, make sure that you do not have any packet filtering rules that deny access to port 6699 or 6697.

- **Why can't I use the ICQ 2000b beta through the ISA Server when I didn't have any problems with the previous versions? And before you ask, yes, I have the ICQ protocol definition enabled on my ISA Server computer.**

  The port number used by the ICQ 2000b beta (TCP port 5190) is the same port that is used by the protocol definition in AOL Instant Messenger. Simply add the AOL Instant Messenger to the list of protocols that are permitted access and you should be able to use the ICQ 2000b beta.

Troubleshooting Authentication

You can configure ISA Server to process inbound and outbound requests such that users are required to get authenticated. If the users aren't successfully authenticated, the Web requests will be automatically denied. Here are some troubleshooting scenarios that pertain to authentication problems.

- **I've configured ISA Server for Integrated Windows authentication, but some clients can't connect to the internal servers from the Internet. Why can't they connect when they are using Windows 2000 Professional to access the network?**

  Windows 2000 supports Basic, Digest, Integrated Windows, and Client Certificate authentication but not all clients support all the authentication methods. Internet Explorer 5.0 or later supports all these methods. Most browsers, including Netscape, support Basic authentication. Your clients may not be using Internet Explorer. Make sure that your clients can use the authentication method that you have configured.

  What if you don't know what browsers the clients might be using? In that case, it's a good idea to use Basic authentication to be on the safe side, because it is supported by most browsers.

> **TIP**
>
> Basic authentication does not encrypt the passwords. Because the passwords are transmitted in clear text, for confidential contents be sure to implement Basic with Secure Socket Layer (SSL).

For more information on IIS 5.0 authentication methods, check out the article "Internet Information Services 5.0 Authentication Methods" at `http://www.win2000mag.com/Articles/Print.cfm?ArticleID=8443`.

- **Why does a user still have access to the Web even though I created a policy that denies him access?**

  Depending on the configuration, you might get some unexpected results. Let's say you have configured three ISA Server rules:

  - A site and content rule that permits everyone access to all the sites.
  - A protocol rule that permits everyone complete access to all the protocols.
  - A custom site and content rule that denies access to a user Shawn.

  If Shawn uses a Firewall client and he is trying to access non-HTTP objects, he will be denied access because the Firewall service will require authentication and Shawn isn't permitted access. So you say that's cool. That's exactly what you wanted. However, if Shawn uses a Firewall client and requests HTTP objects (instead of non-HTTP) he will be permitted access, because for HTTP objects the ISA Server will not require authentication.

  In a third scenario, if Shawn uses a Web Proxy client and requests HTTP objects, he will still be permitted access because the Web Proxy service doesn't require authentication.

  So the moral of the story is this: If you want to ensure that unauthenticated users are denied access for all outgoing Web requests, configure the array as shown in Figure 9.9.

All authentication information is lost when a packet is sent on behalf of a Firewall client from the HTTP Redirector to the Web Proxy service. As a result, when the HTTP redirector filter sends requests from a Firewall client to the Web Proxy service, the requests are handled as unauthenticated. If you are permitting unauthenticated access, obviously the requests will go through. What you need to do is to configure your ISA Server to not permit unauthenticated users access to the Internet. Here's how:

1. In the ISA Management console, right-click the array and click on Properties.
2. On the Outgoing Web Requests tab, check the box that says Ask Unauthenticated Users for Identification.

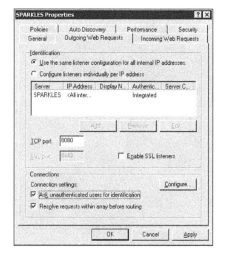

FIGURE 9.9

Forcing authentication on all outbound requests.

- **Why can't a user access his/her Hotmail account from Outlook Express?**

  If the ISA Server is permitting access to only specific users, then Outlook Express might
  not be able to pass the authentication information to the ISA Server. On the client machine,
  enable Web site exceptions to the configured proxy settings in Internet Explorer. Then,
  install the Firewall client software on the machine. Finally, enable the Send to Requested
  Web Server option in the HTTP Redirector Filter on the ISA Server.

To configure the HTTP Redirector Filter option, use the following procedure:

1. In the ISA Server Management console go to Extensions, Application Filters, and double-click HTTP Redirector Filter in the right-hand pane.

2. Make sure the Enable This Filter box is checked on the General tab.

3. On the Options tab, select the option Send To Requested Web Server as shown in
   Figure 9.10.

For more information, please refer to Microsoft Knowledge Base article Q287921. The article also discusses additional methods as a solution.

9

TROUBLESHOOTING

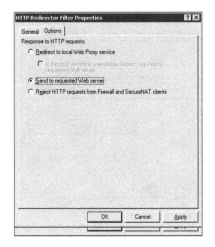

FIGURE 9.10
Configuring the Send to Requested Web Server option.

Troubleshooting Publishing

ISA Server allows you to publish Web servers that are on your internal network to the external clients on the Internet. This is known as Web publishing. You can also publish other servers (such as Exchange), known as server publishing. Here are several scenarios involving publishing.

- **Why can't I send mail from an Exchange Server that is configured as a Firewall client behind an ISA Server?**

  Publishing servers, such as Exchange, are published as SecureNAT clients, and therefore don't require any special configuration in ISA Server environment. This is different than what we used to do in the Proxy Server 2.0 environment. With Proxy Server 2.0, you configured a wspclnt.ini file on the Exchange Server so that it could act as a Winsock Proxy client. In the ISA Server environment, first you need to delete the wspclnt.ini file from your publishing server (as in Exchange Server). Then run the Mail Server Security Wizard.

To run the Mail Server Security Wizard, use the following procedure:

1. In the ISA Server Management console, go to Server Publishing Rules under Publishing.

2. Select the Secure Mail Server option to start the wizard and then follow the instructions.

- **Why am I having occasional communication problems between the Exchange Server and the ISA Server?**

You may be running into some issues with your Exchange Server temporarily losing its connection to your ISA Server. If so, you need to restart Exchange services so they can properly bind to the ISA Server ports.

- **Why are the clients receiving 403 errors when they try to connect to a published Web server?**

Generally this would be a situation where you haven't configured any authentication methods for the listener, even though some access policy rules are requiring authentication. Simply configure an authentication method for the listener.

Troubleshooting Dial-Up

In this last troubleshooting section, let's look at a couple of dial-up scenarios. Although a lot of dial-up problems can be associated with the hardware, such as modems and phone lines, this section addresses problems related to ISA Server configuration.

- **After I make a dial-up connection, it never hangs up. Why does the connection stay active even when there is no dialing activity?**

The ISA Server sends name resolution requests to both internal and external DNS servers, even if the client makes a request for a local computer inside the internal network. To fix this problem, configure the ISA Server to use only internal DNS servers. Make sure that your internal DNS server is an ISA Server client, and then configure it to forward the requests to an external DNS server.

- **Why is dialing out to the Internet failing when manual dial-up is working?**

Your dial-up entry credentials may not be configured properly even though you configured the network dial-up connection properly. Reconfigure the dial-up entries by going to the ISA Management. Here's the procedure:

1. In the ISA Server Management console, go to Server and Arrays.
2. Go to your server, Policy Elements, and select Dial-up Entries.
3. Right-click the dial-up entry that you want to configure and then click on Properties.
4. Go to the Dial-up Entry tab.
5. Under Use the Following Network Dial-up Connection, click Select and choose a network dial-up connection.
6. Under the Network dial-up account, click Set Account and enter a user name and password for the account that you will use for this dial-up connection.

9

TROUBLESHOOTING

TIP

The user name and password that you need to provide with the network dial-up connection should be the same user name and password that you would provide to manually establish a network dial-up connection.

Summary

ISA Server is a complex product with many configuration options. When client access problems arise, don't get overwhelmed! Use your common sense and evaluate the situation. Ask yourself questions such as: "What is the client trying to do?" or "Have I created a rule for that yet?" Sometimes a problem might simply be the result of an oversight. Other times, the issues are much trickier.

Hopefully, the questions and answers in this chapter were helpful in presenting some ideas on how to address particular problems or issues that might come up during (or after) an ISA Server implementation. Note that the answers presented here are not the only ways to solve the problems or to address the issues. Consult the product help, Microsoft TechNet, or try one of the several Web sites for answers to particularly bothersome problems.

TIP

Sometimes you will need to switch between the Taskpad and Advanced view. For example, if you've created a Dial-up entry and you are in the Advanced view, you will not see an option to delete the entry. Select Taskpad from the View menu and you will see a Delete a Dial-Up Entry option in the right-hand pane.

Don't forget to check out the appendices, as they will be beneficial to troubleshooting in many ways. Appendix A covers bug fixes and patches for ISA Server 2000. Appendix B lists Microsoft Knowledge Base articles, also known as Q-articles. Q-articles will assist you in solving known problems and offer you some workarounds. Sometimes just knowing that a problem is a known bug and that the vendor is working on a solution can save you time in the sense that you no longer need to waste precious time in trying to fix a problem that has no known solution.

Appendix C lists TCP/IP port assignments that will help you troubleshoot your Firewall port issues and will also assist in security configuration. The back of the book contains a glossary of common terms used in Windows 2000 that are related to ISA Server 2000.

Bug Fixes and Patches for ISA Server 2000

- Windows 2000 Service Pack 2 Updates for ISA Server 2000   262

- Web Requests Can Cause Access Violations in ISA Server Web Proxy Service   263

- ISA Server 2000 Fix for Packet Filter Log   264

- ISA Server 2000 Fix for UDP Log   264

- Security Mailing Lists and Other Resources   265

Microsoft releases bug fixes and patches for its products on a regular basis. The information listed below is available from Microsoft's Web site and/or Microsoft TechNet. If you wish to receive product security bulletins automatically from Microsoft via e-mail, you can sign up at `http://www.microsoft.com/technet/treeview/default.asp?url=/technet/security/bulletin/notify.asp`.

For additional information on where to find Microsoft security patches, check out `http://www.microsoft.com/technet/treeview/default.asp?url=/technet/columns/security/secpatch.asp`.

Windows 2000 Service Pack 2 Updates for ISA Server 2000

Microsoft Windows 2000 Service Pack 2 contains several fixes for issues related to ISA Server 2000. One of the patches has to do with the Quality of Service (QoS) Packet Scheduler service, which does not classify forwarded IP packets to a traffic control flow. This prevents an application from controlling IP traffic when it uses Windows 2000's routing with QoS Packet Scheduler service. Another fix has to do with the clients leaving a large number of open sockets that are caused by the TIMER_INTERVAL parameter. This typically happens when a client reaches a high open and close connection rate (about 600 connections per second).

- Article Q270921: Windows 2000 Quality of Service Packet Scheduler Service Does Not Filter and Flow Forwarded Traffic.

  The above Q-article is available at `http://support.microsoft.com/support/kb/articles/Q270/9/21.ASP`.

- Article Q270923: Windows 2000 QoS Packet Scheduler Sends Packets with Wrong Checksum on Network Adapters That Enable Hardware Checksum.

  The above Q-article is available at `http://support.microsoft.com/support/kb/articles/Q270/9/23.ASP`.

- Article Q271067: Client Computer with High Connect Rate Opens Many Sockets.

  The above Q-article is available at `http://support.microsoft.com/support/kb/articles/Q271/0/67.ASP`.

You should install the latest service pack for Windows 2000 (Service Pack 2 at the time of writing) to fix these problems. The fix for the English version of Windows 2000 should have the following file attributes or later:

Date	Time	Version	Size	File name
9/27/00	8:05PM	03.60.3714.5	545	Dao360.dll
10/4/00	5:17PM	5.00.2195.2417	65	Ipnat.sys
10/3/00	5:17PM	4.00.4331.7	501	Msexch40.dll
10/3/00	5:17PM	4.00.4431.3	313	Msexcl40.dll
10/3/00	5:17PM	4.00.4331.1	1,469	Msjet40.dll
10/3/00	5:17PM	4.00.4431.4	341	Msjetol01.dll
10/3/00	5:17PM	4.00.4229.0	237	Msjtes40.dll
10/3/00	5:17PM	4.00.4331.3	209	Msltus40.dll
10/3/00	5:17PM	4.00.4331.6	341	Mspbde40.dll
10/3/00	5:17PM	4.00.4325.0	309	Msrd3x40.dll
10/3/00	5:17PM	4.00.4331.0	541	Msrepl40.dll
10/3/00	5:17PM	4.00.4331.5	249	Mstext40.dll
10/3/00	5:17PM	4.00.4331.6	337	Msxbde40.dll
8/28/00	12:48AM	5.00.2195.2104	59	Psched.sys
10/04/00	1:24PM	5.00.2195.2412	304	Tcpip.sys
9/8/00	3:39PM	5.00.2195.2153	121	Wldap32.dl

For information on Installing Windows 2000 and Windows 2000 Hotfixes, check out Article
Q249149 at http://support.microsoft.com/support/kb/articles/Q249/1/49.ASP.

Web Requests Can Cause Access Violations in ISA Server Web Proxy Service

The ISA Server Web Proxy service does not correctly handle some Web requests if they exceed
a certain length. If you try to process these requests, it could cause the Web Proxy service to
fail because of the access violation. You could restart the service, but it will disrupt your Web
Proxy service. However, other services will continue to function normally. Both ISA Server
2000 and Proxy Server 2.0 are affected by this vulnerability. For more information, check out
Article Q295279.

- Version Number 1.0 was released on 4/16/2001.
- Version Number 1.1 was released on 4/17/2001 to address the possibility that an external
  hacker could use HTML e-mail or a Web page to exploit this vulnerability.

The file to download is isahf63.exe (229 KB).

To verify that the above patch has been installed on your computer, ensure that the following registry has been created:

`HKEY_LOCAL_MACHINE\SOFTWARE\Microsoft\FPC\Hofixes\63`

You can also use the date, time, and version information in Knowledge Base article Q295279 to verify the individual files.

This hot fix is available at

`http://www.microsoft.com/technet/treeview/default.asp?url=/technet/security/bulletin/MS01-021.asp.`

ISA Server 2000 Fix for Packet Filter Log

You can block and log all outbound ICMP traffic that is sent from the private network to the public network by modifying the registry. Before you modify the registry, make sure you back up the registry and follow Microsoft's usual cautions in making any changes to the registry. Here's the procedure:

1. Apply the listed download on each ISA Server.
2. Run the registry editor and go to the following key:

    `/HKEY_LOCAL_MACHINE/System/CurrentControlSet/Services/MspFltEx`

3. Add a key called `Parameters`.
4. Add a value under this `Parameters` key called `BlockOutboundICMP` and type `DWORD`.
5. Set this `BlockOutboundICMP` value to any non-zero value.

   - Version Number 1.0 was released on 1/25/2001.

The file to download is `isahf51.exe` (93 KB).

This hot fix is available at `http://www.microsoft.com/downloads/release.asp?ReleaseID=27396.`

ISA Server 2000 Fix for UDP Log

A bug in Microsoft Internet Security and Acceleration (ISA) Server 2000's firewall logging module prevents the logging of the Rule#1 and Rule#2 fields for certain UDP traffic, even if those fields are selected in the logging configuration dialog. This fix adds the two fields for proper logging of UDP traffic.

   - Version Number 1.0 was released on 1/25/2001.

The file to download is `isahf54.exe` (198 KB).

This hot fix is available at `http://www.microsoft.com/downloads/release.asp?ReleaseID=27397`.

Security Mailing Lists and Other Resources

There are numerous resources available to keep up with the bug fixes and security patches. You can join some of the mailing lists to receive automatic security alerts via e-mail. Here are a few security-related Web sites that you will find useful.

- Microsoft Security: `http://www.microsoft.com/security/default.asp`
- TechNet Security Bulletin Search: `http://www.microsoft.com/technet/security/current.asp`
- Security Focus: `http://www.securityfocus.com/`
- Windows IT Security: `http://www.windowsitsecurity.com/`
- SANS Institute: `http://www.sans.org/newlook/home.htm`
- @stake's Security Education Center: `http://www.atstake.com/services/education/index.html`
- The Encyclopedia of Computer Security: `http://www.itsecurity.com/defaultie5.htm`

Microsoft Knowledge
Base Articles

There are a host of Q-articles that you will find useful in configuring, managing, supporting, and troubleshooting ISA Server 2000 available at Microsoft's Knowledge Base. To read these articles, you can go to http://search.support.microsoft.com/kb/c.asp, as seen in Figure B.1, and select Internet Security and Acceleration Server 2000 from the drop-down box in Step 1. Then type ISA in Step 3 to access the relevant articles.

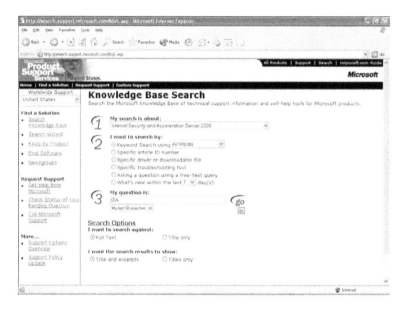

FIGURE B.1
Searching for Q-articles.

TIP

To quickly access a Q-article, type mskb, followed by the article number in the address box of Internet Explorer. For example, to access the article Q-284831, type mskb 284831. Do not type http://, the letter Q before the article number, or anything else in the address box.

The Q-articles are also available on Microsoft's TechNet CD. This listing is sorted by the order of relevance as it appears on Microsoft's Web site.

Q-Article	*Description*
Q284831	**The ISA Server Control Service May Report Event 14158 After You Have Installed ISA Server** http://support.microsoft.com/support/kb/articles/Q284/8/31.ASP

B

Q-Article	Description
Q287921	**ISA Server Configuration Options for Hotmail Access When You Use Outlook Express** http://support.microsoft.com/support/kb/articles/Q287/9/21.ASP
Q288206	**How to Configure the Gatekeeper Service in ISA Server to Allow Inbound Netmeeting Calls** http://support.microsoft.com/support/kb/articles/Q288/2/06.ASP
Q288214	**The ISA Server Array Configuration Cannot Be Restored** http://support.microsoft.com/support/kb/articles/Q288/2/14.ASP
Q288247	**Access Violation in Mspadmin.exe with ISA Server with Multiple IP Addresses on an External Interface** http://support.microsoft.com/support/kb/articles/Q288/2/47.ASP
Q288396	**ISA Server Event 14120 Is Logged and Packet Filter Cannot Be Created** http://support.microsoft.com/support/kb/articles/Q288/3/96.ASP
Q288734	**Real Player Cannot Connect to the Internet Through ISA Server** http://support.microsoft.com/support/kb/articles/Q288/7/34.ASP
Q289858	**ISA Server Pass-Through Authentication Does Not Work with NTLM** http://support.microsoft.com/support/kb/articles/Q289/8/58.ASP
Q290113	**How to Publish Outlook Web Access Behind Internet Security and Acceleration Server** http://support.microsoft.com/support/kb/articles/Q290/1/13.ASP
Q290384	**"ISA Server Cannot Load the Property Page" Error Message with Error Code 0x80004002** http://support.microsoft.com/support/kb/articles/Q290/3/84.ASP
Q291662	**How to Publish Domain Name System Servers with Internet Security and Acceleration Server** http://support.microsoft.com/support/kb/articles/Q291/6/62.ASP
Q292018	**Slow Response from Downstream ISA Server Using Web Proxy Chaining** http://support.microsoft.com/support/kb/articles/Q292/0/18.ASP
Q292569	**How to Set Up Internet Security and Acceleration Server to Host Web Sites by Using the Secure Sockets Layer Protocol** http://support.microsoft.com/support/kb/articles/Q292/5/69.ASP
Q295310	**The Internet Security and Acceleration Server Report Log Is Empty** http://support.microsoft.com/support/kb/articles/Q295/3/10.ASP

Q-Article	Description
Q295386	**PDF Files Are Not Returned from the ISA Server Cache**
	http://support.microsoft.com/support/kb/articles/Q295/3/86.ASP
Q296534	**How to Configure ISA Server to Use a PPPoE Connection**
	http://support.microsoft.com/support/kb/articles/Q296/5/34.ASP
Q296674	**The SecureNAT Clients Cannot Access the Internal Resources That Are Published by Means of ISA Server**
	http://support.microsoft.com/support/kb/articles/Q296/6/74.ASP
Q297080	**Incomplete HTML Pages and Random Authentication Prompts If ISA Server Is Chained to Upstream Proxy**
	http://support.microsoft.com/support/kb/articles/Q297/0/80.ASP
Q297315	**You May Not Be Able to Add New Users After You Run the Secure Your ISA Server Computer Wizard**
	http://support.microsoft.com/support/kb/articles/Q297/3/15.ASP
Q297922	**HOW TO: How to Provide Internet Access Through a Firewall by Using Internet Security and Acceleration Server**
	http://support.microsoft.com/support/kb/articles/Q297/9/22.ASP
Q299673	**HOW TO: Configure ISA Server 2000 and Enterprise Manager to Connect Through ISA to a SQL Server**
	http://support.microsoft.com/support/kb/articles/Q299/6/73.ASP
Q300199	**Packet Filters May Not Apply in ISA Server**
	http://support.microsoft.com/support/kb/articles/Q300/1/99.ASP
Q300435	**HOW TO: Securely Publish Multiple Web Sites Using ISA Server**
	http://support.microsoft.com/support/kb/articles/Q300/4/35.ASP
Q300707	**Invalid Content-Length Header May Cause Requests to Fail Through ISA Server**
	http://support.microsoft.com/support/kb/articles/Q300/7/07.ASP
Q300879	**How to Stop an ISA Server Service by Using a Command-Line Prompt**
	http://support.microsoft.com/support/kb/articles/Q300/8/79.ASP
Q301380	**Some Server Variables Are Not Fully Implemented in ISA Server**
	http://support.microsoft.com/support/kb/articles/Q301/3/80.ASP
Q301425	**ISA Server Does Not Cache Responses That Contain the Location Header**
	http://support.microsoft.com/support/kb/articles/Q301/4/25.ASP
Q301471	**How to Delete the Web Cache on Internet Security and Acceleration Server**
	http://support.microsoft.com/support/kb/articles/Q301/4/71.ASP

Q-Article	Description
Q302372	HOW TO: Configure Logging for Microsoft Internet Security and Acceleration Server
	http://support.microsoft.com/support/kb/articles/Q302/3/72.ASP
Q302529	HOW TO: Monitor Server Activity for Internet Security and Acceleration Server 2000
	http://support.microsoft.com/support/kb/articles/Q302/5/29.ASP
Q250293	ISA Server Error Message "Cannot Save Modifications to LAT" Is Displayed
	http://support.microsoft.com/support/kb/articles/Q250/2/93.ASP
Q270025	Automatic Dial Settings Are Lost After You Upgrade to ISA Server
	http://support.microsoft.com/support/kb/articles/Q270/0/25.ASP
Q270268	NetMeeting Does Not Accept Incoming Calls When Internet Security and Acceleration Server Is Installed
	http://support.microsoft.com/support/kb/articles/Q270/2/68.ASP
Q271270	How to Enable Live Stream Splitting in ISA Server
	http://support.microsoft.com/support/kb/articles/Q271/2/70.ASP
Q271272	How Internet Security and Acceleration Server Handles the Caching of Responses to Requests Received By Web Publishing
	http://support.microsoft.com/support/kb/articles/Q271/2/72.ASP
Q275236	How to Allow Outbound Napster Traffic to Pass Through ISA Server
	http://support.microsoft.com/support/kb/articles/Q275/2/36.ASP
Q300177	How to Publish a Citrix Server Behind ISA Server
	http://support.microsoft.com/support/kb/articles/q300/1/77.ASP
Q303098	XCCC: How to Configure Exchange 2000 Conferencing Server and ISA Server to Allow Audio and Video
	http://support.microsoft.com/support/kb/articles/Q303/0/98.ASP
Q303426	ISA Server Publishing Rule Does Not Include SMTP Outbound Check Boxes
	http://support.microsoft.com/support/kb/articles/Q303/4/26.ASP
Q303530	VPN Clients May Not Work on ISA Server Perimeter Networks
	http://support.microsoft.com/support/kb/articles/q303/5/30.ASP

Q-Article	Description
Q275237	**How to Stop Napster Traffic from Passing Through ISA Server**
	http://support.microsoft.com/support/kb/articles/Q275/2/37.ASP
Q275286	**Windows 2000 Service Pack 2 Updates for Internet Security and Acceleration (ISA) Server**
	http://support.microsoft.com/support/kb/articles/Q275/2/86.ASP
Q279340	**Outgoing ICQ 2000 Traffic Not Passing Through Internet Security and Acceleration Server**
	http://support.microsoft.com/support/kb/articles/Q279/3/40.ASP
Q279347	**Enable IP Routing on ISA Server to Increase Performance**
	http://support.microsoft.com/support/kb/articles/Q279/3/47.ASP
Q279928	**Error Message: ISA Server Cannot Save the Properties. The IP Range Already Exists in the Local Address Table.**
	http://support.microsoft.com/support/kb/articles/Q279/9/28.ASP
Q279964	**Error Message: HTTP 502 Proxy Error; ISA Server Dial-Out Connection Failed**
	http://support.microsoft.com/support/kb/articles/Q279/9/64.ASP
Q279973	**Existing Users Do Not Have Permission to Use the Shared Fax Server and ISA Server if the Servers Are Added After an Initial Install**
	http://support.microsoft.com/support/kb/articles/Q279/9/73.ASP
Q281985	**ISA Server Configuration Changes Are Not Instantaneous**
	http://support.microsoft.com/support/kb/articles/Q281/9/85.ASP
Q282916	**Unable to Configure ISA Server Settings Using Internet Connection Wizard**
	http://support.microsoft.com/support/kb/articles/Q282/9/16.ASP
Q283213	**Blocking and Logging Traffic on ISA Server Internal Interfaces**
	http://support.microsoft.com/support/kb/articles/Q283/2/13.ASP
Q283284	**How to Configure a Tunnel Port Range in ISA Server**
	http://support.microsoft.com/support/kb/articles/Q283/2/84.ASP
Q284499	**Internet Security and Acceleration Server Does Not Work If the Computer Is Moved from a Domain**
	http://support.microsoft.com/support/kb/articles/Q284/4/99.ASP

Q-Article	Description
Q284701	**Firewall Service Stops After You Upgrade ISA Server RC1**
	http://support.microsoft.com/support/kb/articles/Q284/7/01.ASP
Q284761	**Error Message "Could Not Register Smtpfltr.dll" Occurs When You Attempt to Install ISA Server in an Array**
	http://support.microsoft.com/support/kb/articles/Q284/7/61.ASP
Q258237	**All Logs in ISA Server Use GMT (UTC) Times**
	http://support.microsoft.com/support/kb/articles/Q258/2/37.ASP
Q270471	**ISA Server Unable to Redirect a Request to a URL**
	http://support.microsoft.com/support/kb/articles/Q270/4/71.ASP
Q271379	**Q - Receiving Many Simultaneous H.323 Requests Causes a Computer with ISA Server Installed to Hang**
	http://support.microsoft.com/support/kb/articles/Q271/3/79.ASP
Q296638	**Starting Internet Services Manager May Cause Error Message After Installing an ISA Server Hotfix**
	http://support.microsoft.com/support/kb/articles/Q296/6/38.ASP
Q302527	**HOW TO: Set Bandwidth Configuration for Microsoft Internet Security and Acceleration Server**
	http://support.microsoft.com/support/kb/articles/Q302/5/27.ASP
Q302538	**HOW TO: Enable Reporting for Internet Security and Acceleration Server 2000**
	http://support.microsoft.com/support/kb/articles/Q302/5/38.ASP
Q282295	**The Upgrade Method for Beta Versions of Internet Security and Acceleration Server**
	http://support.microsoft.com/support/kb/articles/Q282/2/95.ASP
Q284523	**How to Use Chkwsp32.exe for Winsock Proxy Clients and ISA Server Firewall Clients**
	http://support.microsoft.com/support/kb/articles/Q284/5/23.ASP
Q284605	**The Internet Security and Acceleration Server Reports Cannot Display the Data from Incomplete Days**
	http://support.microsoft.com/support/kb/articles/Q284/6/05.ASP
Q284800	**The Use of Alert Actions in Internet Security and Acceleration Server 2000**
	http://support.microsoft.com/support/kb/articles/Q284/8/00.ASP

Q-Article	Description
Q285812	**Cannot Configure or Use the SMTP Filter If the Decimal Symbol Is Not a Period**
	http://support.microsoft.com/support/kb/articles/Q285/8/12.ASP
Q288236	**Microsoft Web Proxy Event 14120 for Every Web Request**
	http://support.microsoft.com/support/kb/articles/Q288/2/36.ASP
Q288571	**The Report Logs Record Anonymous Logon Attempts When Logging Is Enabled for the Web Proxy Service**
	http://support.microsoft.com/support/kb/articles/Q288/5/71.ASP
Q289581	**How to Configure Internal NetMeeting Clients to Call External Netmeeting Clients**
	http://support.microsoft.com/support/kb/articles/Q289/5/81.ASP
Q292278	**Internet Information Services Simple Mail Transfer Protocol Service May Be Unable to Send Mail**
	http://support.microsoft.com/support/kb/articles/Q292/2/78.ASP
Q294679	**How to Enable External Client Computers Access to a File Transfer Protocol Server**
	http://support.microsoft.com/support/kb/articles/Q294/6/79.ASP
Q260210	**Description of WinSock Proxy Auto Detect Support**
	http://support.microsoft.com/support/kb/articles/Q260/2/10.ASP
Q262366	**The Enterprise or Array Policies Restricting Internet Access Do Not Seem to Work**
	http://support.microsoft.com/support/kb/articles/Q262/3/66.ASP
Q291000	**External MAPI Clients Cannot Connect with RPC**
	http://support.microsoft.com/support/kb/articles/Q291/0/00.ASP
Q291427	**Only the First Web Site Is Returned Using Web Publishing for Multiple Sites**
	http://support.microsoft.com/support/kb/articles/Q291/4/27.ASP
Q292546	**Firewall Service (Wspsrv.exe) Hangs When Handling RTSP Streams**
	http://support.microsoft.com/support/kb/articles/Q292/5/46.ASP
Q295654	**Windows 2000 Server Cannot Join Existing ISA Array**
	http://support.microsoft.com/support/kb/articles/Q295/6/54.ASP
Q296202	**A Proxy Chain Error Message "12206" Is Displayed**
	http://support.microsoft.com/support/kb/articles/Q296/2/02.ASP

Q-Article	*Description*
Q296591	**A Description of the Automatic Discovery Feature**
	http://support.microsoft.com/support/kb/articles/Q296/5/91.ASP
Q296620	**The Internet Clients Cannot Access the Published Web Servers**
	http://support.microsoft.com/support/kb/articles/Q296/6/20.ASP
Q300876	**HOW TO: Safely Connect Your Company to the Internet**
	http://support.microsoft.com/support/kb/articles/Q300/8/76.ASP
Q269556	**DNS Queries Generated When Static Packet Filter Is Removed**
	http://support.microsoft.com/support/kb/articles/Q269/5/56.ASP
Q271471	**Firewall Client-Based Client Computers Are Unable to Access Resources**
	http://support.microsoft.com/support/kb/articles/Q271/4/71.ASP
Q274568	**How to Enable Internet Control Message Protocol Proxy PING Requests**
	http://support.microsoft.com/support/kb/articles/Q274/5/68.ASP
Q275234	**Firewall Clients Are Unable to Use the Upstream Proxy**
	http://support.microsoft.com/support/kb/articles/Q275/2/34.ASP
Q275851	**BUG: Core Interaction Problems Between BizTalk and ISA Servers**
	http://support.microsoft.com/support/kb/articles/Q275/8/51.ASP
Q280249	**The Default Dynamic Host Configuration Protocol Client Filter Is Disabled**
	http://support.microsoft.com/support/kb/articles/Q280/2/49.ASP
Q280437	**Exchange 2000 Server Exchange System Manager Cannot Open Public Folders**
	http://support.microsoft.com/support/kb/articles/Q280/4/37.ASP
Q281106	**How to Use a Certificate for SSL Authentication Within a Web Publishing Rule**
	http://support.microsoft.com/support/kb/articles/Q281/1/06.ASP
Q281242	**Creating Custom HTML Error Messages to Be Returned to Clients**
	http://support.microsoft.com/support/kb/articles/Q281/2/42.ASP
Q282035	**Unable to Control ISA If LAT Configuration Prevents Access to DC**
	http://support.microsoft.com/support/kb/articles/Q282/0/35.ASP

Q-Article	Description
Q284550	**Error Message: Cache Initialization Failure**
	http://support.microsoft.com/support/kb/articles/Q284/5/50.ASP
Q284674	**Error Message "10060 Connection Timed Out" and the Via Header Are Displayed When Web Publishing**
	http://support.microsoft.com/support/kb/articles/Q284/6/74.ASP
Q284688	**The Server Name May Be Overwritten When You Restore the Backup from Another Computer**
	http://support.microsoft.com/support/kb/articles/Q284/6/88.ASP
Q284818	**A Description of the Various Log Files and Fields**
	http://support.microsoft.com/support/kb/articles/Q284/8/18.ASP
Q292013	**Unregistered Fltrsnk1.dll Starts with Inetinfo.exe**
	http://support.microsoft.com/support/kb/articles/Q292/0/13.ASP
Q293161	**"STOP 0x000000D1" When Passing Fragmented Packets Without NAT**
	http://support.microsoft.com/support/kb/articles/Q293/1/61.ASP
Q293427	**Error Message: Page Cannot Be Displayed**
	http://support.microsoft.com/support/kb/articles/Q293/4/27.ASP
Q295090	**Access Violation in W3proxy.exe Because of HTTP VARY Header Processing**
	http://support.microsoft.com/support/kb/articles/Q295/0/90.ASP
Q292014	**Deleting Disabled SMTP Filter Attachment Rule Leaves Corrupted Rule**
	http://support.microsoft.com/support/kb/articles/Q292/0/14.ASP
Q293101	**Error Message: The Microsoft Web Proxy Service Terminated with Service-Specific Error 2148074253**
	http://support.microsoft.com/support/kb/articles/Q293/1/01.ASP

The following is a listing of the above Microsoft Knowledge Base Q-articles sorted numerically by the article number for your convenience.

Q-Article	Description
Q250293	**ISA Server Error Message "Cannot Save Modifications to LAT" Is Displayed**
	http://support.microsoft.com/support/kb/articles/Q250/2/93.ASP

Q-Article	Description
Q258237	All Logs in ISA Server Use GMT (UTC) Times
	http://support.microsoft.com/support/kb/articles/Q258/2/37.ASP
Q260210	Description of WinSock Proxy Auto Detect Support
	http://support.microsoft.com/support/kb/articles/Q260/2/10.ASP
Q262366	The Enterprise or Array Policies Restricting Internet Access Do Not Seem to Work
	http://support.microsoft.com/support/kb/articles/Q262/3/66.ASP
Q269556	DNS Queries Generated When Static Packet Filter Is Removed
	http://support.microsoft.com/support/kb/articles/Q269/5/56.ASP
Q270025	Automatic Dial Settings Are Lost After You Upgrade to ISA Server
	http://support.microsoft.com/support/kb/articles/Q270/0/25.ASP
Q270268	NetMeeting Does Not Accept Incoming Calls When Internet Security and Acceleration Server Is Installed
	http://support.microsoft.com/support/kb/articles/Q270/2/68.ASP
Q270471	ISA Server Unable to Redirect a Request to a URL
	http://support.microsoft.com/support/kb/articles/Q270/4/71.ASP
Q271270	How to Enable Live Stream Splitting in ISA Server
	http://support.microsoft.com/support/kb/articles/Q271/2/70.ASP
Q271272	How Internet Security and Acceleration Server Handles the Caching of Responses to Requests Received By Web Publishing
	http://support.microsoft.com/support/kb/articles/Q271/2/72.ASP
Q271379	Receiving Many Simultaneous H.323 Requests Causes a Computer with ISA Server Installed to Hang
	http://support.microsoft.com/support/kb/articles/Q271/3/79.ASP
Q271471	Firewall Client-Based Client Computers Are Unable to Access Resources
	http://support.microsoft.com/support/kb/articles/Q271/4/71.ASP
Q274568	How to Enable Internet Control Message Protocol Proxy PING Requests
	http://support.microsoft.com/support/kb/articles/Q274/5/68.ASP
Q275234	Firewall Clients Are Unable to Use the Upstream Proxy
	http://support.microsoft.com/support/kb/articles/Q275/2/34.ASP

Q-Article	Description
Q275236	How to Allow Outbound Napster Traffic to Pass Through ISA Server
	http://support.microsoft.com/support/kb/articles/Q275/2/36.ASP
Q275237	How to Stop Napster Traffic from Passing Through ISA Server
	http://support.microsoft.com/support/kb/articles/Q275/2/37.ASP
Q275286	Windows 2000 Service Pack 2 Updates for Internet Security and Acceleration (ISA) Server
	http://support.microsoft.com/support/kb/articles/Q275/2/86.ASP
Q275851	BUG: Core Interaction Problems Between BizTalk and ISA Servers
	http://support.microsoft.com/support/kb/articles/Q275/8/51.ASP
Q279340	Outgoing ICQ 2000 Traffic Not Passing Through Internet Security and Acceleration Server
	http://support.microsoft.com/support/kb/articles/Q279/3/40.ASP
Q279347	Enable IP Routing on ISA Server to Increase Performance
	http://support.microsoft.com/support/kb/articles/Q279/3/47.ASP
Q279928	Error Message: ISA Server Cannot Save the Properties. The IP Range Already Exists in the Local Address Table.
	http://support.microsoft.com/support/kb/articles/Q279/9/28.ASP
Q279964	Error Message: HTTP 502 Proxy Error ; ISA Server Dial-Out Connection Failed
	http://support.microsoft.com/support/kb/articles/Q279/9/64.ASP
Q279973	Existing Users Do Not Have Permission to Use the Shared Fax Server and ISA Server if the Servers Are Added After an Initial Install
	http://support.microsoft.com/support/kb/articles/Q279/9/73.ASP
Q280249	The Default Dynamic Host Configuration Protocol Client Filter Is Disabled
	http://support.microsoft.com/support/kb/articles/Q280/2/49.ASP
Q280437	Exchange 2000 Server Exchange System Manager Cannot Open Public Folders
	http://support.microsoft.com/support/kb/articles/Q280/4/37.ASP
Q281106	How to Use a Certificate for SSL Authentication Within a Web Publishing Rule
	http://support.microsoft.com/support/kb/articles/Q281/1/06.ASP

Q-Article	Description
Q281242	**Creating Custom HTML Error Messages to Be Returned to Clients**
	http://support.microsoft.com/support/kb/articles/Q281/2/42.ASP
Q281985	**ISA Server Configuration Changes Are Not Instantaneous**
	http://support.microsoft.com/support/kb/articles/Q281/9/85.ASP
Q282035	**Unable to Control ISA If LAT Configuration Prevents Access to DC**
	http://support.microsoft.com/support/kb/articles/Q282/0/35.ASP
Q282295	**The Upgrade Method for Beta Versions of Internet Security and Acceleration Server**
	http://support.microsoft.com/support/kb/articles/Q282/2/95.ASP
Q282916	**Unable to Configure ISA Server Settings Using Internet Connection Wizard**
	http://support.microsoft.com/support/kb/articles/Q282/9/16.ASP
Q283213	**Blocking and Logging Traffic on ISA Server Internal Interfaces**
	http://support.microsoft.com/support/kb/articles/Q283/2/13.ASP
Q283284	**How to Configure a Tunnel Port Range in ISA Server**
	http://support.microsoft.com/support/kb/articles/Q283/2/84.ASP
Q284499	**Internet Security and Acceleration Server Does Not Work If the Computer Is Moved from a Domain**
	http://support.microsoft.com/support/kb/articles/Q284/4/99.ASP
Q284523	**How to Use Chkwsp32.exe for Winsock Proxy Clients and ISA Server Firewall Clients**
	http://support.microsoft.com/support/kb/articles/Q284/5/23.ASP
Q284550	**Error Message: Cache Initialization Failure**
	http://support.microsoft.com/support/kb/articles/Q284/5/50.ASP
Q284605	**The Internet Security and Acceleration Server Reports Cannot Display the Data from Incomplete Days**
	http://support.microsoft.com/support/kb/articles/Q284/6/05.ASP
Q284674	**Error Message "10060 Connection Timed Out" and the Via Header Are Displayed When Web Publishing**
	http://support.microsoft.com/support/kb/articles/Q284/6/74.ASP
Q284688	**The Server Name May Be Overwritten When You Restore the Backup from Another Computer**
	http://support.microsoft.com/support/kb/articles/Q284/6/88.ASP

Q-Article	Description
Q284701	**Firewall Service Stops After You Upgrade ISA Server RC1** http://support.microsoft.com/support/kb/articles/Q284/7/01.ASP
Q284761	**Error Message "Could Not Register Smtpfltr.dll" Occurs When You Attempt to Install ISA Server in an Array** http://support.microsoft.com/support/kb/articles/Q284/7/61.ASP
Q284800	**The Use of Alert Actions in Internet Security and Acceleration Server 2000** http://support.microsoft.com/support/kb/articles/Q284/8/00.ASP
Q284818	**A Description of the Various Log Files and Fields** http://support.microsoft.com/support/kb/articles/Q284/8/18.ASP
Q284831	**The ISA Server Control Service May Report Event 14158 After You Have Installed ISA Server** http://support.microsoft.com/support/kb/articles/Q284/8/31.ASP
Q285812	**Cannot Configure or Use the SMTP Filter If the Decimal Symbol Is Not a Period** http://support.microsoft.com/support/kb/articles/Q285/8/12.ASP
Q287921	**ISA Server Configuration Options for Hotmail Access When You Use Outlook Express** http://support.microsoft.com/support/kb/articles/Q287/9/21.ASP
Q288206	**How to Configure the Gatekeeper Service in ISA Server to Allow Inbound Netmeeting Calls** http://support.microsoft.com/support/kb/articles/Q288/2/06.ASP
Q288214	**The ISA Server Array Configuration Cannot Be Restored** http://support.microsoft.com/support/kb/articles/Q288/2/14.ASP
Q288236	**Microsoft Web Proxy Event 14120 for Every Web Request** http://support.microsoft.com/support/kb/articles/Q288/2/36.ASP
Q288247	**Access Violation in Mspadmin.exe with ISA Server with Multiple IP Addresses on an External Interface** http://support.microsoft.com/support/kb/articles/Q288/2/47.ASP
Q288396	**ISA Server Event 14120 Is Logged and Packet Filter Cannot Be Created** http://support.microsoft.com/support/kb/articles/Q288/3/96.ASP
Q288571	**The Report Logs Record Anonymous Logon Attempts When Logging Is Enabled for the Web Proxy Service** http://support.microsoft.com/support/kb/articles/Q288/5/71.ASP

B

Q-Article	Description
Q288734	Real Player Cannot Connect to the Internet Through ISA Server
	http://support.microsoft.com/support/kb/articles/Q288/7/34.ASP
Q289581	How to Configure Internal NetMeeting Clients to Call External Netmeeting Clients
	http://support.microsoft.com/support/kb/articles/Q289/5/81.ASP
Q289858	ISA Server Pass-Through Authentication Does Not Work with NTLM
	http://support.microsoft.com/support/kb/articles/Q289/8/58.ASP
Q290113	How to Publish Outlook Web Access Behind Internet Security and Acceleration Server
	http://support.microsoft.com/support/kb/articles/Q290/1/13.ASP
Q290384	"ISA Server Cannot Load the Property Page" Error Message with Error Code 0x80004002
	http://support.microsoft.com/support/kb/articles/Q290/3/84.ASP
Q291000	External MAPI Clients Cannot Connect with RPC
	http://support.microsoft.com/support/kb/articles/Q291/0/00.ASP
Q291427	Only the First Web Site Is Returned Using Web Publishing for Multiple Sites
	http://support.microsoft.com/support/kb/articles/Q291/4/27.ASP
Q291662	How to Publish Domain Name System Servers with Internet Security and Acceleration Server
	http://support.microsoft.com/support/kb/articles/Q291/6/62.ASP
Q292013	Unregistered Fltrsnk1.dll Starts with Inetinfo.exe
	http://support.microsoft.com/support/kb/articles/Q292/0/13.ASP
Q292014	Deleting Disabled SMTP Filter Attachment Rule Leaves Corrupted Rule
	http://support.microsoft.com/support/kb/articles/Q292/0/14.ASP
Q292018	Slow Response from Downstream ISA Server Using Web Proxy Chaining
	http://support.microsoft.com/support/kb/articles/Q292/0/18.ASP
Q292278	Internet Information Services Simple Mail Transfer Protocol Service May Be Unable to Send Mail
	http://support.microsoft.com/support/kb/articles/Q292/2/78.ASP

Q-Article	Description
Q292546	**Firewall Service (Wspsrv.exe) Hangs When Handling RTSP Streams**
	http://support.microsoft.com/support/kb/articles/Q292/5/46.ASP
Q292569	**How to Set Up Internet Security and Acceleration Server to Host Web Sites by Using the Secure Sockets Layer Protocol**
	http://support.microsoft.com/support/kb/articles/Q292/5/69.ASP
Q293101	**Error Message: The Microsoft Web Proxy Service Terminated with Service-Specific Error 2148074253**
	http://support.microsoft.com/support/kb/articles/Q293/1/01.ASP
Q293161	**"STOP 0x000000D1" When Passing Fragmented Packets Without NAT**
	http://support.microsoft.com/support/kb/articles/Q293/1/61.ASP
Q293427	**Error Message: Page Cannot Be Displayed**
	http://support.microsoft.com/support/kb/articles/Q293/4/27.ASP
Q294679	**How to Enable External Client Computers Access to a File Transfer Protocol Server**
	http://support.microsoft.com/support/kb/articles/Q294/6/79.ASP
Q295090	**Access Violation in W3proxy.exe Because of HTTP VARY Header Processing**
	http://support.microsoft.com/support/kb/articles/Q295/0/90.ASP
Q295310	**The Internet Security and Acceleration Server Report Log Is Empty**
	http://support.microsoft.com/support/kb/articles/Q295/3/10.ASP
Q295386	**PDF Files Are Not Returned from the ISA Server Cache**
	http://support.microsoft.com/support/kb/articles/Q295/3/86.ASP
Q295654	**Windows 2000 Server Cannot Join Existing ISA Array**
	http://support.microsoft.com/support/kb/articles/Q295/6/54.ASP
Q296202	**A Proxy Chain Error Message "12206" Is Displayed**
	http://support.microsoft.com/support/kb/articles/Q296/2/02.ASP
Q296534	**How to Configure ISA Server to Use a PPPoE Connection**
	http://support.microsoft.com/support/kb/articles/Q296/5/34.ASP
Q296591	**A Description of the Automatic Discovery Feature**
	http://support.microsoft.com/support/kb/articles/Q296/5/91.ASP
Q296620	**The Internet Clients Cannot Access the Published Web Servers**
	http://support.microsoft.com/support/kb/articles/Q296/6/20.ASP

Q-Article	Description
Q296638	Starting Internet Services Manager May Cause Error Message After Installing an ISA Server Hotfix
	http://support.microsoft.com/support/kb/articles/Q296/6/38.ASP
Q296674	The SecureNAT Clients Cannot Access the Internal Resources That Are Published by Means of ISA Server
	http://support.microsoft.com/support/kb/articles/Q296/6/74.ASP
Q297080	Incomplete HTML Pages and Random Authentication Prompts If ISA Server Is Chained to Upstream Proxy
	http://support.microsoft.com/support/kb/articles/Q297/0/80.ASP
Q297315	You May Not Be Able to Add New Users After You Run the Secure Your ISA Server Computer Wizard
	http://support.microsoft.com/support/kb/articles/Q297/3/15.ASP
Q297922	HOW TO: How to Provide Internet Access Through a Firewall by Using Internet Security and Acceleration Server
	http://support.microsoft.com/support/kb/articles/Q297/9/22.ASP
Q299673	HOW TO: Configure ISA Server 2000 and Enterprise Manager to Connect Through ISA to a SQL Server
	http://support.microsoft.com/support/kb/articles/Q299/6/73.ASP
Q300177	How to Publish a Citrix Server Behind ISA Server
	http://support.microsoft.com/support/kb/articles/q300/1/77.ASP
Q300199	Packet Filters May Not Apply in ISA Server
	http://support.microsoft.com/support/kb/articles/Q300/1/99.ASP
Q300435	HOW TO: Securely Publish Multiple Web Sites Using ISA Server
	http://support.microsoft.com/support/kb/articles/Q300/4/35.ASP
Q300707	Invalid Content-Length Header May Cause Requests to Fail Through ISA Server
	http://support.microsoft.com/support/kb/articles/Q300/7/07.ASP
Q300876	HOW TO: Safely Connect Your Company to the Internet
	http://support.microsoft.com/support/kb/articles/Q300/8/76.ASP
Q300879	How to Stop an ISA Server Service by Using a Command- Line Prompt
	http://support.microsoft.com/support/kb/articles/Q300/8/79.ASP
Q301380	Some Server Variables Are Not Fully Implemented in ISA Server
	http://support.microsoft.com/support/kb/articles/Q301/3/80.ASP

Q-Article	Description
Q301425	**ISA Server Does Not Cache Responses That Contain the Location Header** http://support.microsoft.com/support/kb/articles/Q301/4/25.ASP
Q301471	**How to Delete the Web Cache on Internet Security and Acceleration Server** http://support.microsoft.com/support/kb/articles/Q301/4/71.ASP
Q302372	**HOW TO: Configure Logging for Microsoft Internet Security and Acceleration Server** http://support.microsoft.com/support/kb/articles/Q302/3/72.ASP
Q302527	**HOW TO: Set Bandwidth Configuration for Microsoft Internet Security and Acceleration Server** http://support.microsoft.com/support/kb/articles/Q302/5/27.ASP
Q302529	**HOW TO: Monitor Server Activity for Internet Security and Acceleration Server 2000** http://support.microsoft.com/support/kb/articles/Q302/5/29.ASP
Q302538	**HOW TO: Enable Reporting for Internet Security and Acceleration Server 2000** http://support.microsoft.com/support/kb/articles/Q302/5/38.ASP
Q303098	**XCCC: How to Configure Exchange 2000 Conferencing Server and ISA Server to Allow Audio and Video** http://support.microsoft.com/support/kb/articles/Q303/0/98.ASP
Q303426	**ISA Server Publishing Rule Does Not Include SMTP Outbound Check Boxes** http://support.microsoft.com/support/kb/articles/Q303/4/26.ASP
Q303530	**VPN Clients May Not Work on ISA Server Perimeter Networks** http://support.microsoft.com/support/kb/articles/q303/5/30.ASP

TCP/IP Port Assignments

TCP/IP port numbers are divided into the following three categories:

- Well-known ports (0–1023)
- Registered ports (1024–49151)
- Dynamic and/or private ports (49152–65535)

Transmission Control Protocol (TCP) is defined in Request for Comment (RFC) 793, STD 7 (`ftp://ftp.isi.edu/in-notes/rfc793.txt`). For the most part, the same port numbers are used with UDP, which is defined in RFC 768 (`ftp://ftp.isi.edu/in-notes/rfc768.txt`). The well-known ports are primarily used by the system and are assigned by the Internet Assigned Numbers Authority (IANA). This appendix covers some of the common TCP/IP port numbers.

Notice that some ports are TCP, while others are UDP. When you are opening ports for a certain service, make sure that you look at all the ports that are required. For example, the printing service requires several ports: 137 UDP, 138 UDP, and 139 TCP. Similarly, WINS requires several ports to function properly. Also notice that some services require a protocol ID in addition to a port. For example, Point-to-Point Tunneling Protocol (PPTP) requires configuring protocol ID 47, in addition to the TCP port 1723.

The following table is sorted by port numbers for your convenience.

TABLE C.1 TCP/IP Port Assignments

Keyword	Port #	Description
echo	7 TCP	Echo
echo	7 UDP	Echo
qotd	17 TCP	Quote of the day
qotd	17 UDP	Quote of the day
ftp-data	20	TCP File Transfer Protocol - data
ftp	21 TCP	File Transfer Protocol - control
telnet	23 TCP	Telnet
smtp	25 TCP	Simple Mail Transfer Protocol
time	37 TCP	Time Server
time	37 UDP	Time Server
nameserver	42 TCP	Host Name server
nameserver	42 UDP	Host Name server
wins	42 TCP	WINS replication
nickname	43 TCP	Whois

TABLE C.1   Continued

Keyword	Port #	Description
domain	53 TCP	Domain Name Server
domain	53 UDP	Domain Name Server
bootps	67 UDP	Bootstrap protocol server, bootp/DHCP server
bootpc	68 UDP	Bootstrap protocol client, bootp/DHCP client
tftp	69 UDP	Trivial File Transfer protocol
gopher	70 TCP	Gopher
finger	79 TCP	Finger
http	80 TCP	HyperText Transport Protocol, world wide web
kerberos	88 TCP	Kerberos v5
kerberos	88 UDP	Kerberos v5
pop3	110 TCP	Post Office Protocol v3
nntp	119 TCP	Network News Transfer Protocol
ntp	123 UDP	Network Time Protocol
wins	135 TCP	WINS manager
dhcp	135 TCP	DHCP Manager
dns	135 TCP	DNS administration
exchange	135 TCP	Exchange administration
client/server	135 TCP	Client/Server communication
rpc	135 TCP	Remote Procedure Call
netbios-ns	137 TCP	NETBIOS name service (WINS) registration
netbios-ns	137 UDP	NETBIOS name service (WINS) registration
printing	137 UDP	Printing
browsing	137 UDP	Browsing
logon	137 UDP	Logon sequence
logon	138 UDP	Logon sequence
browsing	138 UDP	Browsing
replication	138 UDP	NT 4.0 directory replication
printing	138 UDP	Printing
netlogon	138 UDP	Netlogon service
netbios-dgm	138 UDP	NETBIOS datagram service
netbios-ssn	139 TCP	NETBIOS session service

C

**TCP/IP PORT
ASSIGNMENTS**

TABLE C.1   Continued

Keyword	Port #	Description
printing	139 TCP	Printing
replication	139 TCP	NT 4.0 directory replication
event viewer	139 TCP	Event viewer
file sharing	139 TCP	File sharing
perfmon	139 TCP	Performance Monitor
servmgr	139 TCP	NT 4.0 Server Manager
usrmgr	139 TCP	NT 4.0 User Manager
logon	139 TCP	Logon sequence
regedit	139 TCP	Registry Editor
imap	143 TCP	Internet Message Access Protocol v4
pcmail-srv	158 TCP	PCMail server
sqlsrv	156	SQL Service
snmp	161 UDP	Simple Network Management Protocol
snmptrap	162 UDP	SNMP traps
irc	194 TCP	Internet Relay Chat protocol
at	201-208	Various AppleTalk services
ipx	213 UDP	IPX over IP
ldap	389 TCP	Lightweight Directory Access Protocol
https	443 TCP	HTTP Secure (SSL)
directhost	445 TCP	Direct hosting of SMB over TCP/IP
directhost	445 UDP	Direct hosting of SMB over TCP/IP
ipsec	500 UDP	IPSec (ESP: protocol ID 50; AH: protocol ID 51)
nntp	563 TCP	NNTP (SSL)
ldap	636 TCP	LDAP (SSL)
imap	993 TCP	IMAP (SSL)
pop3	995 TCP	POP3 (SSL)
ica	1494 TCP	Citrix ICA client
convoy	1717 UDP	Convoy for cluster control
pptp	1723 TCP	Point-to-Point Tunneling Protocol (protocol ID 47)
wlbs	2504 UDP	Windows Load Balancing Service
rdp	3389 TCP	Microsoft RDP client (Terminal Services)

TABLE C.1   Continued

Keyword	Port #	Description
tsac	3389 TCP	ActiveX client (TSAC)
radius	1812 UDP	RADIUS authentication protocol
radacct	1813 UDP	RADIUS accounting protocol

Here are some additional resources for port assignments. To check out the directory of general assigned numbers and for details on protocol numbers and assignment services, go to IANA's Web site at http://www.iana.org/numbers.htm.

For a list of assigned port numbers, check out the following URLs:

    http://www.iana.org/assignments/port-numbers

    http://info.internet.isi.edu/in-notes/rfc/files/rfc1700.txt

For known TCP/IP ports (TCP and/or UDP) that are used by services within Microsoft Windows NT Version 4.0 and Microsoft Exchange Server Version 5.0, check out http://support.microsoft.com/support/kb/articles/q150/5/43.asp.

C

TCP/IP PORT
ASSIGNMENTS

Default MIME Types in Internet Information Services

The following table lists the default filename extensions that are associated with the MIME types. You can add your own custom associations, as described in the section "Content Groups" found in Chapter 5, "ISA Acceleration Concepts." The table is sorted alphabetically by extensions.

TABLE D.1 IIS Default MIME Types

Common Extensions	Associated MIME Types
.*	application/octet-stream
.323	text/h323
.acx	application/internet-property-stream
.ai	application/postscript
.aif	audio/x-aiff
.aifc	audio/aiff
.aiff	audio/aiff
.au	audio/basic
.axs	application/olescript
.bcpio	application/x-bcpio
.bin	application/octet-stream
.cat	application/vndms-pkiseccat
.cdf	application/x-cdf
.cer	application/x-x509-ca-cert
.clp	application/x-msclip
.cmx	image/x-cmx
.cod	image/cis-cod
.cpio	application/x-cpio
.crd	application/x-mscardfile
.crl	application/pkix-crl
.crt	application/x-x509-ca-cert
.csh	application/x-csh
.dcr	application/x-director
.der	application/x-x509-ca-cert
.dib	image/bmp
.dir	application/x-director
.dll	application/x-msdownload

TABLE D.1   Continued

Common Extensions	Associated MIME Types
.doc	application/msword
.dot	application/msword
.dvi	application/x-dvi
.dxr	application/x-director
.eps	application/postscript
.evy	application/envoy
.exe	application/octet-stream
.fif	application/fractals
.gif	image/gif
.gtar	application/x-gtar
.gz	application/x-gzip
.hdf	application/x-hdf
.hlp	application/winhlp
.hqx	application/mac-binhex40
.hta	application/hta
.htm	text/html
.html	text/html
.htt	text/webviewhtml
.ief	image/ief
.iii	application/x-iphone
.ins	application/x-internet-signup
.isp	application/x-internet-signup
.jfif	image/pjpeg
.jpe	image/jpeg
.jpeg	image/jpeg
.jpg	image/jpeg
.js	application/x-javascript
.latex	application/x-latex
.m13	application/x-msmediaview
.m14	application/x-msmediaview
.m3u	audio/x-mpegurl

D

DEFAULT MIME
TYPES

TABLE D.1   Continued

Common Extensions	Associated MIME Types
.man	application/x-troff-man
.mdb	application/x-msaccess
.me	application/x-troff-me
.mid	audio/mid
.mny	application/x-msmoney
.mp3	audio/mpeg
.mpp	application/vnd.ms-project
.ms	application/x-troff-ms
.mvb	application/x-msmediaview
.nc	application/x-netcdf
.oda	application/oda
.ods	application/oleobject
.p10	application/pkcs10
.p12	application/x-pkcs12
.p7b	application/x-pkcs7-certificates
.p7c	application/pkcs7-mime
.p7m	application/pkcs7-mime
.p7r	application/x-pkcs7-certreqresp
.p7s	application/pkcs7-signature
.pbm	image/x-portable-bitmap
.pdf	application/pdf
.pfx	application/x-pkcs12
.pko	application/vndms-pkipko
.pma	application/x-perfmon
.pmc	application/x-perfmon
.pml	application/x-perfmon
.pmr	application/x-perfmon
.pmw	application/x-perfmon
.pnm	image/x-portable-anymap
.pot	application/vnd.ms-powerpoint
.ppm	image/x-portable-pixmap

TABLE D.1 Continued

Common Extensions	Associated MIME Types
.pps	application/vnd.ms-powerpoint
.ppt	application/vnd.ms-powerpoint
.prf	application/pics-rules
.ps	application/postscript
.pub	application/x-mspublisher
.ra	audio/x-pn-realaudio
.ram	audio/x-pn-realaudio
.ras	image/x-cmu-raster
.rgb	image/x-rgb
.rmi	audio/mid
.roff	application/x-troff
.rtf	application/rtf
.scd	application/x-msschedule
.sct	text/scriptlet
.setpay	application/set-payment-initiation
.setreg	application/set-registration-initiation
.sh	application/x-sh
.shar	application/x-shar
.sit	application/x-stuffit
.snd	audio/basic
.spc	application/x-pkcs7-certificates
.spl	application/futuresplash
.src	application/x-wais-source
.sst	application/vndms-pkicertstore
.stl	application/vndms-pkistl
.stm	text/html
.sv4cpio	application/x-sv4cpio
.sv4crc	application/x-sv4crc
.t	application/x-troff
.tar	application/x-tar
.tcl	application/x-tcl

D

DEFAULT MIME
TYPES

TABLE D.1 Continued

Common Extensions	Associated MIME Types
.tex	application/x-tex
.texi	application/x-texinfo
.texinfo	application/x-texinfo
.tgz	application/x-compressed
.tif	image/tiff
.tiff	image/tiff
.tr	application/x-troff
.trm	application/x-msterminal
.tsv	text/tab-separated-values
.ustar	application/x-ustar
.wav	audio/wav
.wcm	application/vnd.ms-works
.wdb	application/vnd.ms-works
.wks	application/vnd.ms-works
.wmf	application/x-msmetafile
.wps	application/vnd.ms-works
.wri	application/x-mswrite
.xbm	image/x-xbitmap
.xla	application/vnd.ms-excel
.xlc	application/vnd.ms-excel
.xlm	application/vnd.ms-excel
.xls	application/vnd.ms-excel
.xlt	application/vnd.ms-excel
.xlw	application/vnd.ms-excel
.xml	text/xml
.xsl	text/xml
.z	application/x-compress
.zip	application/x-zip-compressed

Glossary

access policy   An access policy consists of site and content rules, protocol rules, and IP packet filters. Access policy rules apply to all three types of ISA Server clients: Firewall, Web Proxy, and SecureNAT.

active caching   Active caching allows the ISA Server to determine which objects in the cache are most commonly used. When the frequently accessed objects in the cache are close to expiration, ISA Server automatically refreshes the items in the cache by updating them from the Internet.

address resolution   Address resolution is the mapping of an Internet Protocol (IP) address to the physical machine address. The machine address is also referred to as a hardware, or media access control (MAC) address.

ARP (Address Resolution Protocol)
Address Resolution Protocol is a TCP/IP protocol that provides IP address-to-MAC address resolution for IP packets.

alerting   Alerting is an ISA Server feature that allows administrators to be notified of any possible security or protocol violations. Administrators can configure events that trigger alerts so they can be notified by various methods, such as by e-mail.

anonymous logon   This feature is used by users on the Internet to remotely access a computer without providing a username or password. When using the anonymous logon authentication method, users access the computer with guest privileges. The

Windows 2000 Guest account doesn't need to be enabled for anonymous logon to work. The account used for anonymous access (IUSR_*<computername>*) automatically becomes a member of the Guests group.

application filter   An application filter offers an extra layer of security for your network by performing application-specific tasks. For example, an HTTP Redirector application filter redirects the requests from the Firewall and SecureNAT clients to the Web Proxy service. Application filters are registered with the Firewall service and are useful in performing tasks such as intrusion detection, authentication, virus checking, and redirection.

array   A group of ISA Server computers that is treated as a single logical entity. An array offers several advantages, such as distributed caching, load balancing, and fault tolerance. In addition, arrays provide centralized management, because all servers in an array share a common configuration. You configure the array once and apply the configuration to all the members of the array. To install ISA Server computer in an array, the server must be a member of a Windows 2000 domain.

array member   An ISA Server computer that is part of an array is known as an array member. An array can have one or more ISA Server computers, and must be installed in a Windows 2000 Active Directory domain. You can apply a single policy to all the members of an array.

authentication   Authentication is the process of validating a user's credentials so he/she can access resources on the network. You can configure different authentication methods for inbound requests and outbound requests. ISA Server supports several authentication methods, such as basic, certificates, digest, and integrated windows.

automatic discovery   Automatic discovery is an ISA Server feature that allows a client to locate an ISA Server computer automatically. This feature is particularly useful for roaming clients, so they can easily discover an ISA Server computer.

bandwidth control   Bandwidth control is responsible for notifying the Windows 2000 QoS packet scheduling service how it should prioritize network connections.

bandwidth priority   Bandwidth priority works with bandwidth rules, and is used to define the priority level that can be applied to connections that pass through ISA Server.

bandwidth rules   Bandwidth rules determine which connections have higher priorities. However, bandwidth rules do not control network bandwidth; they simply notify the Windows 2000 QoS packet scheduling service how it should prioritize network connections.

basic authentication   Basic authentication requires users to enter a username and password before they can connect to the network to access resources. This type of authentication is not secure because the passwords are not encrypted when they travel over the network wire. To protect users' passwords from exposure, administrators typically use SSL (Secure Socket Layer) with basic authentication. Using SSL encrypts all data traveling between client and the server including the users' passwords and data.

cache (Pronounced "cash") A feature used by ISA Server that offers a high-speed storage mechanism in which frequently used objects are duplicated for quick access. The objects might be duplicated in random access memory (RAM), known as RAM caching; or on ISA Server's hard disk, known as Disk caching. Caching speeds up clients' access to frequently used data because the objects can be retrieved from ISA Server's cache instead of the Internet.

cache drive Cache drive refers to the space reserved on an ISA Server hard disk to store frequently accessed (cached) objects. Cache drives can be configured when you install ISA Server either in Cache mode or Integrated mode. A cache drive must be a local drive that is formatted with NTFS.

Cache mode Cache mode is one of the three ISA Server installation modes. Cache mode saves network bandwidth by keeping frequently accessed Web objects in cache for quick retrieval. Network performance is improved because the objects are kept closer to the clients.

cache filtering The capability of ISA Server to control which contents from World Wide Web, FTP, or Gopher sites should be cached. You can configure routing rules for objects that should not be cached.

cache policy Cache policy refers to a set of rules that control how ISA Server cache should be implemented on your ISA Server computers.

CARP (Cache Array Routing Protocol) Cache Array Routing Protocol is a protocol used in ISA Server cache arrays. It uses a hash-based routing algorithm to determine the best path for locating objects in an ISA Server array. This improves performance for the clients. CARP offers several advantages, such as elimination of duplicate contents, evenly distributed cache objects, and a higher level of efficiency with the addition of additional servers to an array.

CERN-compliance CERN, the European Organization for Nuclear Physics, is the world's largest particle physics center. One of its computer scientists wrote the first Web browser in 1990. The original CERN browsers didn't have today's fancy graphical user interface. Instead, they simply offered a line-mode interface. Today, most of the popular browsers, such as Internet Explorer and Netscape, take pride in complying with CERN and are known as CERN-compatible. CERN-Proxy protocol is yet another widely accepted industry standard. ISA Server's Web Proxy services are CERN-compatible.

chaining Chaining is a process of linking multiple ISA Server computers together, in essence to form a chain. The chained computers communicate in a hierarchical order. You can chain individual ISA Server computers, arrays, or use a combination of both servers and arrays.

client address set   A set of one or more client computers that are grouped together for the purpose of applying rules and policies is known as a client address set. Client address sets are one of the seven policy elements in ISA Server.

.cdat   A cache content file that is created by ISA Server when a drive is configured for caching is known as the .cdat file. As objects are cached, they are appended to the file. When the cache file is full, ISA Server removes old objects in the file and replaces them with the new ones. A specific formula is used for this purpose that considers how frequently the object is accessed, in addition to considering the size and age of the object.

default gateway   A default gateway is also referred to as a router in a TCP/IP network. It is a device that forwards (routes) packets from one network to another. TCP/IP hosts that communicate on the Internet use a default gateway to route packets to their destinations.

destination sets   While a destination refers to a computer or an IP address range, destination sets refers to one or more computers. Computers in a destination set are grouped together so you can apply rules and policies to them. Destination sets might be internal, which include groups of computers on your internal network, or external, which include groups of computers on your external network.

DHCP (Dynamic Host Configuration Protocol)   Dynamic Host Configuration Protocol is a Windows 2000 service that provides dynamic assignment of IP addresses to network clients. DHCP eliminates the need to statically configure TCP/IP parameters for network connectivity.

digest authentication   Digest authentication is one of several authentication methods supported by ISA Server. It offers features similar to basic authentication, except that instead of transmitting passwords in clear readable text, it protects the passwords from unauthorized users by securing it with a method known as hashing. Digest authentication only works in Windows 2000 domains.

distributed caching   Distributed caching is the process of spreading (distributing) the cache contents to multiple servers in an array. ISA Server uses CARP and treats all the servers in an array as a single logical cache.

DMZ (Demilitarized Zone)   Demilitarized Zone refers to a network that is separate but connected to your corporate network. A DMZ acts as a buffer or neutral zone to protect your private network from potential Internet intruders. External clients are allowed to enter the DMZ, but cannot penetrate the private network. Many organizations use DMZ to install DNS or Web servers.

DNS (Domain Name System)   A system used on TCP/IP networks (such as the Internet) that maps IP addresses to their domain names. This allows users to locate computers and services on the Internet using easy-to-remember aliases rather than the IP addresses. For example, you can access the domain name Microsoft.com on the Internet by typing `http://www.microsoft.com` instead of `http://208.40.148.152`.

DNS server   A DNS server is a domain name system server that provides IP address-to-domain name mapping. DNS servers maintain a database of computers and services. Computers on the Internet use DNS servers to locate other computers or services.

dynamic IP filtering   Dynamic IP filtering refers to the process of controlling inbound and outbound IP packets on the ISA Server computer by using access policies or publishing rules. This is in contrast to static packet filtering, which is achieved by configuring IP packet filters.

encryption   Encryption is the process of scrambling information so it cannot be deciphered by unauthorized users. ISA Server supports various forms of encryption, such as digital certificates, digest authentication, Secure Socket Layer, and so on.

enterprise   All the arrays in your company together are referred to as an enterprise. You can configure a centralized enterprise policy for all the arrays in your organization.

enterprise policy   The enterprise administrator is responsible for creating and managing an enterprise policy, which consists of site and content rules and protocol rules. You can apply an enterprise policy to all the arrays in the enterprise.

event messages   These are text messages that are generated by the ISA Server computer to assist administrators in monitoring and troubleshooting various services. These event messages are logged in the Event Viewer.

firewall   A firewall is a hardware or software solution that protects an internal network from intruders. ISA Server offers a dedicated firewall service that protects your network from unauthorized access.

Firewall client   A computer that has the ISA Server Firewall client software installed is known as a Firewall client. The Firewall clients run Winsock applications. The Firewall client software is supported on Windows Me, Windows 95/98, Windows NT, and Windows 2000. You can only use the Firewall client when the ISA Server is installed in the Firewall or Integrated mode.

Firewall mode   Firewall mode is one of the three ISA Server installation modes. It allows you to secure your network by configuring rules. In addition, you can securely publish your internal servers to the Internet users in Firewall mode.

Firewall service   Firewall service is a Windows 2000 service that supports requests from Firewall and SecureNAT clients. The service works with Windows Sockets (Winsock) compatible applications, such as Telnet, RealAudio, IRC, or Windows Media.

forward caching   A type of caching that is used when internal clients access information on an external network, such as the Internet. It is the opposite of reverse caching, which implements caching for external Internet clients accessing data on the internally published servers, such as a published Web server.

FTP (File Transfer Protocol) File Transfer Protocol is a TCP/IP protocol used to transfer files between computers. FTP is faster than HTTP protocol because it is a bi-directional file transfer mechanism.

Gatekeeper See H.323 Gatekeeper

H.323 client An H.323 client registers with the H.323 Gatekeeper service to partic-ipate in audio, video, and conferences across firewalls over the Internet. H.323 clients can take advantage of directory services and call routing features of the H.323 Gatekeeper service, and can communicate with other H.323-registered clients easily using well-known aliases, such as e-mail addresses.

H.323 Gatekeeper The H.323 Gatekeeper service works with H.323 protocol and offers registered clients the capability to use real-time multimedia conferencing across the Internet. For example, registered clients can communicate across the Internet using NetMeeting 3.0.

half scan attack An IP half scan attack indicates that someone is trying to scan open ports, because there were repeated attempts to connect to a host, but the host didn't respond with an acknowledgement (ACK). In this type of attack, an intruder can probe the ports without the knowledge of the desti-nation host.

hierarchical caching Hierarchical caching is also known as *chained caching*. It is an extension of distributed caching in which you configure ISA Servers in a hierarchy. For example, you can set up a hierarchy of caches by chaining arrays of ISA Server computers. Clients will access objects on the

server that is closest to them, say in their local branch office, before the requests are forwarded upstream to a corporate ISA Server array. This not only distributes the load to several servers, it also provides fault tolerance.

hit rate Hit rate is the percentage of client requests that the ISA Server was able to ful-fill through cached information compared to the total number of client requests that were processed by the ISA Service.

host name The host name is referred to any device on a TCP/IP network. For exam-ple, computers, servers, or routers are all considered TCP/IP hosts and have a host name and an IP address associated with them. Host name is used to identify a net-work device by a friendly name that is easier to remember. If you do not know the host name, you can still communicate with the host by using its IP address, which is harder to remember.

integrated authentication Integrated authentication is one of the several authenti-cation methods supported by ISA Server. Integrated authentication is secure, unlike anonymous logon, which doesn't require a password; and basic authentication, which requires a password, but the password is not encrypted. Integrated authentication secures your logon credentials so they cannot be read when the information travels over the network wires.

Integrated mode Integrated mode is one of the three installation options offered by ISA Server setup process. With Integrated mode, you get the best of both worlds—all the security and firewall features of Firewall mode, and all the caching features of Cache mode. For example, Firewall mode doesn't support cache configuration; and the Cache mode doesn't support Virtual Private Networks; but Integrated mode supports these and all the rest of the features.

ICMP (Internet Control Message Protocol)   Internet Control Message Protocol is a component of the Internet Protocol that is responsible for errors and informational messages. For example, the PING utility uses ICMP to check the availability of other hosts on the Internet.

IP (Internet Protocol)   Internet Protocol is the IP part of the TCP/IP suite of protocols and is defined in RFC 791. IP uses a connectionless, unreliable packet delivery system. It's connectionless because unlike TCP, IP doesn't establish a session before it communicates with other hosts. It's unreliable because it doesn't guarantee that the IP datagrams will reach the destination. The reliability is left to higher-level protocols such as TCP. IP packets are known as IP datagrams.

ISP (Internet Service Provider)   An Internet Service Provider is an organization that provides Internet access to consumers. In addition to providing a connection to the Internet, some large ISPs such as AOL and MSN offer several additional services, such as instant messaging.

intrusion detection   Intrusion detection filters analyze all incoming traffic for specific intrusions. It can detect when an attack is attempted on a network that is protected by ISA Server.

IP address   An IP address uniquely identifies a host on a TCP/IP network and consists of a network ID and a host ID. IP addresses are 32-bit logical addresses that consist of four octets. An example of an IP address is 192.168.1.200.

IP fragment   Large IP datagrams can be broken down into smaller pieces known as IP fragments. Because fragmented IP packets can be a security risk, ISA Server can drop fragmented IP packets. You should not enable IP fragment filtering on the ISA Server computer if you intend to use streaming audio or video through the ISA Server.

ISA Management console   ISA Management console is a Microsoft Management Console (MMC) tool that the ISA Server administrators use to manage ISA Server computers. The tool can also be used for remote administration on computers that do not have ISA Server installed.

ISA Server schema   ISA Server schema is the configuration information about the ISA Server that is stored in the Active Directory. Before you install an ISA Server in an array, ISA Server schema must be installed in the Active Directory. You must be a member of the Enterprise Admins and Schema Admins group to install schema in the Active Directory. ISA Server provides an Enterprise Initialization utility for installing the schema.

ISA Server Control service   The ISA Server Control service is a Windows 2000 service that is responsible for several services, such as synchronizing configuration information in an array, generating alerts, updating client configuration files, and managing ISA Server services. You cannot use the ISA Management console to start or stop this service. Instead, either use the Services MMC, or use the `net stop` or `net start` at the command prompt. For example, to stop the service, use `net stop isactrl`.

Kerberos   Kerberos version 5 is an industry standard authentication protocol that supports mutual authentication and delegated authentication. With mutual authentication, both the client and the server are authenticated. With delegated authentication, the user's authentication is tracked from end-to-end. Kerberos v5 is the primary authentication method in Windows 2000.

land attack   A land attack is a type of denial-of-service (DoS) attack that occurs when a hacker uses a fake IP address (known as *spoofing*) to establish a TCP connection. The spoofed IP address and the port numbers of the source and destination host match, which can potentially cause a computer to either crash or deny services to legitimate users.

L2TP (Layer Two Tunneling Protocol)   Layer Two Tunneling Protocol is a combination of Layer 2 Forwarding (L2F) and Point-to-Point Tunneling Protocol (PPTP). It's a tunneling protocol that is used with virtual private networks. L2TP relies on IPSec for encryption. L2TP is installed automatically when you install Routing and Remote Access service.

load factor   The load factor is used to distribute client load evenly among the members of an ISA Server array. When you enter a load factor value for a computer in an array, you are configuring the relative cache availability of that particular server, compared to the rest of the members in the array.

LAT (Local Address Table)   The local address table is a table that contains all the internal IP address ranges on your private network, including the IP address of the internal interface of the ISA Server computer. The LAT is used by the internal clients to communicate with external networks. You should never include any IP address ranges in the LAT that are external to your network. For example, you should not include the IP addresses of any computers on the Internet, or the IP address of the external interface of the ISA Server computer to your LAT.

LDT (Local Domain Table)   The Local Domain Table is a listing of domain names that are internal to your network. When Firewall clients need to resolve a domain name, they first check their copy of LDT; if the domain exists in the LDT, it is resolved directly. Otherwise, the request is sent to the ISA Server so it can resolve the request from a DNS server on the client's behalf. SecureNAT clients don't keep a copy of LDT, so they need to have access to DNS servers to resolve internal and external names.

live stream splitting   Live stream splitting is an ISA Server feature that allows a streaming media filter to grab the information from the Internet once and then make it available to the internal clients on a private network via Windows Media technology server.

MIME (Multiple Internet Mail Extensions) Multiple Internet Mail Extensions allow you to exchange information between different computers on the Internet, such as multimedia within e-mail, or various characters sets. Depending on the type of browser you are using, you will notice different MIME types associated with different filename extensions. For example, you might notice that audio/mpeg MIME types are associated with .mp3 filename extensions.

NAT editor A Network Address Translation editor offers translation of the IP, TCP, and UDP headers. A NAT editor is used to make modifications to the IP packet beyond the translation of these headers.

NAT (Network Address Translation) Network Address Translation is a popular industry standard that enables you to use private reserved IP address ranges on your internal network to communicate with computers on the Internet through a NAT Server. The NAT Server translates the network addresses on behalf of the internal clients. ISA Server extends the Windows 2000's NAT functionality with SecureNAT.

NNTP (Network News Transfer Protocol) Network News Transfer Protocol is a component of the TCP/IP suite of protocols responsible for distributing network news messages among news groups on the Internet. Messages are stored on the NNTP servers in a central database and accessed by the NNTP clients (newsreaders).

negative caching Negative caching occurs when a server cannot retrieve an object requested by a client and the response is cached. Negative caching allows you to cache HTTP objects that have a status code of 203, 300, 301, or 410.

NIC (Network Interface Card) Network Interface Card, also known as Network Adapter, is the hardware device that allows you to communicate with other computers on a network. A software component known as a driver allows the NIC to communicate with the operating system.

NTFS (NT File System) An NT File System is an advanced file system used on Windows NT and Windows 2000 computers that offers several advantages over traditional file systems such as the FAT (File Allocation Table) file system. NTFS offers security, built-in compression, encryption, and is more reliable than FAT.

packet When a message is sent over a network, it is broken down into smaller pieces or "packets." Individual packets are not necessarily transmitted in a sequence, or even through the same route. They are marked with information such as the source and destination addresses, and also contain data. When the packets arrive at the destination, they are reassembled. IP packets are known as IP datagrams.

packet filtering Packet filtering is the process of controlling the flow of IP packets that travel through the ISA Server. When packet filtering is enabled, the ISA Server drops all packets except those that are permitted explicitly by packet filters. Even if you don't create packet filters, you still have to create rules that will allow traffic to enter your network, or else all packets will be discarded by the ISA Server computer.

pass-through authentication   Pass-through authentication refers to the process of ISA Server passing the client's authentication information to another server. The pass-through authentication works for Web requests in both directions—inbound and outbound. Kerberos version 5 cannot be used in a pass-through authentication scenario because the client will not be able to identify the authenticating server, which is a Kerberos version 5 requirement.

perimeter network   see DMZ

PING   Packet Internet Groper is a TCP/IP utility that is used to verify network connectivity. It uses ICMP echo and reply messages to verify the availability of a remote host on a TCP/IP network.

ping of death attack   A ping of death is a type of denial-of-service (DoS) attack that occurs when a hacker adds a large amount of data to a ping, more specifically to an ICMP echo request packet. This can cause the computer to stop responding (servicing) to the clients' requests, hence the term denial-of-service.

port scan attack   Ports are entry points into a computer. There are 65,535 TCP/IP ports. See Appendix C, "TCP/IP Port Assignments," for more details. Hackers use port scanners to determine which ports are open on a computer. They can then use one or more of these ports as entry points to attack the computer.

PPTP (Point-to-Point Tunneling Protocol)   Point-to-Point Tunneling Protocol is a protocol used by remote network clients to access a corporate network either dialing in through an ISP using a modem, or connecting directly to the Internet using a digital subscriber line (DSL) or a cable modem. PPTP uses MPPE encryption to secure data. ISA Server supports PPTP for both inbound and outbound connections.

protocol   A set of rules used to communicate over a network. A protocol is analogous to a language. Two devices must use the same protocol to communicate. For example, a client configured with only IPX protocol cannot communicate with a server that is configured only with TCP/IP protocol. However, if the server is running both TCP/IP and IPX, it's sort of "bilingual;" therefore, it will be able to communicate with the client. The protocol used on the Internet is TCP/IP.

publishing rule   Publishing rules determine how ISA Server is going to control inbound requests from external networks. ISA Server supports Web publishing rules to control inbound requests to the internal Web servers and Server publishing rules to control the inbound requests to all other internal servers, such as Exchange or Terminal Server.

Q931 address   H.323 transactions have an originating and a destination endpoint. When an H.323 client registers an endpoint with the H.323 Gatekeeper service, among other attributes, it also provides a list of Q931 addresses. H.323 Gatekeeper service requires that the Q931 addresses be unique.

QoS (Quality of Service)   Quality of Service is a set of quality assurance standards implemented in Windows 2000. QoS-enabled applications can provide efficient use of network bandwidth to assure an adequate level of service.

QoS Admission Control   QoS Admission Control is a Windows 2000 service that allows you to control how network applications are allotted bandwidth. For example, you may configure important corporate applications to have more network bandwidth compared to the less important ones.

QoS Packet Scheduling service   QoS Packet Scheduling service is a Windows 2000 service that is used by ISA Server to control bandwidth priorities, and it works with bandwidth rules. Bandwidth rules determine which connections have higher priorities. However, bandwidth rules do not control network bandwidth; they simply notify the Windows 2000 QoS Packet Scheduling service how it should prioritize network connections.

reverse caching   A type of caching that is used for external Internet clients accessing data on the internally published servers, such as a published Web server. It is the opposite of forward caching, which is used when internal clients access information on an external network, such as the Internet.

routing   Routing is the process of forwarding client requests from one ISA Server to a particular upstream server. For example, when a client requests an object from an ISA Server and the object doesn't exist in the ISA Server's cache, the server can for-ward the request to another upstream server to resolve the client's request.

scheduled cache   An ISA Server feature that lets you schedule the downloading of Web contents at specific intervals. This feature improves cache performance and conserves network bandwidth.

secondary connection   When working with protocol definitions, you create a primary connection by specifying a port number, a low-level protocol (TCP or UDP), and a direction. After an initial connection has been made, you can create additional secondary connections.

Secure HTTP (HTTPS)   Secure HTTP is a protocol that is used for secure HTTP communications. It utilizes Secure Socket Layer (SSL) to encrypt HTTP packets.

SecureNAT clients   Secure Network Address Translation clients are one of the three types of clients supported by ISA Server. They do not require installation of any client software, but they do require that you configure a default gateway that points to the ISA Server computer, either directly or indirectly through a router.

sockets   Sockets are a common set of APIs that use a TCP/IP address and a port (TCP or UDP) number to communicate. Socket-based applications allow the data to be sent and received and then close the communication channel when the transmission is complete. Microsoft has its own implementation of sockets known as Winsock.

SSL (Secure Sockets Layer)   Secure Sockets Layer is an industry standard that secures network communications by encrypting all information that travels between computers; for example, between a client browser and a Web server. It uses a combination of a public and a private key to secure data.

server certificate   A server certificate identifies a server to the client. During SSL communications, when a client requests SSL objects from the server, the server uses a server certificate to authenticate itself to the client.

server publishing rule   An ISA Server rule that controls how inbound requests to internal servers on the private network should be handled is known as a server publishing rule. These rules filter traffic going through the ISA Server. For example, you can configure a server publishing rule for an FTP server on your internal network to grant access to Internet users dynamically.

SMTP (Simple Mail Transport Protocol) Simple Mail Transport Protocol is part of the TCP/IP suite of protocols that is responsible for exchanging e-mail between message transfer agents on the Internet.

SNMP (Simple Network Management Protocol)   Simple Network Management Protocol is part of a TCP/IP suite of protocols that is responsible for managing TCP/IP networks. SNMP hosts (for example, routers, servers, computers) provide status information to third party SNMP management systems (for example, Hewlett Packard's OpenView) to help you manage your network. Microsoft doesn't provide an SNMP management system (that is, an SNMP Server) but Windows 2000 computers can be configured as SNMP clients.

SSL bridging   Secure Socket Layer bridging is responsible for encrypting and decrypting client requests at the ISA Server before they are forwarded to their destination. SSL bridging is different than SSL tunneling. SSL bridging is used when the server starts or ends an SSL connection. For example, if an external client requests an SSL object on an internal Web server, the ISA Server can close the client's SSL connection and then open a new connection to the internal Web server. This is known as SSL bridging.

SSL tunneling   Secure Socket Layer tunneling is used when a client requests an SSL object on a Web server on the Internet. The request goes through the ISA Server, which establishes the connection for the client on the Web server's SSL port 443. The client can then directly communicate with the Web server on the Internet by using this SSL tunnel.

standalone server   Standalone servers are Windows 2000 Servers that do not belong to a domain. When you install ISA Server, you can choose to install it as a standalone server, in which case it will not belong to an ISA Server array. You would install an ISA Server as a standalone server if you do not expect your network to grow. In all other scenarios, you should install it in an array.

Time-to-Live (TTL)   A custom value that determines how long an HTTP object should live before it is discarded in ISA Server's cache. Longer TTL values will improve a client's access to the objects for a longer time, but the information may not be as fresh. Shorter TTL values will cause more network traffic because the objects will have to be downloaded more frequently from the

Internet; however, the objects will be more up-to-date.

TCP (Transmission Control Protocol) Transmission Control Protocol is the TCP component of the industry standard TCP/IP suite of protocols. It provides a reliable, connection-oriented communication mechanism between computers. It's reliable because it uses acknowledgements to confirm that the packets have arrived at their destination. It's connection-oriented because it establishes a TCP session to communicate.

TCP/IP (Transmission Control Protocol/Internet Protocol) TCP/IP is an industry standard that consists of several protocols and utilities, known collectively as a TCP/IP suite. TCP/IP is used as the standard protocol for communication across the worldwide network of computers (the Internet). Network administrators and support personnel require a solid understanding of TCP/IP to implement and support networks and operating systems such as Windows 2000.

UDP bomb attack If a UDP packet contains an illegal value in certain fields, it can cause some operating systems to crash. A UDP bomb attack can cause problems on the network. Administrators can configure the ISA Server's firewall service to notify them of such attacks.

verbose logging An option used when logging ISA Server events in the event log. The standard logging option includes certain events in the logs. With verbose logging, you get additional information that is helpful in troubleshooting or analyzing the events.

VPN (Virtual Private Network) A network that extends the functionality of a private network across a public network such as the Internet, while maintaining its security is known as a virtual private network. ISA Server supports VPN functionality with PPTP or L2TP protocols.

Web Proxy client A Web Proxy client is a computer that is configured to use ISA Server's Web Proxy service. Web Proxy clients use CERN-compatible Web browser applications that comply with the HTTP 1.1 standard to communicate with the Web Proxy service on the ISA Server computer. Web Proxy clients include most of the common operating systems, such as Windows 95/98, Windows Me, Windows NT, Windows 2000, UNIX, and Macintosh.

Web Proxy service (w3proxy) Web Proxy service is a Windows 2000 service that retrieves objects from the Internet for clients running a Web browser. It supports the HTTP, HTTPS, FTP, and Gopher protocols.

Web publishing rule An ISA Server rule that determines how inbound Web requests to an internal Web server should be handled by the ISA Server, without compromising network security. There is a default Web publishing rule that discards all inbound requests. This rule is applied after all the other rules are applied. In addition, the default rule cannot be modified or deleted.

well-known ports Well-known ports refer to TCP/IP port numbers 0-1023. They are primarily used by the system and are assigned by the Internet Assigned Numbers

Authority (IANA). See Appendix C, "TCP/IP Port Assignments," for more details.

Winsock (Windows Socket)   Sockets are a common set of APIs that use an IP address and a port number to communicate. Socket-based applications allow the data to be sent and received and then close the communication channel when the transmission is complete. Winsock, short for Windows Socket, is Microsoft's flavor of the industry standard sockets. It's an inter-process communication (IPC) mechanism between applications. Examples of Winsock applications include FTP, RealAudio, and IRC.

INDEX

A

acceleration concepts. *See* caching
acceleration updates, from Proxy 2.0 Server, 4-5
    RAM caching, 5
    scheduled content downloads, 5-6
    streaming media support, 6
access, PPTP, allowing outbound, 93
Access Control feature, 50
access policies, troubleshooting, 252-255
accessing Internet from ISA Server computer, 63
active caching
    configuring, 132
    functions of, 133
    overview, 131-132
Active Directory
    replication, 36
    sites, 10
Add/Remove programs (Control Panel), 37
Address Mapping screen (New Server Publishing Rule Wizard), 187
address sets, client
    creating, 150
    deleting, 152
    editing, 150
    overview, 149-150
Administrative Tools
    Custom installation option, 40
    DHCP management console, 18
    DNS management console, 17
alerts, ISA Server, 214-215
    Alerts feature, 50
    configuring
        actions, 221
        conditions, 221
        thresholds, 219-220
    creating, 215-218
    editing, 219
Allow filters, 101

application filters, 25
built-in, 108
FTP access filter, 110-111
H.323 filter, 114-115
HTTP redirector, 108, 110
intrusion detection filters,
117-118
RPC filter, 111
SMTP filter, 111-114
SOCKS filter, 111
streaming media filters,
115-117
overview, 107
types of, 108
application usage reports,
234
architecture, ISA Server
Enterprise Edition servers,
9-12
importance of, 7-8
Standard Edition servers, 9-12
Array Level Policy Rules That
Restrict Enterprise Policy
check box (Autorun con-
sole), 36
arrays
advantages over standalone
servers, 9-10
array policy, 10
defined, 9
example setup, 10
installing ISA Server in, 41-43
cache mode, 44
Custom Enterprise Policy
Settings, 42
Default Enterprise Policy
Settings, 42
firewall mode, 43
integrated mode, 44
minimum requirements, 32
site and content security rules,
74
attacks, intrusion detection,
26
authentication, troubleshoot-
ing, 255-257
autodiscovery protocol. See
WPAD

Autorun console, 33
Array-Level Policy Rules
That Restrict Enterprise
Policy check box, 36
installation choices, 34
Microsoft ISA Server Setup
screen
custom installation, 38-40
license agreement, 38
Product ID, 38
Run ISA Server Enterprise
Initialization option, 35
Use This Enterprise Policy
radio button, 35

B

bandwidth
priorities
complainers, 145
creating, 146-149
deleting, 149
editing, 149
overview, 145
QoS (Quality of Service),
145
purchasing, 5
security rules, 79-82
bastion host, 94
batch updates, 123
Block filters, 101

C

Cache Array Routing
Protocol. See CARP
Cache Directory Tool, 123-
124
Cache Hit Ratio (%), moni-
toring, 209
cache mode, arrays,
installing ISA Server in, 44
caching
active caching, configuring,
132
functions of, 133
overview, 131-132
cache drives, requirements,
140-141

CARP (Cache Array Routing
Protocol), 23, 122, 137
advantages of, 138
distributed caching and,
140
enabling in ISA Server,
139-140
hierarchical caching and,
140
ICP and, differences
between, 138
locating objects with, 139
overview, 138
distributed caching, 135-136
forward caching
advantages of, 123
hardware requirements,
122
Microsoft requirements, 31
overview, 122
procedural scenario,
126-127
TTL (Time-To-Live),
124-126
Microsoft requirements, 31
hierarchical caching
overview, 136
procedural scenario,
136-137
negative caching
configuring, 134-135
overview, 133-134
RAM caching, 5
reverse caching
hardware requirements,
127-128
overview, 127
scheduled caching
advantages of, 131
download job, creating,
128-131
overview, 128
server mode, 13
size, adjusting, 142
troubleshooting, 246-249
Web caching services, 21-22
distributed caching, 23
forward caching, 22
hierarchical caching, 23-24

reverse caching, 22
scheduled caching, 23
CARP (Cache Array Routing Protocol), 23, 122, 137
advantages of, 138
distributed caching and, 140
enabling in ISA Server, 139-140
hierarchical caching and, 140
ICP and, differences between, 138
locating objects with, 139
overview, 138
CERN compliance, 16
chained caching. *See* hierarchical caching
client address sets
creating, 150
deleting, 152
editing, 150
overview, 149-150
Client configuration feature, 50
client server modes, 14
comparisons between, 16
firewall client, 14
secureNAT client, 14-15
Web Proxy client, 15-16
client sessions, troubleshooting, 249-250
Client Sets screen (New Server Publishing Rule Wizard), 188
Client Type screen
New Server Publishing Rule Wizard, 188
New Web Publishing Rule Wizard, 178
clients, configuring, 54
Direct Access, 62
firewall clients, 54-59
SecureNAT clients, 59-61
Web Proxy clients, 61-62
commands
New menu, Filter, 101
View menu, Advanced, 101
complainers, 145
compliance, CERN, 16

configuring
active caching, 132
alerts
actions, 221
conditions, 221
thresholds, 219-220
cache options, 45-46
DHCP, for automatic discovery, 18-20
Direct Access, 62
DNS, for automatic discovery, 17
firewall clients, 54-56
ISA Server, configuring for, 56-58
on client computer, 59
Web browser settings on ISA Server computer, 58-59
H.323 filters, 115
H.323 Gatekeeper service, 64-66
on ISA Server computer, 66-67
permissions, 68-69
traffic, controlling, 68
HTTP redirector filter, 110
IIS, to run on ISA Server computer, 196
LAT options, 46-48
listeners for inbound Web requests, 193-195
Message Screener, 200-202
negative caching, 134-135
Outlook Express, to run on ISA Server computer, 197-198
policy elements, 144
bandwidth priorities, 145-149
client address sets, 149-152
content groups, 152-155
destination sets, 156-158
dial-up entries, 158-159
protocol definitions, 159-169
schedules, 170-172
protocol for IP filter, 104-106

SecureNAT clients, 59-61
security levels, 73
Server publishing, 187
SMTP filters, 112-114
streaming media filters, 116-117
TTL values
for FTP objects, 125-126
for HTTP objects, 124-125
Web Proxy clients, 61-62
connections, troubleshooting, 250-252
content groups
adding, 154
deleting, 155
editing, 155
overview, 152-154
Content screen (Scheduled Content Download Job Wizard), 130
Control Panel, Add/Remove programs, 37
creating
packet filters, 196
Server publishing rules, 187-188
Web publishing rules, 178-179
Custom Enterprise Policy Settings, 42
Custom Installation box, 38
Add-in Services option, 39-40
Administration Tools options, 40
options, list of, 39

D

databases, logging to, 226-227
dedicated security level (ISA Server Security Wizard), 71
Default Enterprise Policy Settings, 42
deleting
Server publishing rules, 189
Web publishing rules, 180
demilitarized zones. *See* DMZs,

destination sets
  creating, 156-157
  deleting, 158
  editing, 157
  overview, 156
  rules, 156
Destination Sets screen (New Web Publishing Rule Wizard), 178
DHCP (Dynamic Host Configuration Protocol), 17
  configuring, for automatic discovery, 18-20
  management console, Administrative Tools, 18
dial-up entries
  active, setting up, 159
  creating, 158
  deleting, 159
  editing, 159
  overview, 158
dialog boxes, SMTP Properties, 112
Digital Subscriber Lines. See DSL
Direct Access, configuring, 62
disabling
  Server publishing rules, 189
  Web publishing rules, 180
Disk Failure Rate, 212
disk space, monitoring, 210
distributed caching, 23
  CARP and, 140
  overview, 135-136
DMZs (demilitarized zones), 70
  back-to-back firewall configuration, 96
  sample configuration, 94-95
  scenarios, 95
  three-homed firewall configuration, 95-96
DNS (Domain Name System),
  configuring, for automatic discovery, 17
  intrusion filters, 117
  management console, Administrative Tools, 17

  Web publishing issues, 180-181
Domain Name System. See DNS
downloading
  download jobs, scheduled cache, creating, 128-131
  scheduling, 5-6
  service packs, 38
drives, cache drives, 140-141
DSL (Digital Subscriber Lines), 94
Dynamic Host Configuration Protocol. See DHCP
dynamic packet filtering versus static filtering, 107

E

editing
  Server publishing rules, 189
  Web publishing rules, 180
enabling
  Server publishing rules, 189
  Web publishing rules, 180
end user license agreement (EULA), 38
Enterprise Edition
  hardware requirements, 30
  servers, 9-12
ErrorHtmls folder, 135
errors. See troubleshooting
EULA (end user license agreement), 38
Event Viewer, troubleshooting events with, 243
  event messages, 245-246
  sample warning event message, 243-244
  security levels, 244-245
events, troubleshooting, 243
  event messages, 245-246
  sample warning event message, 243-244
  security levels, 244-245
extensibility (ISA Server), 4

F

features, new, ISA Server, 5
  RAM caching, 5
  scheduled content downloads, 5-6
  streaming media support , 6
Filter Mode screen (New IP Packet Filter Wizard), 190
Filter Settings screen (New IP Packet Filter Wizard), 190
Filter Type screen (New IP Packet Filter Wizard), 190
filtering
  application filters, 25, 108
    FTP access filter, 110-111
    H.323 filter, 114-115
    HTTP redirector, 108, 110
    intrusion detection filters, 117-118
    overview, 107
    RPC filter, 111
    SMTP filter, 111-114
    SOCKS filter, 111
    streaming media filters, 115-117
    types of, 108
  IP packet filters
    access characteristics, 100
    Allow filters, 101
    applying to server, 103
    Block filters, 101
    configuring protocol for, 104-106
    creating, 101-103
    overview, 100
    requirements, 100
    static versus dynamic, 107
  packet filtering, 24-25
firewall clients, configuring, 54-56
  arrays, installing ISA Server in, 43
  client software on client computer, 59

ISA Server, configuring for, 56-58

Web browser settings on ISA Server, 58-59

firewall mode, arrays, installing ISA Server in, 43

firewall services, 24

application filtering, 25

intrusion detection, 26

packet filtering, 24-25

stateful inspection, 25

troubleshooting, 241-242

VPN support, 25-26

forward caching, 22

advantages of, 123

authors recommendations, 31

hardware requirements, 122

Microsoft requirements, 31

overview, 122

procedural scenario, 126-127

TTL (Time-To-Live)

overview, 124

values, configuring for FTP objects, 125-126

values, configuring for HTTP object, 124-125

Frequency screen (Scheduled Content Download Job Wizard), 129

FTP

access filters, 110-111

objects, configuring TTL values for, 125-126

G–H

Getting Starting Wizard, accessing, 48

H.323 filters

configuring, 115

overview, 114

H.323 Gatekeeper, 39-40

adding to ISA, 66-67

configuring, 64

on ISA Server computer, 66-67

permissions, 68-69

traffic, controlling, 68

destination endpoint, 64

H.323 Registration, 69

incoming/outgoing traffic, controlling, 68

origination endpoint, 64

overview, 64, 66

troubleshooting, 242

hard disks, monitoring considerations, 212-213

hardware

ISA Server installation requirements, 30-32

arrays, author recommendations for, 32

author forward caching recommendations, 31

Microsoft forward caching requirements, 31

services, displayed, 32-33

requirements

cache drives, 140-141

forward caching, 122

reverse caching, 127-128

Server publishing, 176

Web publishing, 176

hierarchical caching, 23-24

CARP and, 140

overview, 136

procedural scenario, 136-137

hosting services, 27

HTTP

configuring, 110

objects, configuring TTL values for, 124-125

redirector filters

configuring, 110

overview, 108-110

requests, redirecting, 184-185

I

IANA (Internet Assigned Named Authority), 26

ICP (Internet Cache Protocol)

CARP and, differences between, 138

overview, 137

IIS (Internet Information Services),

configuring, to run on ISA Server computer, 196

publishing services, stopping, 45

installation modes

caching mode, 13

client modes, 14

comparisons between, 16

firewall client, 14

secureNAT client, 14-15

Web Proxy client, 15-16

comparisons between, 12

firewall mode, 12-13

integrated mode, 13

switching modes, 13

installing

ISA Server

array selection, 41-44

Autorun console, 33-34

cache configuration, 45-46

custom installation, 38-40

Getting Started Wizard, 48

hardware requirements, 30-33

IIS publishing services, stopping, 45

LAT configuration, 46-48

license agreement, 38

on Terminal Server, 37

pre-installation considerations, 33-35

Product ID, 38

reinstalling, 49-50

schema, 35-37

Service Pack 1, running, 37

uninstalling, 49-50

Terminal Services, 33

integrated mode, arrays, installing ISA Server in, **44**

integrated server mode, **13**

International Telecommunication Union. *See* ITU

Internet, accessing from ISA Server computer, **63**

Internet Assigned Named Authority. *See* IANA

Internet Cache Protocol. *See* ICP

Internet Explorer, configuring for Web Proxy service, **62**

Internet Information Services. *See* IIS, **196**

intrusion detection, **26**
    DNS intrusion filter, 117
    IANA, 26
    POP intrusion filter, 118

IO failure, **212**

IP packet filters
    access characteristics, 100
    Allow filters, 101
    applying to server, 103
    Block filters, 101
    configuring protocol for, 104-106
    creating, 101-103
    overview, 100
    requirements, 100
    static versus dynamic, 107

IPSec (IP Security protocol), **88-89**

ISA Management console, Servers and Arrays, **124-125**

ISA Server
    acceleration concepts, 122
    active caching, 131-133
    cache drives, 140-141
    cache files, 141-142
    CARP (Cache Array Routing Protocol), 137-140
    distributed caching, 135-136
    forward caching, 122-127
    hierarchical caching, 136-137
    negative caching, 133-135
    reverse caching, 127-128
    scheduled caching, 128-131

add-on projects, 4

alerts, 214-215
    actions, configuring, 221
    conditions, configuring, 221
    creating, 215-216, 218
    editing, 219
    thresholds, configuring, 219-220

architecture
    Enterprise Edition servers, 9-12
    importance of, 7-8
    Standard Edition servers, 9, 11-12

Cache Directory Tool, 123-124

computer, publishing Web servers on, 182-184

computers, configuring IIS to run on, 196

computers, configuring Outlook Express to run on, 197-198

computers, Server publishing on, 192-193

Control service, troubleshooting, 239-240

default settings
    Access Control, 50
    Alerts, 50
    Caching, 50
    Client configuration, 50
    LAT, 50
    packet filtering, 51
    Publishing, 51
    Routing, 51

firewall services, 24
    application filtering, 25
    intrusion detection, 26
    packet filtering, 24-25
    stateful inspections, 25
    VPN support, 25-26

H.323 Gatekeeper, adding, 66-67

hosting services, 27

installation modes
    caching mode, 13
    client modes, 14-16
    comparisons between, 12
    firewall mode, 12-13
    integrated mode, 13
    switching modes, 13

installing
    array selection, 41-44
    Autorun console, 33-34
    cache configuration, 45-46
    custom installation, 38-40
    Getting Started Wizard, 48
    IIS publishing services, stopping, 45
    LAT configuration, 46-48
    license agreement, 38
    on Terminal Server, 37
    pre-installation considerations, 33-35
    Product ID, 38
    reinstalling, 49-50
    schema, 35-37
    Service Pack 1, running, 37
    uninstalling, 49-50

logging feature, 222-223
    configuring, 223-225
    logging to databases, 226-227
    logging to files, 225

new features, 4-5
    RAM caching, 5
    scheduled content downloads, 5-6
    streaming media support, 6

NLB features, 7

performance, monitoring, 206
    active sessions, 209
    active TCP connections, 209

active UPD connections, 209

baseline, establishing, 206-207

Cache Hit Ratio (%), 209

client bytes, total/sec, 209

counters, 207-208

current users, 210

disk space, 210

dropped packets, 211

hard disk considerations, 212-213

memory cache allocated space, 210

memory considerations, 212

memory usage ratio percent, 210

milliseconds/request, 210

network-related issues, 213-214

processor considerations, 213

requests/sec, 210

SecureNAT mappings, 211

tips, 211

URL commit rate, URL/sec, 211

URLs, cached, 210

Proxy Server 2.0, acceleration updates from, 5

reports, 227, 233

application usage, 234

generating, 228, 230-232

managing, 232-233

security, 235

summary, 233-234

traffic, 234-235

utilization, 234-235

viewing, 228, 230-232

Web usage, 234

Routing and Remote Access, 7

security concepts, 70, 74

bandwidth rules, 79-82

DMZ, 70, 94-96

ISA Server Security Wizard, 71-73

network security, 70-71

protocol rules, 77-79

publishing policy rules, 82-86

security solution comparisons, 93-94

site and content rules, 74-77

VPN support, 87-93

Web caching services, 21-22

distributed caching, 23

forward caching, 22

hierarchical caching, 23-24

reverse caching, 22

scheduled caching, 23

Windows 2000 services, extending, 6-7

WPAD

configuring DHCP for, 18-20

configuring DNS for, 17

publishing, 20

WPAD (Web Proxy Autodiscovery Protocol), 17

WSPAD (Winsock Proxy Autodetect), 17

ISA Server Management console, Servers and Arrays, 20

ITU (International Telecommunication Union), H.323 Gatekeeper Server and, 64

L

L2TP (Layer 2 Tunneling Protocol), 88-89

LAT (Local Address Table), configuring, 46-48

LDT (Local Domain Table), 62

license agreement, setting, 38

limited services security level (ISA Server Security Wizard), 71

Links and Downloaded screen (Scheduled Content Download Job Wizard), 130

listeners

defined, 193

establishing for inbound Web requests, 193-195

live stream splitting, 6, 115

Local Address Table. *See* **LAT**

Local Computer screen (New IP Packet Filter Wizard), 191

Local Domain Table. *See* **LDT**

Local ISA VPN Wizard, 26

LocalLAT.txt file, 56

logging, ISA Server, 222-223

configuring, 223

ISA Server file format, 224

ODBC format, 225

W3C extended log file format, 224

to databases, 226-227

to files, 225

M

Mail Server, publishing, 198-202

memory

cache allocated space, monitoring, 210

minimum requirements, 32

monitoring considerations, 212

usage ratio percent, monitoring, 210

Message Screener, configuring, 200-202

Microsoft, forward caching requirements, 31

Microsoft Point-to-Point Encryption. *See* **MPPE**

Microsoft Web site, 4

Microsoft Windows Media. *See* **MMS**

migration, Proxy Server 2.0

effects of, 52-53

from Windows 2000, 53

from Windows NT, 51-52

mixed policy, enabling, 35
MMS (Microsoft Windows Media), streaming media support, 6
monitoring, ISA Server performance, 206
    active sessions, 209
    active TCP connections, 209
    active UDP connections, 209
    baseline, establishing, 206-207
    Cache Hit Ratio (%), 209
    client bytes, total/sec, 209
    counters, 207-208
    current users, 210
    disk space, 210
    dropped packets, 211
    hard disk considerations, 212-213
    memory cache allocated space, 210
    memory considerations, 212
    memory usage ratio percent, 210
    milliseconds/request, 210
    network-related issues, 213-214
    processor considerations, 213
    requests/sec, 210
    SecureNAT mappings, 211
    tips, 211
    URL commit rate, URL/sec, 211
    URLs, cached, 210
MPPE (Microsoft Point-to-Point Encryption), 89
MsISAund.ini file, 49-50
mspclnt.ini file, 55
msplat.txt file, 55

N

NAT (Network Address Translation), 7
negative caching
    configuring, 134-135
    overview, 133-134

Network Address Translation. *See* NAT
Network Load Balancing. *See* NLB
networks
    perimeter network, 94
    security, 70-71
    VPNs, 7
New Alert Wizard, 215
New Alias (DNS management console), 17
new features, ISA Server, 5
    RAM caching, 5
    scheduled content downloads, 5-6
    streaming media support, 6
New IP Packet Filter Wizard, 101, 190
New Server Publishing Rule Wizard, 187
New Web Publishing Rule Wizard, 178
NLB (Network Loading Balancing), Windows 2000 Advanced Server configured with, 7

O-P

Outlook Express, configuring, 197-198

packet filtering, 24-25, 51
    application. *See* application filtering
    creating, 196
    IP. See IP packet filters, 100
performance, ISA Server, monitoring, 206
    active sessions, 209
    active TCP connections, 209
    active UDP connections, 209
    baseline, establishing, 206-207
    Cache Hit Ratio (%), 209
    client bytes, total/sec, 209

    counters, 207-208
    current users, 210
    disk space, 210
    dropped packets, 211
    hard disk considerations, 212-213
    memory cache allocated space, 210
    memory considerations, 212
    memory usage ratio percent, 210
    milliseconds/request, 210
    network-related issues, 213-214
    processor considerations, 213
    requests/sec, 210
    SecureNAT mapping, 211
    tips, 211
    URL commit rate, URL/sec, 211
    URLs, cached, 210
perimeter network, 94
permissions, H.323 Gatekeeper, configuring, 68-69
PNM (Progressive Networks) protocol, streaming media support, 6
Point-to-Point Tunneling Protocol. *See* PPTP
policy element configuration, 144
    bandwidth priorities, 145
        creating, 146-149
        deleting, 149
        editing, 149
    client address sets
        creating, 150
        deleting, 152
        editing, 150
        overview, 149-150
    content groups
        adding, 154
        deleting, 155
        editing, 155
        overview, 152-154

destination sets
    creating, 156-157
    deleting, 158
    editing, 157
    overview, 156
    rules, 156
dial-up entries, 158
    active, setting up, 159
    creating, 158
    deleting, 159
    editing, 159
overview, 144
protocol definitions
    adding, 168
    built-in, list of, 160-168
    deleting, 169
    editing, 169
    overview, 159-160
schedules
    adding, 170
    deleting, 172
    editing, 170-171
    overview, 170
POP intrusion filters, 118
**PPTP (Point-to-Point
    Tunneling Protocol), 88-89**
    access, allowing outbound, 93
    overview, 88-89
**private networks, publishing
    Web server inside, 181-182**
**processors, monitoring con-
    siderations, 213**
Product ID, setting up, 38
**Progressive Networks proto-
    col. See PNM**
protocol definitions
    adding, 168
    built-in, list of, 160-168
    deleting, 169
    editing, 169
    overview, 159-160
protocol security rules, 77-79
**Protocol Settings screen
    (New Server Publishing
    Rule Wizard), 188**

Proxy Server 2.0
acceleration updates from, 4-5
    RAM caching, 5
    *scheduled content down-
        loads, 5-6*
    *streaming media support,
        6*
migrating
    effects of, 52-53
    from Windows 2000, 53
    from Windows NT, 51-52
tasks performed, comparisons
    to ISA Server 2000, 53-54
**PSTN (public switched tele-
    phone network), 64**
publishing
automatic discovery, on ISA
    Server, 20
Mail Server, 198-202
Server publishing
    concepts of, 186
    configuring, 187
    defined, 176
    *hardware requirements,
        176*
    *listeners, establishing for
        inbound Web requests,
        193, 195*
    *on back-to-back DMZ net-
        work, 192*
    *on ISA Server computer,
        192-193*
    *on three-homed DMZ net-
        work, 189-192*
    rules, creating, 187-188
    rules, deleting, 189
    rules, disabling, 189
    rules, editing, 189
    rules, enabling, 189
    rules, overview, 187
troubleshooting, 258-259
Web publishing
    concepts of, 177
    defined, 176
    DNS issues, 180-181
    *hardware requirements,
        176*

    *HTTP requests, redirect-
        ing, 184-185*
    *inside private networks,
        181-182*
    *on ISA Server computer,
        182-184*
    rules, creating, 178-179
    rules, deleting, 180
    rules, disabling, 180
    rules, editing, 180
    rules, enabling, 180
    rules, overview, 177
    *SSL requests, redirecting,
        185-186*
Publishing feature, 51
**publishing policy security
    rules, 82**
    server publishing, 82-84
    Web publishing, 84-86
**purchasing ISA Server 2000,
    11-12**

Q–R

**Qos (Quality of Service),
    bandwidth priorities, 145**

**RAID (Redundant Array of
    Inexpensive Disks), 32**
RAM, caching, 5
**Real Time Streaming
    Protocol. See RTSP**
redirecting
    HTTP requests, 184-185
    SSL requests, 185-186
**Redundant Array of
    Inexpensive Disks. See
    RAID**
registering endpoints, 69
reinstalling ISA Server, 49-50
**Remote Computers screen
    (New IP Packet Filter
    Wizard), 191**
Remote ISA VPN Wizard, 26

reports, 227
   generating, 228-232
   managing, 232-233
   viewing, 228-233
      application usage, 234
      security, 235
      summary, 233-234
      traffic, 234-235
      utilization, 234-235
      Web usage, 234
reverse caching, 22
   hardware requirements,
      127-128
   overview, 127
**Routing and Remote Access,
   7**
routing feature, 51
RPC filters, 111
**RTSP (Real Time Streaming
   Protocol), streaming media
   support, 6**
**Rule Action screen (New
   Web Publishing Rule
   Wizard), 179**
rules, Web publishing
   creating, 178-179, 187-188
   deleting, 180, 189
   disabling, 180, 189
   editing, 180, 189
   enabling, 180, 189
   overview, 177, 187
**Run ISA Server Enterprise
   Initialization option
   (Autorun console), 35**

S

**saving cache contents to
   files, 124**
scheduled caching, 23
   advantages of, 131
   download job, creating,
      128-131
   overview, 128
**Scheduled Content
   Download Job Wizard, 129**
   Content screen, 130
   Frequency screen, 129

   Links and Downloaded
      screen, 130
   Start Time screen, 129
**scheduled content down-
   loads, 5-6**
schedules
   adding, 170
   deleting, 172
   editing, 170-171
   overview, 170
**schema, ISA Server,
   installing, 35-37**
screened subnet, 94
**SDK (Software Development
   Kit), 4**
**secure security level (ISA
   Server Security Wizard), 72**
**Secure Sockets Layer. See
   SSL, 27**
SecureNAT
   client server modes and,
      14-15
   clients, configuring, 59-61
   mappings, monitoring, 211
security
   application filters, 108
      FTP access filter, 110-111
      H.323 filter, 114-115
      HTTP redirector, 108, 110
      *intrusion detection,
         117-118*
      overview, 107
      RPC filter, 111
      SMTP filter, 111-114
      SOCKS filter, 111
      streaming media, 115-117
      types of, 108
   DMZs (demilitarized zones),
      70
      *back-to-back firewall con-
         figuration, 96*
      *sample configuration,
         94-95*
      scenarios, 95
      *three-homed firewall con-
         figuration, 95-96*

   IP packet filters
      access characteristics, 100
      Allow filters, 101
      applying to server, 103
      Block filters, 101
      *configuring protocol for,
         104-106*
      creating, 101-103
      overview, 100
      requirements, 100
      static versus dynamic, 107
   ISA server rules, 74
      bandwidth, 79-82
      protocol, 77-79
      publishing policy, 82-86
      site and content, 74-77
   ISA Server Security Wizard,
      71
      *security levels, configur-
         ing, 73*
      *security levels, list of,
         71-72*
      warning against, 72-73
   network security, 70-71
   reports, 235
   security solution comparisons,
      93-94
   VPN support, 87-88
      *IPSec (IP Security
         Protocol), 89*
      *L2TP (Layer 2 Tunneling
         Protocol), 89*
      *PPTP (Point-to-Point
         Tunneling Protocol),
         88-89, 93*
      VPN client requests, 92-93
      *VPN servers, local, setting
         up, 89-92*
      *VPN servers, remote, set-
         ting up, 92*
Server publishing
   concepts of, 186
   configuring, 187
   defined, 176
   hardware requirements, 176
   listeners, establishing for
      inbound Web requests,
      193-195

on back-to-back DMZ net-
work, 192
on ISA Server computer,
192-193
on three-homed DMZ net-
work, 189-192
rules, 82-84
creating, 187-188
deleting, 189
disabling, 189
editing, 189
enabling, 189
overview, 187
troubleshooting, 258-259
servers
local ISA VPN, setting up,
89-92
remote ISA VPN, setting up,
92
standalone, example of, 9
**Servers and Arrays (ISA
Server Management con-
sole), 20**
**Servers and Arrays com-
mand, Cache configuration,
124-125**
**Servers screen (New IP
Packet Filter Wizard), 190**
Service Pack 1, running, 37
**services, troubleshooting,
238**
Firewall, 241-242
H.323 Gatekeeper service, 242
ISA Server Control service,
239-240
service restarts, 239
Web Proxy service, 241
sessions
monitoring, 209
troubleshooting, 249-250
**Set Predefined Options
(DHCP management con-
sole), 18**
**site and content security
rules, 74-77**

SMTP filters
configuring, 112-114
overview, 111-112
SOCKS filter, 111
Software Development Kit.
See **SDK**
**SSL (Secure Sockets Layer),
27**
**SSL requests, redirecting,
185-186**
**standalone server, example
of, 9**
Standard Edition
hardware requirements, 30
servers, 9-12
**Start Time screen (Scheduled
Content Download Job
Wizard), 129**
stateful inspection, 25
**static packet filtering *versus*
dynamic packet filtering,
107**
streaming media
filters, 115-117
live-stream splitting, 6
protocol supporting, 6
summary reports, 233-234
switching server modes, 13
system performance. *See*
performance

T

**TCP connections, monitoring,
209**
**Terminal Server, installing
ISA Server on, 37**
**Terminal Services, installing,
33**
Time-To-Live. *See* **TTL**
traffic reports, 234-235
troubleshooting, 238
access policies, 252-255
authentication, 255-257
caching, 246-249
connections, 250-252

events, 243
event messages, 245-246
*sample warning event mes-
sage, 243-244*
security levels, 244-245
ISA Server
hard disk issues, 212-213
memory, 212
*network-related issues,
213-214*
performance, memory, 212
processors, 213
publishing, 258-259
services, 238
Firewall service, 241-242
*H.323 Gatekeeper service,
242*
*ISA Server Control ser-
vice, 239-240*
service restarts, 239
Web Proxy service, 241
sessions, 249-250
Web publishing, 258-259
TTL (Time-To-Live)
configuring
*values, for FTP objects,
125-126*
*values, for HTTP objects,
124-125*
overview, 124

U–V

**UDP connections, monitor-
ing, 209**
**Uninstalling, ISA Server,
49-50**
**Use This Enterprise Policy
radio button (Autorun console), 35**
users, monitoring, 210
**Users and Groups screen
(New Web Publishing Rule
Wizard), 178**
utilization reports, 234-235

View menu command, Advanced command, 101

Virtual Private Network. *See* **VPN**

VPN (Virtual Private Network), 7

firewall services, 25-26

security support, 87-88

   IPSec (IP Security Protocol), 89

   L2TP (Layer 2 Protocol), 89

   PPTP (Point-to-Point Tunneling Protocol), 88-89, 93

   VPN client requests, 92-93

   VPN server, local, setting up, 89-92

   VPN server, remote, setting up, 92

technology, 26

W

W3C, log file format, 224

W3SVC, stopping message, 45

Web caching services, 21-22

distributed caching, 23

forward caching, 22

hierarchical caching, 23-24

reverse caching, 22

scheduling caching, 23

Web Proxy

client server modes and, 15-16

clients, configuring, 61-62

service, troubleshooting, 241

Web Proxy Autodiscovery Protocol. *See* **WPAD**

Web publishing

concepts of, 177

defined, 176

DNS issues, 180-181

hardware requirements, 176

HTTP requests, redirecting, 184-185

inside private networks, 181-182

on ISA Server computer, 182-184

rules

   creating, 178-179

   deleting, 180

   disabling, 180

   editing, 180

   enabling, 180

   overview, 177

security rules, 84-86

SSL requests, redirecting, 185-186

troubleshooting, 258-259

Web usage reports, 234

Windows 2000

migrating Proxy Server 2.0 from, 53

service packs, downloading, 38

services, 6-7

Terminal Server, installing ISA server on, 37

Windows NT, migrating Proxy Server 2.0 from, 51-53

Windows sockets. *See* **Winsock**

Winsock (Windows sockets), 24

Winsock Proxy Autodetect. *See* **WSPAD**

wizards

Getting Started Wizard, accessing, 48

ISA Server Security Wizard, 71

   security levels, configuring, 73

   security levels, list of, 71-72

   warning against, 72-73

Local ISA VPN, 26

New Alert, 215

New IP Packet Filter, 101, 190

New Server Publishing Rule, 187

New Web Publishing Rule, 178

Remote ISA VPN, 26

Scheduled Content Download Job, 129

   Content screen, 130

   Frequency screen, 129

   Links and Downloaded screen, 130

   Start Time screen, 129

WPAD (Web Proxy Autodiscovery Protocol), configuring

configuring

   DHCP for, 18-20

   DNS for, 17

publishing on ISA Server, 20

WSPAD (Winsock Proxy Autodetect), 17

www.ingramcontent.com/pod-product-compliance
Lightning Source LLC
Chambersburg PA
CBHW062058050326
40690CB00016B/3137